DATE DUE

Treatment of Obsessive Compulsive Disorder

TREATMENT MANUALS FOR PRACTITIONERS
David H. Barlow, *Editor*

TREATMENT OF OBSESSIVE COMPULSIVE DISORDER
Gail S. Steketee

PROBLEM DRINKERS
GUIDED SELF-CHANGE TREATMENT
Mark B. Sobell and Linda C. Sobell

INSOMNIA
PSYCHOLOGICAL ASSESSMENT AND MANAGEMENT
Charles M. Morin

PSYCHOLOGICAL MANAGEMENT OF CHRONIC HEADACHES
Paul R. Martin

TREATING PTSD
COGNITIVE–BEHAVIORAL STRATEGIES
David W. Foy, *Editor*

PREVENTING PHYSICAL AND EMOTIONAL ABUSE OF CHILDREN
David A. Wolfe

SEXUAL DYSFUNCTION
A GUIDE FOR ASSESSMENT AND TREATMENT
John P. Wincze and Michael P. Carey

SEVERE BEHAVIOR PROBLEMS
A FUNCTIONAL COMMUNICATION TRAINING APPROACH
V. Mark Durand

DEPRESSION IN MARRIAGE
A MODEL FOR ETIOLOGY AND TREATMENT
Steven R. H. Beach, Evelyn E. Sandeen, and K. Daniel O'Leary

TREATING ALCOHOL DEPENDENCE
A COPING SKILLS TRAINING GUIDE
Peter M. Monti, David B. Abrams, Ronald M. Kadden, and Ned L. Cooney

SELF-MANAGEMENT FOR ADOLESCENTS
A SKILLS-TRAINING PROGRAM
MANAGING EVERYDAY PROBLEMS
Thomas A. Brigham

PSYCHOLOGICAL TREATMENT OF PANIC
David H. Barlow and Jerome A. Cerny

Treatment of Obsessive Compulsive Disorder

GAIL S. STEKETEE
Boston University

Series Editor's Note by David H. Barlow

THE GUILFORD PRESS
New York   London

© 1993 The Guilford Press
A Division of Guilford Publications, Inc.
72 Spring Street, New York, NY 10012

Printed in the United States of America

This book is printed on acid-free paper.

Last digit is print number: 9   8   7   6   5   4   3   2   1

Library of Congress Cataloging-in-Publication Data
Steketee, Gail.
        Treatment of obsessive compulsive disorder / Gail S. Steketee.
        p.   cm. — (Treatment manuals for practitioners)
        Includes bibliographical references and index.
        ISBN 0-89862-184-4
        1. Obsessive–compulsive disorder—Treatment. 2. Behavior therapy.
    I. Title. II. Series: Treatment manuals for practitioners.
        [DNLM: 1. Obsessive–Compulsive Disorder—therapy. WM 176 S8237t
    1993]
    RC533.S74 1993
    616.85'2270651—dc20
    DNLM/DLC
    for Library of Congress   93-15832
                                                                        CIP

Acknowledgments

I owe a debt of gratitude to many people who have directly or indirectly helped in the writing of this book. First are the many clients with obsessive compulsive symptoms from whom I have learned much about when and how to use behavioral treatment strategies and about the importance of the therapeutic relationship. I have often admired the courage of those whose lives were filled with the intense frustration of coping with persistent and debilitating obsessions and rituals. Had I not seen substantial improvement in the lives of many of these clients, I would not have written such a book.

Two colleagues in particular have played important roles in the generation of this book. Many of the behavioral treatment strategies were developed under the expert mentorship of Edna B. Foa, PhD. Kerrin White, MD, was kind enough to improve upon an earlier draft of Chapter 5 and on my discussion of biological issues.

Finally, I am grateful for my husband, Brian's, tolerance of seemingly endless periods of my distraction while I wrote the book or tried to clear away enough current business to be able to write.

GAIL S. STEKETEE

Series Editor's Note

Recent epidemological studies have revealed a surprisingly high prevalence of obsessive compulsive disorder (OCD). The evidence indicates that OCD is more prevalent than even panic disorder, and yet knowledge of effective treatment is woefully inadequate. Based on my experience at a large anxiety disorders clinic, if patients come in from the community badly diagnosed, chances are they have OCD. If patients have experienced a variety of pharmacological and psychosocial treatments with no improvement whatsoever, they probably have OCD. And, if individuals with an anxiety disorder need hospitalization because they are utterly unable to function, most likely the diagnosis is OCD. In view of the high prevalence, the marked severity in many patients, and the shocking lack of knowledge of effective treatments for this disorder among clinicians, this volume by Gail Steketee is very timely indeed. In this volume, Dr. Steketee, one of the world's leading experts on OCD, brings us up-to-date on the latest developments concerning this difficult disorder. More importantly, she illustrates, in gratifying detail, a step-by-step treatment approach that should be invaluable to any clinician who comes in contact with these cases. Particularly important are some recent advances in the conceptualization and treatment of OCD, including directly assessing and treating cognitive rituals, handling the noncompliant patient, and dealing with strongly held ideas about danger as well as other personality characteristics that might interfere with successful treatment. The role of the family in treatment is also addressed in an important way, as it must be for anyone attempting to treat these problems. This book is a notable addition to the treatment manuals comprising this series. Since it is so tragically difficult for people with OCD to find appropriate treatment, many clinicians who undertake to utilize these procedures and incorporate them into their practice will have the opportunity to relieve considerable suffering that would otherwise continue for years or even a lifetime.

DAVID H. BARLOW
University at Albany
State University of New York

Contents

Appendices

NOTE ABOUT PHOTOCOPY RIGHTS

The publisher grants book purchasers permission to reproduce handouts
and forms in this book—with the exception of those reprinted from other
publications—for professional use with their clients.

Treatment of Obsessive Compulsive Disorder

1

Introduction

How to Use This Book

This book is intended for the mental health professional who wishes to undertake behavioral treatment of those who suffer from obsessive compulsive disorder (OCD). Because of wide variations in personality styles, symptomatic behaviors, and functioning levels of individuals with this disorder, substantial clinical judgment is often required to deliver this treatment effectively. Toward that end, chapters in this volume are designed to provide educational background for the clinician, as well as step-by-step guidelines for conducting exposure and response prevention treatment. Detailed suggestions for implementation are given, along with some verbatim material designed to provide guidelines for how to introduce various aspects of the treatment method to clients. Chapter contents and strategies for use of this book by readers with varying levels of clinical experience are described below.

The book begins with didactic material organized into chapters on the nature of obsessions and compulsions (Chapter 2), behavioral models and research findings regarding behavioral treatments (Chapter 3), cognitive theory and treatment (Chapter 4), and biological models and treatment (Chapter 5). Clinicians who feel well grounded in these models and the empirical findings regarding treatments for OCD derived from them are invited to go directly to Chapter 6 on assessment of OCD, and to proceed from there through the treatment and relapse prevention material. Chapters 6 and 7 address planning aspects of treatment, including clinical treatment considerations based on client characteristics and available resources; methods for standardized assessment of OCD symptoms; and methods for introducing clients to behavioral treatment. Chapters 8, 9, and 10 address the implementation of direct exposure, imaginal exposure, and preventing rituals. Chapter 11 is intended to help clinicians assist clients in maintaining treatment gains during follow-up. Case examples illustrating behavioral assessment and treatment are given throughout Chapters 6 to 11. In addition to the forms for assessment and treatment contained in several of the chapters, appendices are included to provide relevant assessment forms for measuring symptomatology and assessing progress during the treatment program.

Some clinicians who are familiar with the basics of exposure methods and with prevention of avoidance and ritualistic behavior will want pointers on complications in treatment and management of coexisting problems and potential relapse concerns. These experienced therapists are encouraged to skim Chapters 6 through 11 for specific sections of particular interest to them. In particular, aspects of treatment requiring more careful consideration include identification and treatment of cognitive rituals and of reassurance seeking; motivational and compliance difficulties; overvalued ideas and problematic attitudes and beliefs that interfere with progress; comorbidity complications; involvement of family members in treatment; and relapse prevention planning.

For clients and family members who would like reading material that provides them with basic knowledge about their disorder and about the behavioral treatment process, clinicians can recommend *When Once Is Not Enough* (Steketee & White, 1990), published by New Harbinger Press, Oakland, CA. Written as a "self-help" book, it can readily be used as a companion volume for the educational and behavioral treatment phases, since it follows the format of the present volume fairly closely. Several other excellent self-help books have been published recently and can also be recommended to interested clients and family members (e.g., Baer, 1991; Foa & Wilson, 1991; Neziroglu & Yaryura-Tobias, 1990).

Premises for This Book

Particular biases influence the approach outlined here in treatment of anxious clients. These biases are evident in the organization of this volume, as well as in the prescriptions for treatment strategies contained here. In this section I try to articulate the ones I am aware of, in the hope that readers may be attuned to attitudinal similarities and differences they may wish to consider in planning and implementing therapy with OCD clients.

As a clinical researcher, I believe that clinicians should be reasonably knowledgeable about research findings that pertain to the symptoms of OCD and to their treatment. There are several advantages to having this knowledge readily available during clinical interviews. Clients ask many questions: how OCD symptoms develop, especially their biological underpinnings; the probable outcome of treatments proposed; what to expect after treatment ends; and so forth. It is relatively easy to offer private opinions or to be glibly reassuring in answer to these questions, but it is far more compelling for clients to hear well-considered answers derived from current research findings. After all, are we not reassured when our physicians mention recent research findings relevant to treatment of our medical conditions? As clinicians feel competent in providing information, clients gain respect for the clinician and confidence in the upcoming treatment. Clinicians who have up-to-date information about symptoms and treatment are also more likely to evaluate their clients' specific needs critically and to deliver treatment effectively. There is nothing quite so satisfying as substantial improvement in clients' symptoms that persists over time and is directly attributable, at least in part, to the therapist's knowledge and skill in treatment efforts.

With respect to clients' behaviors during treatment, I believe, with many of my behavioral colleagues, that people do the best they can to help themselves manage difficult internal and external situations. If their behavior does not accord with the clinician's ideas of the "best" strategy under the circumstances, chances are that the clients do not understand what to do or how to do it differently, or are unable to implement more effective behaviors for any of a variety of legitimate reasons. Clients' noncompliance or "resistance" merely implies a failure in understanding or in their ability to act differently. The clinician's task is to identify the source of the difficulty without blaming or judging clients. This is sometimes quite difficult, since clinicians do not like all clients equally well, and certain behaviors (e.g., passive–aggressive ones) are very difficult to tolerate.

Holding a nonjudgmental attitude does not mean that every client with OCD, if evaluated carefully, will eventually improve with behavioral treatment or other adjunctive methods. If we are honest with those we treat, we will readily admit at the outset that not all people with OCD respond to exposure and prevention of rituals, and that we do not always know why. Certainly our skills as clinicians are limited, and we are obliged to search first for our own errors. In addition, as noted later in this book, some clients do not appear able to comply with instructions as requested—whether because they believe treatment will not help, or they are unwilling to expend extensive effort or to tolerate unpleasant feelings, or they stand to lose some current benefit the symptoms afford, or for other reasons. As soon as this becomes apparent, clients should be discouraged from continuing further in behavioral treatment, lest more damage to the credibility of the therapy (and the clients) be done and until such time as the difficulty is resolved or the contingencies change. This dismissal must be framed positively to allow the clients to feel welcome to pursue behavioral treatment in future.

A last comment on language use in this volume is in order. The term "client," rather than "patient," is used throughout to describe the individual seeking treatment for OCD symptoms. Both terms are interchangeable from my point of view, though the latter usually denotes a psychiatric setting and often a medical model of illness and treatment. For variety, I have occasionally used the term "obsessive compulsive" to refer to a person who has OCD. It is certainly not meant to imply that obsessive compulsive symptoms are the defining characteristic of the person, or that they will always be present. This book is focused entirely on OCD, not on obsessive compulsive personality disorder, both defined according to current diagnostic nomenclature. This distinction is discussed in detail in Chapter 2.

With the caveats above, readers are encouraged to peruse this guide for practitioners, in the hopes that they will find information directly helpful in treating those who suffer most unfortunately from OCD symptoms. I also encourage clinicians who regularly treat this disorder to consider membership in the OC Foundation (P.O. Box 9573, New Haven, CT 06535; telephone: 203-772-0565), established by individuals with firsthand experience of OCD symptoms for dissemination of information about the disorder and its treatment. The *OC Newsletter* published by the Foundation provides very useful information on a variety of topics pertaining to symptoms and treatment, as well as about upcoming or ongoing research projects, lectures, and the like. There are two additional sources of information about OCD for the professional. Dr. John Greist and his colleagues at the University of Wisconsin have organized a library of published materials about OCD, available to the public on request. The address is OC Information Center (OCIC), Dean Foundation for Health, Research and Education, 8000 Excelsior Dr., Suite 203, Madison, WI 53717. In addition, the American OCD Professional Association (AOCPA) (P.O. Box 11837, Alexandria, VA 22312) provides information (library resources, computer bulletins, and E-mail) and consultation to professional members.

2

The Nature of Obsessions
and Compulsions

This chapter is intended to provide the clinician with detailed information about typical and not-so-typical manifestations and characteristics of OCD—information that is likely to prove useful as a knowledge base during assessment of individuals with this disorder. The more solid the clinician's foundation of basic knowledge about this disorder, the better he or she will be able to evaluate particular clients relative to others, to perceive important details that may affect treatment outcome, and to respond knowledgeably to clients' questions about their symptoms and prognosis.

Definition

OCD is characterized by recurrent obsessions or compulsions that provoke distress and often interfere significantly with everyday functioning. The defining features of OCD, according to the draft criteria for the fourth edition of the *Diagnostic and Statistical Manual of Mental Disorders* (DSM-IV; American Psychiatric Association, 1993), are given in Table 2.1. "Obsessions" are intrusive thoughts, images, or impulses that the individual perceives as senseless. "Compulsions" or "rituals" are repetitive intentional behaviors or mental acts performed in response to an obsession. They are specifically designed to suppress or neutralize discomfort or to prevent a dreaded event, although this intention may not always be apparent to an observer.

Like obsessions, rituals are usually recognized by the client as unreasonable or excessive. Most often the ritualistic activity is directly related to the obsessive discomfort, such as washing rituals designed to remove "contamination," or checking compulsions that relieve fears that something dangerous may happen unless extra care is taken. In some cases, compulsions may not be directly connected to what they are designed to prevent, but still are clearly

5

TABLE 2.1. DSM-IV Draft Criteria for Obsessive Compulsive Disorder (OCD)

A. Either obsessions or compulsions:

⋇ Obsessions as defined by (1), (2), (3), and (4):
  (1) recurrent and persistent ideas, thoughts, impulses, or images that are ex-
      perienced, at some time during the disturbance, as intrusive and in-
      appropriate, and cause marked anxiety or distress
  (2) the thoughts, impulses, or images are not simply excessive worries about
      real-life problems
  (3) the person attempts to ignore or suppress such thoughts or impulses or to
      neutralize them with some other thought or action
  (4) the person recognizes that the obsessional thoughts, impulses, or images are
      the product of his or her own mind (not imposed from without as in thought
      insertion)

⋇ Compulsions as defined by (1) and (2):
  (1) repetitive behaviors (e.g., handwashing, ordering, checking) or mental acts
      (e.g., praying, counting, repeating words silently) that the person feels driven
      to perform in response to an obsession, or according to rules that must be
      applied rigidly
  (2) the behaviors or mental acts are aimed at preventing or reducing distress or
      preventing some dreaded event or situation; however, these behaviors or
      mental acts either are not connected in a realistic way with what they are
      designed to neutralize or prevent, or are clearly excessive

B. At some point during the course of the disorder, the person has recognized that the
    obsessions or compulsions are excessive or unreasonable. Note: this does not apply
    to children.

C. The obsessions or compulsions cause marked distress; are time-consuming (take
    more than an hour a day); or significantly interfere with the person's normal
    routine, occupational functioning, or usual social activities or relationships with
    others.

D. If another Axis I disorder is present, the content of the obsessions or compulsions is
    not restricted to it (e.g., preoccupation with food in the presence of an Eating
    Disorder; hair pulling in the presence of Trichotillomania; concern with appear-
    ance in the presence of Body Dysmorphic Disorder; preoccupation with drugs in
    the presence of a Substance Use Disorder; preoccupation with having a serious
    illness in the presence of Hypochondriasis; or guilty ruminations in the presence of
    Major Depressive Disorder).

E. Not due to the direct effects of a substance (e.g., drugs of abuse, medication) or a
    general medical condition.

Specify if **Poor Insight Type:** if, for most of the time during the current episode, the
person does not recognize that the obsessions and compulsions are excessive or
unreasonable

Note. From American Psychiatric Association (1993). Copyright 1993 by the American Psychiatric Association. Reprinted by permission.

excessive and recognized by clients as unreasonable. For example, an ordinary action may be performed repetitively in order to magically or superstitiously prevent harm from occurring.

According to several studies of intrusive thoughts exhibited by ordinary individuals, clinical obsessions are quite similar in content to those of normals, but provoke more anxiety and are less easily dismissed (Dent & Salkovskis, 1986; Rachman & DeSilva, 1978; Salkovskis & Harrison, 1984). To illustrate the similarities of "normal" obsessions and clinical ones, Table 2.2 includes an abbreviated list of typical intrusive thoughts of normal individuals from a study by Rachman and DeSilva (1978).

Described in the psychiatric literature since the 19th century (Esquirol, 1838), OCD can be clearly identified from written accounts many centuries earlier. However, this condition was not formally documented or defined until the beginning of this century (Janet, 1903; Lewis, 1936; Schneider, 1925). Famous sufferers include writer John Bunyan (the author of *Pilgrim's Progress*), religious reformer Martin Luther, and multimillionaire Howard Hughes (see Fowler, 1986). Among fictional characters, Shakespeare's Lady Macbeth exclaims, "Out, damn'd spot!" as she washes her hands repeatedly; she undoubtedly exhibits obsessive and compulsive symptoms, though arguably delusional in nature.

Manifestations of OCD

Because of their observable nature, rituals and avoidance behaviors are often the most readily apparent features of OCD. Compulsive rituals take a variety of forms, both behavioral and mental, with many clients having more than one type. The most common clinical forms are washing and cleaning rituals designed to remove "contamination" from a specific source, such as germs or chemicals. Typically the individual fears some general or specific consequence of contamination, including becoming ill or dying, or causing someone else to do so. Types of feared contaminants have varied with cultural concerns and with current medical knowledge. For example, in the United States during the last 20 years, obsessive concerns about sexual contamination shifted from syphilis and gonorrhea to genital herpes when this disease was highly publicized in the early 1980s, and more recently to AIDS. Likewise, an upsurgence in fears of environmental contaminants, such as PCBs, asbestos, and pesticides, has appeared to follow scientific findings transmitted by the mass media. Thus, the fears expressed by those with OCD are often exaggerated versions of normal concerns.

Other common manifestations of OCD are checking rituals intended to prevent particular catastrophes, such as burglary, fire, harming someone, social embarrassment, or rejection. The situations checked are directly related

TABLE 2.2. Obsessions Reported by a Nonclinical Sample

Impulse to hurt or harm someone
Thought of intense anger toward someone, related to a past experience
Thought of accident occurring to a loved one
Impulse to say something nasty and damning to someone
Thought of harm to, or death of, close friend or family member
Thought of acts of violence in sex
Thought that something is wrong with her health
Impulse to physically and verbally attack someone
Thought of harm befalling her children, especially accidents
Thought that probability of air crash accident to herself would be minimized if a
    relative had such an accident
Thought whether an accident had occurred to a loved one
Thought that she, her husband, and her baby (due) would be greatly harmed because
    of exposure to asbestos, with conviction that there are tiny asbestos dust particles
    in the house
Thought whether any harm has come to his wife
Impulse to shout at and abuse someone
Impulse to harm, or be violent toward children, especially smaller ones
Impulse to crash car when driving
Impulse to attack and violently punish someone—e.g., to throw a child out of a bus
Impulse to say rude things to people
Thought about accidents or mishaps, usually when about to travel
Impulse to push people away and off, in a crowd—e.g., a queue
Impulse to attack certain persons
Impulse to say inappropriate things—"wrong things at wrong place"
Impulse—sexual impulse toward attractive females, known and unknown
Thought—wishing that someone disappeared from the face of the earth
Thought of "unnatural" sexual acts
Thought—wishing and imagining that someone close to her was hurt or harmed
Thought of experiences many years ago when he was embarrassed, was humiliated, or
    was a failure
Impulse to violently attack and kill someone
Thought that she might do something dramatic like trying to rob a bank
Impulse to jump from top of a tall building or mountain/cliff
Impulse to sexually assault a female, known and unknown
Impulse to say rude and unacceptable things
Impulse to engage in certain sexual practices that involve pain to the partner
Impulse to jump off the platform when a train is arriving
Thought of physically punishing a loved one

Note. Adapted from Rachman and DeSilva (1978). Copyright 1978 by Pergamon Press, Ltd.
Adapted by permission.

to the obsessive fears. For example, checking door and window locks relieves burglary fears; checking heaters and electrical appliances relieves the fear of fire; examining envelopes, bags, or pockets reduces the likelihood of forgetting something important; and retracing an auto route verifies that no pedestrian has been hit. Idiosyncratic obsessive concerns are illustrated by the case of a client who collected nails or sticks in the road that might puncture the tire of an unsuspecting driver and cause an accident. Checking may also be employed in response to contamination fears, as in the case of another client who checked her daughter's head carefully for lice, and a third who checked repeatedly for red spots on her clothing to make sure she had not been exposed to blood, which she equated with AIDS. Both these clients feared contamination and relied primarily on washing and cleaning rituals to reduce discomfort.

Several other compulsions are less commonly observed. Repeating rituals can be likened to superstitions in which ordinary actions (e.g., crossing a threshold, touching something, sitting down and getting up, tying a shoelace, etc.) are repeated to prevent an imagined disaster (e.g., having a loved one die in an accident, going to hell). Ordering rituals require the arrangement of objects to produce a satisfying symmetry or balance. This compulsion is often done to alleviate a general feeling of discomfort or dread, rather than to prevent a particular catastrophe.

Although Greenberg (1987) has differentiated hoarders from other types of obsessionals, such excessive collecting or saving appears to be another type of ritual, which serves to prevent the loss of potentially important objects or information. Saved items often include written information (e.g., newspapers, magazines, scraps of paper, bills, etc.). One client filled her apartment with cases of beer to ensure that she always had some on hand in case of emergency. This began when she had returned home late one night after an upsetting argument, which led her to feel she needed a drink to calm her nerves. The house was empty of beer and all liquor stores were closed. To prevent a recurrence of this situation, she began purchasing increasing amounts of beer, far more than she could possibly drink or store comfortably in her apartment.

Many clients report mental rituals or cognitive compulsions that, like overt ones, are designed to reduce discomfort provoked by obsessive fears. Examples include counting to a "safe number," praying in a "sincere" way to obtain forgiveness for an error, making mental lists to avoid forgetting important events, and forming a corrective image to counteract a catastrophic one (e.g., the image of one's mother walking down the street to replace the image of one's mother in the hospital). Because they are not overt behaviors, mental rituals often go unreported unless clients are specifically queried about such events.

Other illusory forms of compulsive behaviors include repeated requests for reassurance of "experts" or family members. Examples include calling poison control hotlines over and over to gain assurance that one's child is safe, asking repeatedly whether an object is "safe" to touch, and asking for repetition of a statement or instruction to ensure correct understanding.

A rare category of "obsessional slowness" has been suggested by Rachman and Hodgson (1980). They described clients whose daily grooming activities were carried out with meticulous care, requiring many hours of effort. Since such behaviors are not usually associated with anxiety or other negative emotional states, they appear to be an atypical form of OCD, requiring a very different treatment approach from that appropriate for anxiety-based obsessions and compulsions. Interested readers are referred to Rachman and Hodgson's (1980) account of treatment for obsessional slowness, using a gradual method of time reduction for specified activities such as toothbrushing, hair combing, washing, and the like.

The Yale–Brown Obsessive Compulsive Scale (YBOCS) Symptom Checklist (Goodman, Price, Rasmussen, Mazure, Fleischman, et al., 1989) is included in this book (see Appendix A) as a comprehensive list of the many types of obsessions and compulsions, both behavioral and mental, exhibited by most clients. Use of this instrument during assessment (see Chapter 6) makes it far less likely that therapists will fail to identify important OCD symptoms requiring consideration when planning treatment.

Classification

Several writers have attempted to provide classification systems for OCD symptoms, based on the form or the content (e.g., religious, aggressive) of the obsessions and compulsions (Akhtar, Wig, Verma, Pershad, & Verma, 1975; Capstick & Seldrup, 1973; Dowson, 1977; Goodman, Price, Rasmussen, Mazure, Fleischman, et al., 1989). Such taxonomies have not been generally adopted, because they appear to have little direct relationship to treatment strategies. By contrast, Foa and Tillmanns (1980) have proposed a classification based on the functional relationship between obsessive compulsive symptoms and anxiety. They have defined obsessions or ruminations as thoughts, images, or actions that generate anxiety. These may be prompted by external (environmental) or by internal (thoughts, images) fear cues, and may or may not include fears of potential disasters. To relieve anxiety, individuals can simply avoid the feared situation or stimuli (passive avoidance), or else perform overt (behavioral) or covert (mental) rituals (both labeled as "active avoidance" mechanisms) to restore safety or prevent harm (Rachman, 1976b). This definition is consistent with DSM-IV criteria, as well as with behavioral models of OCD and treatment interventions derived from them (see Chapter 3).

Prevalence and Course of OCD

Although early surveys estimated the prevalence rate of OCD in the general population at 0.05% (Rudin, 1953; Woodruff & Pitts, 1964), the recent Epidemiologic Catchment Area survey indicated that the lifetime prevalence of OCD was 2.5% (1 in 40 people) and the 6-month point prevalence was 1.6%, making it the fourth most common psychiatric disorder in the United States (Karno, Golding, Sorenson, & Burnam, 1988). Other studies have reported similar figures (e.g., Henderson & Pollard, 1988). OCD afflicts males nearly as often as females. Calculations for over 1500 clients in various studies indicate that the proportion of males to females is a nearly identical 1.0 to 1.1 (White, Steketee, & Julian, 1992), though the ratio varied widely across studies from a high of 1.0 to 0.4 (Lo, 1967; Gojer, Khanna, & Channabasavanna, 1987) to a low of 1.0 to 1.8 (Rasmussen & Tsuang, 1986). A considerable range of severity is evident, from minimal interference with daily functioning to extreme disability (Myers et al., 1984; Rasmussen & Tsuang, 1984). No difference in racial distribution has been observed (Myers et al., 1984), though OCD clients from minority backgrounds rarely appear among clinic populations. A review by Neal and Turner (1991) of research on anxiety disorders in African-Americans failed to locate any such studies for OCD.

Mean age of onset is quite consistent across studies, ranging from 19.3 to 25.6 years (Karno et al., 1988; Lo, 1967; Rasmussen & Tsuang, 1984; Thyer, 1985; Welner, Reich, Robins, Fishman, & Van Doren, 1976). On average, 65% of OCD cases become symptomatic before the age of 25, with about 30% reporting symptoms as children (Ingram, 1961; Lo, 1967). Fewer than 15% developed symptoms after age 35 (Goodwin, Guze, & Robins, 1969; Rasmussen & Tsuang, 1984, 1986; Thyer, 1985). Unfortunately, many studies do not distinguish onset of current type or episode of OCD symptoms from onset of earlier episodes or other manifestations of obsessions and rituals. Thus, for example, a client whose current washing rituals began at age 22 may not have reported engaging in repeating rituals at age 10. Clinical impression suggests that early histories of changing symptoms are common. Hafner's (1988) finding of a relatively younger mean age of onset (18.4 years) in members of a self-help group suggests that as OCD sufferers become more fully educated about their illness, they may recollect earlier instances of such symptoms.

Males appear to acquire symptoms earlier than females, often beginning in early adolescence (White et al., 1992; Rasmussen & Eisen, 1989). That OCD symptoms interfere with an individual's capacity to form successful marital relationships is evident from the low marriage rates, ranging from 32% to 61% for males and from 58% to 75% for females, as shown in Table 2.3 (Ingram, 1961; Khanna, Kaliaperumal, & Channabasavanna, 1986;

TABLE 2.3. Marital Relationships in OCD

Study	% married	Marital quality
Ingram (1961)	32% (M), 60% (F)	
Khanna et al. (1986)	39% (M), 75% (F)	
Kringlen (1965)	61% (M), 62% (F)	46% unhappy
Lo (1967)	39% (M), 58% (F)	
Welner et al. (1976)	61% (young sample)	35% unhappy
Coryell (1981)	28%	
Hafner (1988)	33%	
Emmelkamp et al. (1990)		50% unhappy
Balslev-Olesen & Geert-Jorgensen (1959)		Generally happy
Steketee et al. (1985)		Normal scores[a]
Steketee (1987)	40%	Normal scores[b]

[a]Marital Adjustment Test.
[b]Dyadic Adjustment Scale.

Kringlen, 1965; Lo, 1967). For those who do marry, the quality of their marital relationships does not appear to be worse than that of marriages in the general population (Steketee, Kozak, & Foa, 1985; Steketee, 1987).

Relatively little is known about the course of OCD in the general population. Interestingly, in one study, diagnosis of OCD in children could be confirmed 2 years later in only one-third of the cases (Berg et al., 1989), indicating that for most children OCD symptoms disappear without treatment. Findings from adult clinic samples indicate that chronic or deteriorating courses are most typical, occasionally punctuated by periods of partial remission (Rasmussen & Tsuang, 1984). Such chronic fluctuating courses appear both prior to treatment and after hospital discharge (Goodwin et al., 1969; Pollitt, 1957; Rasmussen & Tsuang, 1986). Gojer et al. (1987) found a primarily deteriorating course after discharge in 53 OCD clients, with 66% deteriorating, 17% fluctuating, 11% remaining the same, 2% improving, and 4% not identifiable.

Clients in most treatment studies report 10- to 12-year average symptom durations, indicating that many have suffered for long periods before seeking relief. Interestingly, married clients sought treatment later than unmarried ones, according to one study (Khanna et al., 1986); perhaps the marital relationships provided these clients with emotional support, delaying the need for treatment. Alternatively, clients who are able to marry may have less severe symptoms, though this has not been studied.

OCD symptoms do not appear to occur commonly among immediate family members, suggesting that neither genetic transmission nor direct modeling can easily account for their appearance in children. As shown in Table 2.4, three studies reported no cases of OCD among parents of clients, and one reported an 8% incidence in fathers and 12% in mothers. Five of six studies using diagnostic criteria based on DSM-III indicated that the incidence of OCD among relatives was considerably less than 10% (Black, Noyes, Goldstein, & Blum, 1992). Only one study indicated that 25% of parents of OCD children had diagnosable OCD, with father–son pairs predominant (Swedo, Rapoport, Leonard, Lenane, & Cheslow, 1989). Interestingly, symptoms often were not similar in type between the generations (e.g., washing in parent and checking in child).

Although OCD is not frequently diagnosed among parents of OCD clients, obsessional personality traits have been found in up to 40% of

TABLE 2.4. Percentage of Obsessive Compulsive (OC) Symptoms and Personality Traits in Parents of Individuals with OCD

Study	OC symptoms	OC personality traits
Lewis (1936)		37% obsessional
Balslev-Olesen & Geert-Jorgensen (1959)		45% perfectionistic
Kringlen (1965)	8% fathers 12% mothers	
Lo (1967)	8%	9% obsessional 26% perfectionistic 13% overprotective 16% rejecting
Carey & Gottesman (1981)	6% (OCD diagnosis)	8% obsessional symptoms
Coryell (1981)	0	
Insel et al. (1983)	0	30% obsessional (Leyton Obsessional Inventory)
Rasmussen & Tsuang (1986)	2% fathers 7% mothers	
Lenane et al. (1990)	29% fathers 9% mothers	
Honjo et al. (1989)	0	42% obsessional (mothers) 53% perfectionistic (fathers) 13% overprotective (mothers)
Swedo et al. (1989)	25%	
Riddle et al. (1990)	19% (OCD diagnosis)	52% obsessional symptoms
Pauls et al. (1991)	22%	

mothers, according to findings from studies listed in Table 2.4. Clinical impressions correspond with these findings; clients often report that one or both of their parents have obsessional traits that are ego-syntonic and therefore not experienced as problematic. In addition to obsessional traits, perfectionism appeared in up to half of the parents in this research, and overprotection was found in more than 10%. Social isolation of those suffering from OCD has also been noted. Kringlen (1965) found that 40% of clients lived with little contact with friends or relatives because of their symptoms. Compared with population-norms, social support networks for OCD clients were smaller and perceived by clients as less adequate (Steketee, 1987).

Precipitating Factors

Several investigators have pointed to the lack of conclusive information about precipitating factors for the development of OCD (McKeon, Bridget, & Mann, 1984; Khanna et al., 1986; Rasmussen & Tsuang, 1986). However, arguments for clear precipitants (e.g., sexual trauma, medical events, childbirth) in about 60% of cases have been advanced in several studies (Ingram, 1961; Lo, 1967; Pollitt, 1957; Rasmussen & Tsuang, 1984). Although Goodwin et al. (1969) observed that nearly half of their OCD sample could identify precipitants, these were considered to have doubtful significance. Almost all clients related increases in symptoms in response to life stresses, and one group of researchers observed that those with abnormal personality characteristics seemed to require fewer stressful life events to bring about onset of their illness (McKeon et al., 1984).

It seems likely that some studies have confounded precipitants for *exacerbation* with those for *onset*, clouding the picture of possible etiological factors. This seems particularly likely in view of the difficulty in separating first-time occurrences from recurrences with new obsessions or compulsions. It is clear, however, that the environmental factors involved in the etiology of OCD are uncertain. The identification of a particular event as a precipitant for OCD often represents speculation on the part of client, family members, and clinician. Such identifications may depend heavily on individuals' "theories" regarding what they believe may "cause" onset of OCD.

Relationships to Other Disorders

Several disorders have been likened to OCD and may respond favorably to treatments appropriate for this disorder. The somatic preoccupations and repeated requests for medical reassurance found in hypochondriasis closely resemble the obsessive fears and compulsive rituals of OCD (Salkovskis &

Warwick, 1986; Tynes, White, & Steketee, 1990). Some clients, such as those who compulsively search for medical abnormalities (e.g., breast cancer), lie on the border between obsessive and hypochondriacal. Whether clients are perceived as having illness obsessions (e.g., fear of AIDS or cancer) or hypochondriasis may depend more on where they first seek treatment—a psychiatric versus a medical clinic—than on the actual clinical picture.

Anorexics' fears of becoming fat and their discomfort with fullness resemble obsessions. Likewise, bulimics' vomiting and purging constitute a type of active avoidance or ritual that relieves discomfort about gaining weight. Supporting an association of OCD with these two eating disorders are findings of a 33% lifetime prevalence of OCD (unrelated to food) in bulimic subjects (Hudson, Pope, Yurgelun-Todd, Jonas, & Frankenburg, 1988) and a 13% current incidence of OCD in anorexic and bulimic clients (compared with general population rates of 2.5% lifetime and 1.6% current) (Laessle, Wittchen, Fichter, & Pirke, 1989). Furthermore, drug and behavioral treatments similar to those found effective for OCD have also proven useful for anorexia and bulimia (e.g., Rosen & Leitenberg, 1982; Salkovskis, 1989).

Although body dysmorphic disorder (BDD) has recently drawn attention as an OCD-like syndrome (e.g., Brady, Austin, & Lydiard, 1990; Hollander, Liebowitz, Winchel, Klumker, & Klein, 1989), a noteworthy difference is the ego-syntonic nature of the ruminations of BDD clients (like those of anorexic clients). Medications helpful for OCD have also been useful for BDD (Hollander et al., 1989), and Phillips (1990) concludes that there is a convincing association with OCD, at least for some cases.

Trichotillomania has also been likened to OCD, primarily because of the feeling of "compulsion" to pull hair and the response of trichotillomania clients to serotonergic drugs, which are also effective for OCD symptoms (Swedo, Lenane, Leonard, & Rapoport, 1990). However, this disorder lacks the characteristic obsessive thought, and hair pulling is typically experienced as pleasurable or satisfying (positively reinforcing), rather than only discomfort-reducing (negatively reinforcing), as in OCD. Similar comments may be made about other "compulsive" disorders, such as gambling and kleptomania. Unless more convincing findings appear, these problems should probably be considered habit or impulse control disorders (Mansuedo & Goldfinger, 1990).

Comorbidity

Comorbidity in OCD is the rule more than the exception, according to most studies. Although Rasmussen and Tsuang (1986) reported that on admission to their clinic, 48% of adult OCD clients had no other current Axis I disorder, investigators of childhood OCD have observed comorbidity of up to 74%

(Swedo et al., 1989). It is noteworthy that mania and antisocial personality disorder have rarely co-occurred with OCD (Karno et al., 1988). Several types of comorbidity are identified below and listed in Table 2.5. Several are likely to present problems for treatment, as noted in Chapters 7 and 11.

Anxiety Disorders

Anxiety appears to be the most prevalent mood state in OCD, characterizing at least 75% of clients (Farid, 1986). Indeed, OCD is classified in DSM-IV as an anxiety disorder and is also commonly comorbid with several other anxiety disorders, although such anxiety comorbidity has not been identified as having any prognostic significance thus far. The lifetime risk for simple phobia is quite high, ranging from 50% to 77% (Karno et al., 1988; Rasmussen & Tsuang, 1986), but is considerably lower for social phobia (18%) and agoraphobia (9%) (Rasmussen & Tsuang, 1986). The frequency with which OCD and panic disorder co-occur ranges from 11% to 27% (Breier, Charney, & Heninger, 1986; Cloninger, Martin, Guze, & Clayton, 1981; Karno et al., 1988; Katon, 1984; Mellman & Uhde, 1987; Rasmussen & Tsuang, 1986). Clients with comorbid OCD and panic disorder are more symptomatic and more functionally impaired at different follow-up intervals than clients with panic disorder alone.

Among children and adolescents with OCD, comorbidity with other anxiety disorders (38–60%) is more common than with affective disorders (0–35%) (Last & Strauss, 1989; Riddle et al., 1990; Swedo et al., 1989). The most common comorbid anxiety disorders are simple phobia (17%) and overanxious disorder (16%) (Swedo et al., 1989). Anxiety disorders are also more common than affective disorders in first-degree relatives of OCD children (Last & Strauss, 1989).

Depression

Perhaps more than any other anxiety disorder, OCD is often complicated by depression (Barlow, DiNardo, & Vermilyea, 1986; Steketee et al., 1985). Depressed mood state appears to be extremely common (characterizing 45% of clients, according to Farid, 1986). A diagnosis of major depression has been found in 28–38% of OCD clients (Barlow et al., 1986; Karno et al., 1988; Rasmussen & Tsuang, 1986). The prevalence of all diagnosable depressive disorders (e.g., dysthymia, intermittent depressive disorder) has not been reported, but is likely to be considerably higher. Despite the high rate of depression, however, OCD clients appear to attempt suicide or report suicidal ideation only rarely (Coryell, 1981; Gittelson, 1966; Lewis, 1936). However,

TABLE 2.5. Comorbidity in OCD

	Study				
Type of disorder	Rasmussen & Tsuang (1986) (n = 44)	Katon (1984) (n = 55)	Barlow et al. (1986) (n = 13)	Karno et al. (1988) (n = 468)	Rasmussen & Eisen (1989) (n = 100)
Simple phobia	27%	—	—	48%	7%
Social phobia	18%	—	15%	16%	11%
Panic and agoraphobia	9%	—	30%	—	—
Panic disorder	14%	11%	15%	12%	6%
Generalized anxiety disorder	—	—	8%	—	—
Post-traumatic stress disorder	—	—	—	—	—
Tourette's syndrome	5%	—	—	—	5%
Major depression	30%	—	38%	28%	31%
Substance abuse	—	—	—	24%	8%
Eating disorders	—	—	—	—	8%

one study found that those whose obsessions had become delusional in nature lost the "protective" effect of obsessions against suicide (Gittelson, 1966).

With respect to course of illness, depression typically follows the onset of OCD symptoms, probably because of the debilitation these symptoms cause. One study showed that 38% of 150 hospitalized OCD clients reported depression following OCD onset, with only 11% showing depression prior to OCD, and 13% having concurrent onset (Welner et al., 1976). Karno et al. (1988) have confirmed the tendency of OCD to precede onset of depression in an epidemiological sample. Whether the presence of depression threatens effective therapy is discussed further in Chapters 7 and 11.

Personality Disorders

It is not surprising that OCD has often been associated with the personality disorder that bears the same name (see Table 2.6 for the DSM-IV definition of obsessive compulsive personality disorder [OCPD]). However, fewer than 25% of those with OCD actually qualify for a diagnosis of OCPD, according to most studies (Black, 1974; Joffee, Swinson, & Regan, 1988; Mavissakalian,

TABLE 2.6. DSM-IV Draft Criteria for Obsessive Compulsive Personality Disorder (OCPD)

A pervasive pattern of preoccupation with orderliness, perfectionism, and mental and interpersonal control, at the expense of flexibility, openness, and efficiency, beginning by early adulthood and present in a variety of contexts, as indicated by at least four of the following:
(1) preoccupation with details, rules, lists, order, organization, or schedules to the extent that the major point of the activity is lost
(2) perfectionism that interferes with task completion (e.g., inability to complete a project because one's own overly strict standards are not met)
(3) excessive devotion to work and productivity to the exclusion of leisure activities and friendships (not accounted for by obvious economic necessity)
(4) overconscientiousness, scrupulousness, and inflexibility about matters of morality, ethics, or values (not accounted for by cultural or religious identification)
(5) inability to discard worn-out or worthless objects even when they have no sentimental value
(6) reluctant to delegate tasks or to work with others unless they submit to exactly his or her way of doing things
(7) adopts a miserly spending style toward both self and others; money is viewed as something to be hoarded for future catastrophes
(8) rigidity and stubbornness

Note. From American Psychiatric Association (1993). Copyright 1993 by the American Psychiatric Association. Reprinted by permission.

Hamann, & Jones, 1990; Steketee, 1990). Perhaps the primary feature distinguishing between these two disorders is that the repetitive acts of clients with OCD are ego-alien and typically resisted (at least in the initial phases of the disorder), whereas in OCPD they are typically ego-syntonic. Several traits of OCPD, including orderliness, rigidity, indecisiveness, and perfectionism, have commonly been found in clients with OCD (e.g., McKeon et al., 1984; Rasmussen & Eisen, 1989; Steketee, 1990).

Interestingly, Rasmussen and Tsuang (1986) have identified common *premorbid* personality traits that may have a bearing on the development of OCD. These include separation anxiety, resistance to change or novelty, risk aversion, ambivalence, excessive devotion to work, magical thinking, hypermorality, and perfectionism. OCD subjects had much higher scores on a measure of avoidance of harm than did nonpsychiatric controls (Pfohl, Black, Noyes, Kelley, & Blum, 1990). We (Frost, Steketee, Cohn, & Griess, 1991) have also identified perfectionism as a trait found in individuals with subclinical levels of OCD. To date, however, no systematic study of personality traits (as opposed to disorders) in OCD has been conducted, leaving considerable uncertainty about their potential role in the development and treatment of this disorder.

According to recent studies, the personality disorders that most frequently co-occur with OCD (see Table 2.7) are avoidant, dependent, and histrionic (Baer et al., 1990; Mavissakalian, Hamann, & Jones, 1990; Steketee, 1990). Schizotypal personality disorder appeared to be the predominant personality disorder in one sample—it was found in 32% of 43 clients (Jenike, Baer, Minichiello, Schwartz, & Carey, 1986)—though other studies have usually recorded lower frequencies (Joffee et al., 1988). Since poor outcome following behavioral and pharmacological treatment has been linked to some personality disorders, such as passive–aggressive (Steketee, 1990) and schizotypal (Minichiello, Baer, & Jenike, 1987), their diagnosis during the assessment process is important.

Psychosis

In 1878, Westphal noted the distinction between obsessive and psychotic thinking, describing the former as "abortive insanity," much like the French clinician Esquirol's (1838) term "insanity with insight." Several early studies (Ingram, 1961; Kringlen, 1965; Lo, 1967; Pollitt, 1957; Rosen, 1957) found schizophrenia developing in 0.6–6% of clients with OCD; the highest rate of 5–6% was derived from inpatient studies (Ingram, 1961; Kringlen, 1965). Karno et al. (1988) observed an unusually high rate of 12% comorbidity of OCD with schizophrenia. From a clinical standpoint, a decade or two ago it was not uncommon for clients with apparently straightforward "neurotic"

TABLE 2.7. Percentages of OCD Patients with Personality Disorder Diagnoses

Personality disorder	Baer et al. (1990) (n = 96; SIDP)	Rasmussen & Tsuang (1986) (n = 44; DSM-III Checklist)	Steketee (1990) (n = 26; PDQ-R [relatives])	Black et al. (1989) (n = 21; PDQ)	Joffee et al. (1988) (n = 23; MCMI)	Sanderson et al. (in press) (n = 21; SCID-II)	Stanley et al. (1990) (n = 25; SCID-II)
Dependent	18	5	39	24	56	5	4
Compulsive	14[a]	55	4	0	4	5	28
Avoidant	14	0	27	0	56	5	12
Passive-aggressive	1	0	8	0	61	0	0
Histrionic	13	9	31	24	17	5	12
Borderline	5	0	12	24	39	5	0
Narcissistic	0	0	0	0	9	0	0
Antisocial	0	0	0	0	13	0	0
Schizotypal	10	0	35	14	17	0	8
Paranoid	7	0	12	0	17	0	4
Schizoid	3	7	0	0	26	5	4
None	48	34	50	67	17	76	52

Note. SIDP, Structured Interview for Diagnosis of Personality Disorders; DSM-III *Diagnostic and Statistical Manual of Mental Disorders*, third edition; PDQ, Personality Diagnostic Questionnaire (-R, —Revised); MCMI, Millon Clinical Multiaxial Inventory; SCID-II, Structured Clinical Interview for DSM-III-R Personality Disorders.

[a]Baer et al. reported that according to SIDP-R criteria for DSM-III-R, this figure increased to 25%.

OCD symptoms to have received prior diagnoses of schizophrenia. Results of personality tests (such as the Minnesota Multiphasic Personality Inventory [MMPI] or Rorschach) and the seemingly peculiar content of their obsessions and compulsions undoubtedly misled diagnosing clinicians. Clinical experience with hundreds of clients seeking *outpatient* treatment for OCD suggests that psychotic symptoms occur infrequently in this group, and that transformations of nondelusional symptoms into delusional ones during therapy are also rare.

However, a small proportion of otherwise nonpsychotic OCD clients appear to display delusional or "overvalued" thinking, with little insight into the unreasonable nature of their obsessions and compulsions (Foa, 1979; Insel & Akiskal, 1986; McKenna, 1984; Perse, 1988). Suggestions for classification of these clients range from placing them in a separate diagnostic category somewhere between OCD and psychoses (Perse, 1988) to specifying their place along a continuum from typical OCD to "obsessive compulsive psychosis" (Ballerini & Stanghellini, 1989; Insel & Akiskal, 1986). Such clients have failed to respond to behavior therapy (Foa, 1979) or to anti-depressant medication (Perse, 1988), but may respond to cognitive therapy directed at negative automatic thoughts associated with obsessive fears (Salkovskis & Warwick, 1986). Chapter 4 addresses this issue further.

These clients with "overvalued" obsessive fears should not be confused with the many clients who, when stressed and highly anxious, report confusion about the reality of their fears. During assessment, many clients comment that they are embarrassed to describe their obsessions and compulsions because these are so obviously unreasonable and ridiculous. Nonetheless, during anxiety-provoking exposure to feared situations, these same individuals often express uncertainty about whether their feared disaster is likely to occur (e.g., whether touching pizza sauce is safe, since it might actually be blood and lead to their contracting AIDS). The distinction between overvalued ideas and apparently "normal" uncertainty under duress is discussed further in Chapter 6 on assessment and in Chapter 8 on implementation of direct exposure sessions.

Alcoholism

Recent studies suggest that OCD occurs in 6–12% of alcohol-dependent clients—a rate substantially higher than expected from population prevalence rates (Eisen & Rasmussen, 1989; Riemann, McNally, & Cox, 1992). On the other hand, OCD clinic clients do not have higher-than-expected rates of alcohol dependence; they may in fact have lower rates, according to most studies (Barlow et al., 1986; Hasin & Grant, 1987; Karno et al., 1988; Rasmussen & Tsuang, 1986; Riemann et al., 1992; Welner et al., 1976), although some reports are contradictory (Eisen & Rasmussen, 1989; Mellman & Uhde, 1987; Zohar & Insel, 1986). A 24% rate of alcohol abuse was found by Karno et al. (1988) in a large epidemiological study of a population sample meeting criteria for OCD. Alcohol abuse typically followed the reported onset of OCD, suggesting that alcohol may serve as self-medication for anxiety. Regardless of the uncertainty evident in these data, identifying those who are abusing alcohol or drugs is likely to assist in improving clinical outcome, since substance abuse will undoubtedly adversely affect compliance with treatment regimens and maintenance of gains after therapy ends.

Other Disorders

An overlap between Gilles de la Tourette's syndrome and OCD has been repeatedly observed, with most researchers agreeing that there is a genetic link between these two disorders (see Green & Pitman, 1991). However, the frequency of obsessive and compulsive symptoms in clients with Tourette's (up to 68%) is considerably higher than the presence of motor and vocal tics in individuals with OCD (5%) (e.g., Rasmussen & Eisen, 1990).

Comment

Methods for assessment of OCD symptoms, comorbidity, personality traits and disorders, and substance use are detailed in Chapters 6 and 7. Readers may wish to proceed directly to those chapters for details, returning later to Chapters 3, 4, and 5 for a review of theoretical models and treatment findings for OCD.

3

Behavioral Conceptualization and Treatment of OCD

Early Treatments

Early conceptualizations of the development of OCD were based primarily on psychodynamic models derived from Freud's (1924) theories (e.g., the "Rat Man") and elaborated by other psychoanalytic theorists such as Fenichel (1945). However, treatments derived from these models and implemented in inpatient and outpatient settings did not lead to substantial improvement. For example, reports of 138 psychoanalytically treated cases of "compulsion neurosis" showed only 20% "apparently cured" after follow-up at variable intervals (Knight, 1941). An early study of 60 patients with "obsessional states" treated with psychotherapy found 15% "much improved" and 42% "improved" immediately after treatment, and 32% and 20%, respectively, at a 3-year follow-up (Luff & Garrod, 1935). Similarly, Coryell (1981) observed that OCD patients were less likely to experience remission after discharge than were depressed patients (22% vs. 64%). Although results of follow-up studies indicated that outpatients benefited more than inpatients, the average figures of approximately 60% improved were not considered impressive (Black, 1974; Cawley, 1974).

Not surprisingly, OCD gained a reputation as an intractable disorder. It was not until the late 1960s and early 1970s that newly developed intensive behavioral treatments showed considerable promise. Known as "exposure" and "response (ritual) prevention," these strategies were largely derived from learning theory models, discussed below.

Behavioral Theory

Mowrer's two-stage theory for the acquisition and maintenance of fear and avoidance behavior has been commonly adopted to account for the development of anxiety disorders (Dollard & Miller, 1950; Mowrer, 1960), though most agree that the model is inadequate as it stands. This theory has been refined more recently by others (e.g., Rachman, 1971, 1977; Foa & Kozak, 1986). In the first of the two stages, the fear acquisition phase, the theory posits that a neutral event becomes associated with fear by being immediately paired with an aversive stimulus that automatically provokes discomfort or anxiety. Obsessive fears are hypothesized to begin as do phobias—that is, via an association of a particular cue with a traumatic event. For example, concrete neutral objects (e.g., knives, toilets, or electrical appliances), as well as specific thoughts and images (e.g., the number 13 or an image of the devil), may acquire the ability to produce discomfort by being paired with an aversive experience.

The evidence used to support this fear acquisition stage of the model has been found to be inadequate (e.g., Rachman & Wilson, 1980). Many, if not most, patients cannot recall specific conditioning events associated directly with symptom onset. It seems likely that other modes of acquisition, such as observation (modeling) or informational learning, are needed to account for the onset of OCD (see Rachman, 1977; Foa & Kozak, 1986). An example of the former is found in the case of one woman who recalled, after she had already touched blood in a hospital sink, that many of the children who used the bathroom were from drug-abusing families at high risk for AIDS. Modeling is evident in the numerous clients who report that their fears and behaviors are similar to parental patterns of behavior, though it is noteworthy that parents afflicted with OCD often have rituals differing from those of their children (Swedo et al., 1989). Similar patterns are evident in hoarding rituals that mimic the excessive saving by parents of unneeded objects in case they might be useful someday.

Although onset often follows very stressful life events, it rarely does so *immediately*, as postulated by the traumatic-onset theory. Watts (1971) has suggested that stressful events may serve to sensitize the individual to cues that have an innate tendency to elicit fear. Similarly, other theorists have proposed that anxiety responses learned during early aversive or traumatic experiences may be enhanced by stress (Teasdale, 1974), and that individuals may experience heightened arousal when certain thoughts have special cultural or historical significance (Rachman, 1971). Historical and cross-cultural accounts of OCD clearly implicate the environmental milieu as an important determinant of the types of OCD symptoms manifested. For example, as noted in Chapter 2, sexual contamination fears associated with syphilis and gonorrhea in the early 1970s were replaced in the 1980s by fears of herpes, and in the 1990s by AIDS obsessions. Similarly, cultural influences on obsessions are evident in the preponderance of cleaning rituals in Egypt, which are presumably attributable to Moslem religious rites (Okasha, Kamel, & Hassan, 1968); in the phenomon of *koro*, a fear of penile shrinkage found

in Chinese cultures (Lo, 1967); and fears of "bad
tuberculosis or leprosy, in northern Sudan (Elsarrag,

In the second proposed stage of symptom developn.
Miller's (1950) model, any actions (escape, avoidance, i
obsessive fear or discomfort are negatively reinforced, becau.
an unpleasant event and are very likely to be repeated i.
situations. For many clients with OCD, both external cues (o
tions) and internal triggers (thoughts, images, or impulses) a.
producing fear. Because many of these cannot be avoided eas   .en as
going to the bathroom or having to lock the front door on leaving the house,
passive avoidance behaviors are often ineffective in controlling anxiety. Un-
like phobics, who can often simply avoid feared situations, obsessive compulsives need more active avoidance or escape strategies (compulsions) to
prevent perceived future harm or restore a feeling of safety (Rachman, 1976a).

There is substantial evidence that obsessions increase discomfort and
compulsions reduce it. Ruminative (obsessive) thoughts have been found to
increase heart rate and skin conductance more than neutral thoughts
(Boulougouris, Rabavilas, & Stefanis, 1977; Rabavilas & Boulougouris,
1974). Similarly, direct contact with substances believed to be contaminated
has resulted in increased subjective anxiety, heart rate (Hodgson & Rachman,
1972), and skin conductance (Hornsveld, Kraaimaat, & van Dam-Baggen,
1979). As hypothesized, performance of rituals leads to reductions in anxiety
in most instances (Hodgson & Rachman, 1972; Hornsveld et al., 1979; Roper
& Rachman, 1976; Roper, Rachman, & Hodgson, 1973). Some clients with
a chronic history of OCD report an increase rather than a decrease in
discomfort following compulsions; however, this experience can be ascribed
readily to these clients' immediate frustration with their inability to control
time-consuming and obviously unwanted rituals. In general, then, the two-
stage theory is supported more with respect to maintenance of OCD symptoms than to their onset.

According to the behavioral model described above, treatment can be
considered effective only if it (1) disconnects obsessions from their associated
discomfort and (2) eliminates ritualistic behaviors that negatively reinforce
obsessive fears. Reduction in obsessions alone may resolve the fears of those
with recently acquired OCD symptoms (Walton & Mather, 1963). However,
for those with chronic symptoms, rituals may have acquired functional
autonomy, maintained by stress, mood state, and multiple environmental
cues (Foa, Steketee, & Milby, 1980). That is, after a period of time, rituals
may serve to reduce negative feelings in general, regardless of their source.
Indeed, many clients have commented that they tend to ritualize in reaction
to stress that is unrelated to obsessive fears (e.g., after marital arguments or job
difficulties, before a menstrual period).

Because rituals terminate exposure to feared obsessive situations and efore interfere with habituation of anxiety, they must be prevented during treatment. However, merely blocking rituals without also exposing clients to the sources of obsessive anxiety is unlikely to be helpful. Although prohibiting rituals (e.g., handwashing) may force some clients into random contact with feared situations (e.g., supposed contaminants), it is likely simply to increase avoidance. Without direct and prolonged exposure to discomfort-provoking cues, it seems unlikely that obsessive fears will dissipate substantially.

Behavioral Treatment

Strategies for accomplishing the therapeutic tasks of exposure and ritual prevention for OCD clients have included various exposure methods and blocking strategies. Exposure techniques require clients to confront anxiety-evoking material, either directly (*in vivo*) or in imagination, and include systematic desensitization, paradoxical intention, satiation/habituation training, and imaginal or *in vivo* flooding. Blocking, on the other hand, interrupts clients' ruminations or ritualistic behaviors via methods such as thought stopping, aversion therapy via electrical shock or other methods, distraction, and ritual (response) prevention. These methods and their efficacy are discussed below.

Exposure Procedures

One procedure to reduce anxiety, systematic desensitization, consists of the pairing of a relaxed state with very brief presentations (up to 1 minute) of anxiety-evoking items arranged in a hierarchical order; treatment begins with the least threatening and progresses up the hierarchy only when relaxation can be maintained (Wolpe, 1958). Ritualistic behavior is typically not addressed. Multiple-case studies using desensitization have yielded consistently poor results: Only 30–40% were improved with imaginal desensitization procedures (Beech & Vaughn, 1978; Cooper, Gelder, & Marks, 1965). Desensitization in actual practice (*in vivo*) led to more improvement, with 7 of 11 clients (64%) benefiting (Beech & Vaughn, 1978). Although this method has been unhelpful with chronic cases of OCD, it may be more successful with symptoms of very recent onset (Walton & Mather, 1963). Unfortunately, most reports have indicated that desensitization is not an efficient treatment, requiring an average of 25 sessions (Steketee & Lam, 1993).

Several procedures utilizing prolonged exposure have been employed with OCD clients. Noonan (1971) successfully employed "induced anxiety," requiring his client to experience intense anxiety and to describe the images that arose spontaneously. A similar approach, paradoxical intention, involves instructing clients to deliberately evoke problematic obsessive thoughts or behaviors, often with the addition of humor (e.g., a client may be told to try to be the "biggest mistake maker in the world"). Gertz (1966) reported that all 6 of his patients improved or recovered with this method, but in a larger study of 10 patients, only 5 improved (Solyom, Garza-Perez, Ledwidge, & Solyom, 1972).

In another prolonged exposure procedure, satiation, patients are asked to repeat their ruminations aloud, in writing, or by listening to audiotapes for periods of an hour or more. In two series of cases, only 3 of 10 patients improved with satiation (Emmelkamp & Kwee, 1977; Stern, 1978). However, when combined with aversion relief, satiation led to a better response (Solyom, Zamanzadeh, Ledwidge, & Kenny, 1971). This treatment consisted of a taped narrative of obsessions periodically interrupted by brief silences, which were followed by a mild electric shock. When the patient terminated the shock, the taped obsessional material resumed. Thus, the onset of obsessions was associated with relief from shock (negative reinforcement). In contrast to the effects of satiation alone, all four patients improved after the combined method and were recovered at follow-up. Recent investigations of the manner of presenting obsessional material during satiation have demonstrated that audiotaped exposure is more effective in reducing obsessions than just verbalizing the thoughts is (Salkovskis & Westbrook, 1989). Interestingly, exposure to videotaped repeated verbalizations of obsessions was successful in one case, and the effects generalized to untreated OCD symptoms (Milby, Meredith, & Rice, 1981).

In summary, variations of prolonged exposure seem to have limited effects on obsessions, unless they are of very recent onset. Positive results have been obtained with a combination of satiation and aversion relief procedures. Effects of exposure on ritualistic behavior appear to be very limited.

Blocking Procedures

Theoretically, if compulsions are carried out primarily because they reduce discomfort, they should disappear if they lead to an immediate increase rather than a decrease in discomfort. Following this model, aversion relief paradigms somewhat similar to those employed by Solyom et al. (1971) have been tried. In these paradigms, rituals were followed by shock, which ended as soon as the patient directly touched contaminants. Compulsions improved but were not eliminated in case studies (Marks, Crowe, Drewe, Young, & Dewhurst, 1969; Rubin & Merbaum, 1971). In a more typical aversive procedure (i.e., one employing aversion treatment without relief), three of five patients improved when obsessions and compulsions were divided into component steps that were then imagined by patients and followed by shock (Kenny, Mowbray, & Lalani, 1978). These methods have not been studied adequately, but it appears that aversive methods have generally yielded good results in case studies. However, merely punishing the ritualistic behavior associated with negative affect may result in relapse, according to findings by Walton (1960), who reported relapse in cases in which only the behavioral responses and not the obsessions were treated.

Aversive procedures have also been employed to reduce disturbing obsessions. Both shock and snapping a rubber band against the wrist have been successful in case studies (Bass, 1973; Mahoney, 1971; McGuire & Vallance, 1964). However, no group studies have been conducted that support these methods. Another blocking technique used for obsessions is thought stopping. In this method, obsessions are arranged from least to most disturbing, and clients are instructed to shout "Stop!" as soon as intrusive ruminations are evoked. The usefulness of thought stopping in reducing OCD symptoms appears to be limited even in case studies, and only one-third of clients participating in group trials have benefited from this procedure (Emmelkamp & Kwee, 1977; Stern, 1978; Stern, Lipsedge, & Marks, 1975). No studies of the effect of thought stopping on rituals, especially mental rituals, has been reported, though some researchers have proposed that it may be helpful (e.g., Salkovskis & Westbrook, 1989; Steketee & Cleere, 1990). Covert sensitization, another aversive method in which clients are asked to conjure up an extremely unpleasant image immediately following a ritual, has been used successfully in case studies (for a review, see Foa & Steketee, 1979).

Comparisons between Exposure and Blocking Procedures

To date, three studies have compared the effects of exposure and blocking treatments with "pure obsessionals" (i.e., patients with obsessions but with no apparent rituals; such patients are discussed in more detail later in the chapter). Systematic desensitization was found to be equivalent to covert sensitization, an aversive procedure (Kazarian & Evans, 1977). Likewise, thought stopping proved as effective as prolonged imaginal exposure to obsessions; both led to improvement in three of five clients (Emmelkamp & Kwee, 1977). When Stern (1978) compared satiation with thought stopping in a crossover design, again procedures were equivalent, but only two of seven clients improved.

It is noteworthy that in the efforts described earlier, treatments that addressed both obsessions and compulsions were more effective (e.g., aversion relief). The research findings suggest that applications of single treatments to single symptoms of OCD were only mildly to moderately helpful. Furthermore, with few exceptions, these investigations have failed to distinguish between antiobsessional and anticompulsive effects; without such information, it is difficult to determine the differential usefulness of each procedure. In view of the two-stage theoretical model described above, the absence of substantial benefit from unidimensional treatments does not seem surprising. Consistent with the theoretical model, considerable improvement in therapy outcome has come with the systematic application of exposure to obsessions and blocking or prevention to compulsions.

Treatment by Combined Exposure and Response Prevention

The combination of exposure procedures for obsessions and blocking methods for compulsions has proved to be extremely successful in reducing both types of symptoms immediately after treatment, as well as months and years later. Methods for implementing this combined treatment are detailed extensively in Chapters 8 through 10. Studies that have investigated the outcome of this behavioral therapy are described below.

Studies of Outcome

The combining of exposure for obsessions with response prevention for compulsions was first attempted by Meyer and his colleagues with hospitalized patients who had contamination fears and washing or cleaning rituals (Meyer & Levy, 1973; Meyer, Levy, & Schnurer, 1974). In this program, rituals were prevented by nursing staff, with the help of a hospital environment in which plumbing was turned off in OCD patients' rooms; all washing was strictly supervised. For several hours daily, patients were exposed directly to feared contaminants of increasing difficulty, with the encouragement of the hospital staff. Of 15 patients treated in this way, 10 were rated much improved or symptom-free, and the remaining 5 were rated moderately improved. Only 2 relapsed after 5 to 6 years. These remarkable results generated great interest in this combined treatment program. In another case series, Catts and McConaghy (1975) reported excellent results with six OCD clients, all of whom improved. After treatment, four were rated as improved on ritualistic behavior, one was judged much improved, and one became asymptomatic. Further improvement in both rituals and obsessions was noted at follow-up evaluations 9 to 24 months later.

To date, 25 open trials and controlled studies representing over 500 clients with OCD from several countries have examined the effects of exposure combined with prevention of rituals. Results of these studies are summarized in Table 3.1 and discussed below.

TABLE 3.1. Percentages of OCD Patients Improved with Combined Exposure and Ritual Prevention

Study	n	% subjects improved (much improved)			
		Posttest		Follow-up	
Meyer et al. (1974)	15	100	(67)	84	(67)
Marks et al. (1975)	20	75	(40)	75	(70)
Roper et al. (1975)	10	80	(50)	80	(40)
Rabavilas et al. (1976)	12	83	(50)	83	(50)
Boersma et al. (1976)	13	—	—	77	(54)
Foa & Goldstein (1978)	21	95	(81)	87	(74)
Foa, Grayson, et al. (1983)	50	76	(38)	76	(59)
Julien et al. (1980)	18	94	(67)	83	(60)
Emmelkamp et al. (1985)	42	81	(38)	81	(57)
Foa et al. (1984)	12	70	(60)	88	(44)
Hoogduin & Hoogduin (1984)	25	84	(80)	84	(80)
Emmelkamp et al. (1988)	18	89	(22)	100	(22)
Marks et al. (1988)	12	—	—	80	(50)
Emmelkamp et al. (1989)	14	86	(57)	79	(57)
Foa et al. (1992)	38	97	(97)	82	(82)

A series of studies was conducted on OCD inpatients at the Maudsley Hospital in London, providing considerable additional information about the effectiveness of exposure *in vivo* (flooding) and of response prevention that involved blocking rituals and avoidance behaviors (Hodgson, Rachman, & Marks, 1972; Marks, Hodgson, & Rachman, 1975; Rachman, Hodgson, & Marks, 1971; Rachman, Marks, & Hodgson, 1973). Variants of direct exposure were compared with relaxation training, both combined with response prevention, for 20 patients. After 15 daily sessions (3 weeks) of the exposure regimen, 8 patients were much improved, 7 were improved, and 5 failed to show change. By contrast, relaxation training had almost no effect. At a 2-year follow-up, 14 patients remained much improved, 1 was improved, and 5 were unchanged (Marks et al., 1975).

Comparable results with 10 washers were reported by Roper, Rachman, and Marks (1975), who again used a 15-session treatment over a 3-week period. Five patients who observed the therapist modeling exposure to disturbing objects (passive modeling) were compared with five control subjects who received relaxation exercises. Again, relaxation had little effect on OCD symptoms. Both groups were then given 15 additional daily sessions of *in vivo* exposure (participant modeling) and prevention of rituals. At the end of treatment, three patients were much improved, five were improved, and two remained unchanged, with very similar results evident at follow-up. These studies from the Maudsley Hospital indicate that approximately 75–80% of subjects benefited substantially after 15 sessions of exposure and ritual prevention.

In two studies by Greek investigators (Boulougouris & Bassiakos, 1973; Rabavilas, Boulougouris, & Stefanis, 1976), an average of 11 sessions combining *in vivo* and imaginal exposure with response prevention produced very good results: 13 patients (87%) improved after treatment, whereas only 2 remained unchanged. However, a long-term follow-up of these patients 2 to 5 years later was somewhat disappointing: 6 of the 15 patients (40%) failed to maintain their gains (Boulougouris, 1977).

Emmelkamp and his colleagues in the Netherlands conducted three studies with OCD outpatients, using 10–15 sessions of *in vivo* exposure and blocking of compulsions. In the first study, 7 of 13 clients treated in their homes were symptom-free, 3 were improved, and 3 were unchanged after therapy; similar findings were obtained at follow-up (Boersma, Den Hengst, Dekker, & Emmelkamp, 1976). Emmelkamp and Kraanen (1977) reported a significant mean reduction in symptoms for their 13 clients, with only 2 failing to benefit and 6 requiring additional sessions. Emmelkamp, van der Helm, van Zanten, and Plochg (1980) treated 15 OCD clients in 10 sessions, obtaining significant gains comparable to those reported in the Maudsley studies. Slight relapse was evident at follow-up, and on average clients required an additional 15 treatment sessions; these findings suggest that 10 sessions may be too few to lastingly reduce obsessions and rituals.

In France, Julien, Rivière, and Note (1980) provided further support for the effectiveness of direct exposure and response prevention. Of their 20 patients, 2 dropped out of treatment, 12 were much improved, 5 improved moderately, and 1 remained unchanged. Overall, then, 15 of the original 20 (75%) improved at least moderately. Follow-up findings were similar to those of Emmelkamp and colleagues (1980): Assessments conducted 6 months to 3 years after treatment indicated moderate relapse.

Effects on Obsessions and on Compulsions

Somewhat more detailed information about the separate effects of exposure and response prevention on obsessions and on compulsions was provided by Foa and Goldstein's (1978) study of 21 clients in the United States. Most were treated on an outpatient basis, though a few who lived considerable distances from the clinic or who had no supervisory support at home were admitted to the hospital. Treatment consisted of 10 sessions of combined imaginal and *in vivo* exposure to feared obsessive situations, with supervised prevention of rituals. Two weeks of information gathering by the therapist to plan treatment had no effect on obsessions or compulsions, whereas very substantial changes

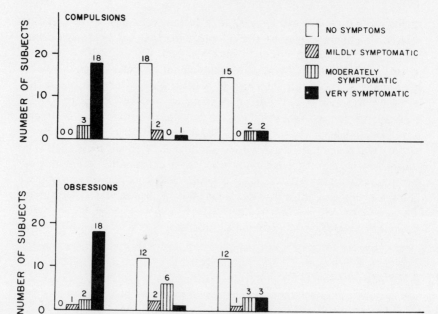

FIGURE 3.1. Changes in the frequency distribution of four categories reflecting severity of compulsions (upper part) and of obsessions (lower part). Follow-up data refer to the most recent observation. From Foa and Goldstein (1978). Copyright 1978 by the Association for Advancement of Behavior Therapy. Reprinted by permission.

occurred after behavioral therapy. Figure 3.1 illlustrates the findings: 18 (86%) stopped ritualizing after treatment, with only 3 relapses an average of 1.5 years later. Somewhat less positive results were obtained for obsessions: 12 clients (57%) were asymptomatic after treatment, and 2 clients relapsed at follow-up. These results suggest that compulsions respond more readily to exposure and response prevention than do obsessions—a finding that has been borne out in subsequent studies of both exposure therapy and pharmacotherapy.

Comparisons with Other Procedures

As noted earlier, combined exposure and prevention of compulsions were shown to be more effective than relaxation therapy (Hodgson et al., 1972; Rachman et al., 1971). The combination also proved superior to marital therapy in a study of 11 patients (Cobb, McDonald, Marks, & Stern, 1980). Marital treatment improved marital problems but not OCD symptoms, whereas the combined treatment improved both the OCD symptoms and marital satisfaction. Although the combination of exposure and response prevention has not been compared to combinations of other exposure and blocking treatments (e.g., desensitization or paradoxical intention and thought stopping or aversion therapy), it is doubtful that these treatments could improve upon its success rate. Nor does it seem likely that expectancy alone could account for the success of exposure and response prevention. The Maudsley studies did not assess this issue. However, in a study examining the separate and combined effects of exposure and response prevention, we (Steketee, Foa, & Grayson, 1982) controlled for expectancy, as well as for frequency and duration of treatment. None of these accounted for the superior results obtained by the combined procedure.

Degree of Improvement

In summary, in numerous studies conducted in various centers around the world, combined exposure and response prevention produced significant and substantial improvement in most measures of OCD symptoms over time. Not surprisingly, the most positive results were evident in measures of target obsessions and compulsions, where the average benefit ranged from 40% to 75%. On standardized paper-and-pencil measures, such as the Maudsley Obsessional–Compulsive Inventory (MOC) and the Compulsive Activity Checklist (CAC), the degree of improvement was only slightly lower. The Leyton Obsessional Inventory (LOI), arguably a less adequate measure of OCD symptoms (see Chapter 7), showed a somewhat lower range of 35–52% average improvement across six studies. At follow-ups ranging from 3 months to 6 years, treatment gains were in the 45–70% range for target symptoms, with questionnaire measures showing slightly more decline: MOC scores and CAC scores averaged 50% improvement. Overall, then, most measures indicated that OCD symptoms were 50–70% improved following behavioral treatment.

With respect to the number of subjects who were improved after behavioral treatment, many investigators defined their categories of improvement quite differently, making it difficult to compare results across studies. On average, however, roughly 85% of clients were at least "improved," and about 55% fell into the "much improved" or "very much improved" categories (meaning that target symptoms improved by more than half) (see Table 3.1). At follow-up, the percentage of subjects who were at least "improved" was quite high, averaging about 75%, and approximately 50% of clients were "much improved" or "very much improved." Thus, results were largely maintained, though some relapse was evident and some clients needed additional therapy (Emmelkamp, Visser, & Hoekstra, 1988; Foa & Goldstein, 1978). The extent of improvement and the consistency of these results across multiple treatment sites and countries are quite impressive. There can be little doubt that the combination of exposure and ritual prevention is a powerful treatment for OCD symptoms.

Use of Exposure and Response Prevention in Clinical Practice

That this research-based treatment is transferable to routine clinical practice has been demonstrated by Kirk (1983), who reported on 36 clinic outpatients treated with combined exposure and ritual prevention. Of these clients, 58% achieved their goals and 17% were moderately improved, leaving 25% with unsatisfactory outcomes. Modifications to research-based treatments in this study included greater reliance on homework assignments than on accompanied direct practice, unless the therapist's presence was required to facilitate progress. In addition, relatives or friends played an important part in treatment in one-third of cases. Additional treatments, such as assertiveness training and marital therapy, were used in several cases. Finally, treatment was relatively brief, with more than half of the clients having 10 or fewer sessions specifically directed at the OCD symptoms.

Efficiency of Treatments

In addition to its superior performance in treating OCD symptoms, the combination of exposure and response prevention appears to be somewhat more cost-effective than other behavioral methods. Usually, it has been administered in 10–20 sessions applied over 4–12 weeks. Thus, a greater frequency of sessions, ranging from two to five times per week, is typical of this therapy. As O'Sullivan, Noshirvani, Marks, Monteiro, and Lelliott (1991) observed, better long-term gains were associated with longer trials of exposure therapy. The combined method so far best combines efficiency and effectiveness.

Differential Effects of Exposure and Response Prevention

Meyer's original treatment consisted of two basic components: exposure to discomfort-provoking cues, and prevention of ritualistic responses. These treatments have typically been employed in tandem, preventing examination of the separate effect of each procedure. Theoretically, exposure should be necessary to reduce anxiety associated with obsessions. Because ritualistic behavior terminates confrontation with the anxiety-evoking stimuli, it should be simultaneously blocked to permit extinction of anxiety reactions.

In multiple-case studies, response prevention was found to reduce compulsions, whereas exposure alone had little effect on rituals (Mills, Agras, Barlow, & Mills, 1973). Furthermore, the addition of exposure after rituals had already been prevented for a period of time did not further reduce them (Turner, Hersen, Bellack, Andrasik, & Capparell, 1980). With regard to obsessional anxiety, some reduction was evident during response prevention, with further improvement resulting from exposure. We (Foa, Steketee, & Milby, 1980) investigated this question in a between-subjects design, assigning eight clients with washing rituals to 10 sessions of either exposure alone or response prevention alone, both groups receiving combined treatment thereafter. Not surprisingly, exposure affected subjective anxiety (obsessions) more than it did rituals, whereas response prevention reduced rituals more than it did obsessions. The addition of the missing component led to improvement in both symptoms. A second study was then conducted to compare these single treatments with combined therapy in three separate groups; this permitted examination of the effects of single components at follow-up (Foa, Steketee, Grayson, Turner, & Latimer, 1984). Again, anxiety in reaction to supposed contaminants was reduced mainly by exposure, whereas ritualistic behavior was affected more by response prevention. Combined treatment led to superior results after treatment and at follow-up 1 year later. Thus, findings from case and group studies support the suggestion that exposure and prevention of rituals operate by separate mechanisms.

Processes during Exposure

Findings from several clinical studies point to particular processes underlying the effectiveness of exposure treatment. These include physiological and subjective activation of anxiety during exposure (reactivity), and the gradual decrease (habituation) of these reactions within and between exposure sessions (Foa & Kozak, 1986).

Reactivity

Foa, I, and our colleagues observed that the greater the initial subjective reaction to obsessive situations, the less clients habituated during exposure treatment (Foa, Grayson, et al., 1983). In addition, heart rate reactivity was positively correlated with outcome (Kozak, Foa, & Steketee, 1988). Surprisingly, in the latter study, subjective anxiety ratings taken at the same time were not significantly associated with outcome—possibly because nearly all clients reported very high anxiety levels, reducing the range of scores on this variable.

Habituation

With regard to *in vivo* exposure, we (Grayson, Foa, & Steketee, 1982) reported gradual heart rate reduction for obsessive compulsive washers exposed to feared contaminants for 90 minutes. Similar habituation of physiological and self-reported anxiety within a single session has also been reported in other studies (Foa, Grayson, & Steketee, 1982; Shahar & Marks, 1980), with faster reduction evident in later exposure sessions (Likierman & Rachman, 1982). Interestingly, subjective discomfort decreased more rapidly than urges to wash in the first few sessions, suggesting that obsessive fears and compulsive urges do not necessarily decline in synchrony during exposure and response prevention treatment. Higher levels of discomfort may require a longer period to decline.

A decrease in subjective and physiological anxiety has also been observed between (across) sessions (Shahar & Marks, 1980). Such a decrement has been observed even when increasingly difficult situations were added in the course of exposure treatment (Foa & Chambless, 1978; Hafner & Marks, 1972). Not surprisingly, greater habituation between sessions was associated with more change following treatment (Foa, Steketee, Grayson, & Doppelt, 1983; Kozak et al., 1988). The above-discussed reports argue for the need of clinicians to attend to subjective and physiological habituation processes as an indicator of the efficacy of exposure treatment.

Distraction and Attention Focusing

Grayson, Foa, and I observed that more habituation of heart rate occurred when attention was focused on the feared object rather than distracted from it (Grayson et al., 1982; Grayson, Steketee, & Foa, 1986). Although no other studies of OCD have examined this issue, these findings suggest that greater benefit will accrue from focusing on feared situations or thoughts than from avoiding them. Thus, therapists should request in standard clinical practice that clients concentrate on obsessive situations during exposure, avoiding distracting circumstances that might interfere with processing of fearful information.

Generalization of Exposure Effects to Related Obsessions

Very little information is available regarding generalization of habituation effects. One single-case study showed that habituation to the visual form of the number 13 generalized to auditory, behavioral, and cognitive forms of the same number (Moergen, Maier, Brown, & Pollard, 1987). Further information about factors affecting generalization of exposure benefits to similar and to different obsessional fears is needed. For example, some clients show a chronic symptom course in which the content of obsessive fears periodically changes. Will successful exposure to current obsessive fears generalize to other potential fear stimuli? If not, will exposure to any general themes underlying the fears (e.g., risk taking, perfectionism) lead to longer-lasting gains?

Problems in the Treatment of Pure Obsessives

Many investigators have puzzled over the question of why exposure reduces obsessions in ritualizers, but fails to do so consistently in obsessive clients who have no apparent rituals. Recall that satiation (prolonged exposure to obsessions) has led to little more than 50% improvement in such "pure obsessionals" (e.g., Emmelkamp & Kwee, 1977; Stern, 1978). One possibility is that although they do not display overt compulsions, these clients do have mental rituals that remain undetected and therefore are not treated with response prevention (Rachman, 1971; Robertson, Wendiggensen, & Kaplan, 1983; Salkovskis & Westbrook, 1989; Steketee & Foa, 1985). That is, anxiety-evoking obsessive thoughts are interspersed with cognitions that briefly reduce discomfort.

Prolonged exposure to the entire chain in such cases may fail in two ways. First, rituals may be strengthened rather than reduced, since they are repeatedly evoked during exposure and therefore continue to maintain obsessions. In fact, Salkovskis and Westbrook (1989) reported preliminary results demonstrating that following an obsessive thought with a "neutralizing" (compulsive) one designed to reduce anxiety actually *increased* discomfort. This accords with Wegner's (1989) findings that efforts to suppress even neutral thoughts produce a rebound effect of actually increasing them. Second, the frequent interruption of the obsessions by cognitive rituals may prevent prolonged exposure and thus may interfere with habituation. Unfortunately, there are as yet no data pertaining to this issue for mental rituals, though findings regarding duration of exposure for obsessions with overt compulsions support this notion (Rabavilas et al., 1976).

These speculations suggest that for effective treatment, exposure should be applied only to anxiety-provoking thoughts, and mental rituals should be blocked—perhaps via thought stopping, distraction, or direct substitution of nonritualistic thoughts. Indeed, several researchers have demonstrated the success of this latter strategy (Headland & MacDonald, 1987; Rachman, 1971; Salkovskis, 1983; Salkovskis & Westbrook, 1989), particularly with the use of uninterrupted audiotaped exposures to narrated obsessions.

Summary

Psychotherapeutic treatments for OCD based on psychodynamic models of this disorder have not been adequately studied; however, reports on outcome for inpatients are consistently negative, and those for outpatients leave room for improvement. Behavioral treatments have improved the picture some-what, but many of these methods, such as systematic desensitization, para-doxical intention, satiation, thought stopping, and aversion therapy, have provided limited benefits. Combined strategies that address obsessive fears as well as compulsive rituals are more effective. Among such combined methods, exposure and ritual prevention have consistently led to substantial improvement in both obsessions and compulsions, with relatively few treat-ment sessions. The differential effects of exposure on obsessive thoughts, images, or impulses, and of response prevention on frequency and duration of rituals, have been demonstrated in several studies.

The transferability of exposure and ritual prevention from research settings to the clinic has been demonstrated, with some modifications that are discussed in later chapters. Treatment for pure obsessives has been less successful than that for obsessive clients who also have overt rituals. A more careful assessment of covert or mental rituals is needed to determine how to apply exposure and blocking methods for pure obsessionals. Cognitive and biological models and their treatments for OCD are presented in the next two chapters.

4

Cognitive Theory and Treatment

OCD is fundamentally a disorder of cognitive processing, in that individuals experience intrusive unwanted thoughts, ideas, images, and impulses that provoke discomfort and are difficult to dismiss. It is important to note here that cognitive intrusions are reported by 80–99% of the general population, and therefore that such mental phenomena must be considered "normal" (e.g., Edwards & Dickerson, 1987; Niler & Beck, 1990; Parkinson & Rachman, 1981; Rachman & DeSilva, 1978). However, those who develop OCD experience more discomfort in response to these intrusions and have more difficulty dismissing them (Rachman & DeSilva, 1978).

Several researchers have investigated various cognitive features of those with OCD, but at present this research is still in its infancy. Thus, cognitive models to explain OCD symptoms, especially obsessive phenomena, are not well developed at this time, nor have treatments derived from such models been adequately tested. Of cognitive treatments tested, one (rational–emotive therapy, or RET) has shown promise in relieving symptoms in two trials by Emmelkamp and his colleagues (Emmelkamp & Beens, 1991; Emmelkamp et al., 1988). Cognitive treatments according to Beck's model (Beck, Emery, & Greenberg, 1985) remain untested except in case studies (e.g., Salkovskis & Warwick, 1986).

Despite the limitations of the research literature at this time, it seems clinically apparent that people with OCD often exhibit mental phenomena (e.g., overvalued ideas, perfectionistic attitudes) that may have abetted the development of the disorder and certainly interfere with treatment benefits. Modification of these thoughts or ideas seems needed, though the best method for doing so is unknown. Because of the apparent importance of such mental processes, a review and discussion of cognitive features and models for OCD are presented below, along with treatment findings and implications. Suggestions for managing cognitive complications during therapy are included as appropriate throughout the chapters on treatment implementation (see especially Chapter 11).

Cognitive Features of OCD

While assessing and treating obsessions and compulsions, clinicians can readily observe the cognitive distortions evident in many OCD clients. Several types of cognitive errors or irrational beliefs have been identified in the literature, and can be categorized as follows:

1. Risk/harm—overestimation of risk or harm, high negative valence associated with harm, risk aversion.
2. Doubt/uncertainty/decision making—doubting perceptions and memory, a need for certainty, difficulty making decisions or trusting them, difficulty categorizing and discriminating.
3. Perfectionism—perfectionistic attitudes.
4. Guilt/responsibility/shame—excessive feelings of responsibility, guilt or shame about thoughts or behaviors.
5. Rigidity/morality—moralistic attitudes, rigid rules (e.g., religious beliefs and practices).

Although this list does not include all possible cognitive features associated with OCD, it serves to organize the increasing information about beliefs and attitudes of those who suffer with this disorder. Obviously, some of these attitudes, such as difficulty making decisions and perfectionism, may be interdependent.

Risk/Harm

Several writers have pointed out that many OCD clients overestimate the risk of negative consequences for many actions (Foa & Kozak, 1985; Salkovskis, 1985; Steiner, 1972). Recently, investigators from Canada also identified overestimation of harm as a feature of volunteer subjects who complained of obsessive and compulsive symptoms (Freeston, Ladouceur, Gagnon, & Thibodeau, 1993). OCD clients often appear to exaggerate the probability or seriousness of ordinary concerns about health, safety, death, others' welfare, sex, morality, religious matters, and scrutiny by others (Carr, 1974).

McFall and Wollersheim (1979) have suggested that erroneous perceptions of threat that derive from perfectionistic ideals provoke anxiety in individuals with OCD. Tendencies to devalue their ability to deal adequately with such threats (which are consistent with their tendency to overestimate their likelihood of making mistakes; Walker, 1967) result in feelings of pervasive uncertainty, discomfort and helplessness. Rituals, McFall and Wollersheim have proposed, are viewed by clients as the only available methods for coping with the perceived threat, since other more appropriate coping resources are lacking. Similarly, Salkovskis (1985) has proposed that OCDs may not actually overestimate risk or harm, but rather overestimate their *responsibility* or blame for harm as a result of the basic assumptions they hold.

Kozak, Foa, and McCarthy (1987) have also noted that people with OCD appear to have difficulty with epistemological reasoning related to their excessive fear of harm. Instead of using the more common logic that a situation is safe unless it has been determined to be dangerous, they tend to assume that it is dangerous until proven safe. Since it is often difficult to demonstrate safety, those with OCD tend to seek extensive information about possible harm to assuage their fears.

Doubt/Uncertainty/Decision Making

Guidano and Liotti (1983) have suggested that because those with OCD tend to believe that every situation has a "correct" solution, they search for certainty. Along these lines, Beech and Liddell (1974) have proposed that ritualistic behaviors are maintained not only to reduce immediate discomfort, but also to address the obsessive compulsive's need for certainty before terminating an activity. Experimental findings lend some support to these assertions. Perhaps because of their need for certainty, obsessive compulsives appear to catalogue events in discrete categories, without being able to link concepts integratively. According to Makhlouf-Norris and colleagues, they create "islands of certainty" amidst confusion, in an effort to control and predict events (Makhlouf-Norris, Jones, & Norris, 1970; Makhlouf-Norris & Norris, 1972). Reed found that obsessive compulsives' thinking was characterized by underinclusion or overspecification of concepts (Reed, 1969), perhaps because of their intolerance of ambiguity (Reed, 1985).

Kozak et al. (1987), among others, have noted indecision as a cognitive feature in those with OCD. Reed (1968) attributed their doubt and indecision to a distrust of their own conclusions. Consistent with these findings, Persons and Foa (1984) observed that OCD clients utilized overly specific concepts (too many categories) in their thought patterns with respect to both obsessive and neutral word cues. More than other psychiatric clients, they requested a repetition of information before rendering a decision (Milner, Beech, & Walker, 1971); they also required more evidence before making a decision (Volans, 1976) and more time (Persons & Foa, 1984). In addition, they demonstrated more uncertainty and doubt about decisions already made than did phobics and nonpsychiatric controls (Sartory & Master, 1984; Volans, 1976). Pitman (1987) has suggested that OCD clients' pervasive sense of incompleteness and doubt may be attributable to an excess of "error signals" to the brain, resulting from neuroanatomical abnormalities.

From a different perspective, findings from analogue studies of compulsive checkers indicate that memory deficits more than perfectionistic attitudes may motivate repetitive checking behavior (Sher, Frost, & Otto, 1983; Sher, Mann, & Frost, 1984). In another analogue study, Freeston et al. (1993) identified intolerance of uncertainty as an important area of cognitive attitudes. It is clear from these studies of clinical and nonclinical populations that OCDs have difficulty making decisions and trusting those they have made.

Perfectionism

McFall and Wollersheim (1979) have also emphasized the erroneous beliefs of obsessive compulsives, especially the ideas that one must be perfectly competent in all endeavors and that failure to live up to perfectionistic ideas should be punished. Such mistaken beliefs, they have suggested, lead to erroneous perceptions of threat as discussed above, which provoke fear and overconcern with precision (Reed, 1985). Pitman (1987) has suggested that commonly observed perfectionistic actions of those with OCD illustrate an excess of control behavior, in which individuals attempt to match their perceptions to particular mental referents. A study of a nonclinical sample showed that overall perfectionism, and particularly scores on subscales measuring concern over mistakes and doubting of actions, were significantly related to obsessionality (Frost et al., 1991).

Guilt/Responsibility/Shame

Freeston, Ladouceur, Thibodeau, and Gagnon (1992) demonstrated that perceived responsibility and guilt were associated with compulsive activities in nonclinical subjects. Niler and Beck (1980) also found that guilt was the strongest predictor of the content of obsessive thoughts and compulsive rituals in a college student sample. Among clinical subjects, my colleagues and I (Steketee, Quay, & White, 1991) examined the roles of guilt and religiosity in OCD. We observed that guilt scores, as assessed by the Problematic Situations Questionnaire (Klass, 1987), were not higher in OCD subjects than in anxious controls; nor were OCDs more religious than anxious clients. However, severity of OCD symptoms (but not mood state) was positively correlated with both guilt and religiosity, which were also strongly related to each other, but only in the OCD clients. Not surprisingly, OCDs who were more religious also reported more religious obsessions.

Rigidity/Morality

Relatively little has been written about the seemingly rigid and often moralistic thinking that many OCD subjects display in their obsessive concerns. Most commentary pertains to religious rigidity in the form of scrupulosity. The findings reported above (Steketee et al., 1991) suggest that the type of religion in which individuals are raised probably plays a relatively small role in development of psychiatric symptomatology, though the rigidity of religious teachings and rules for behavior may do so. The similarities between rituals in religious practices and obsessions and compulsions in the context of religious beliefs have gained recent attention (e.g., Fitz, 1990; Greenberg, Witztum, & Pisante, 1987; Suess & Halpern, 1989).

In summary, these findings suggest that obsessive compulsives are more fearful of harm, reluctant to take risks, rigid, perfectionistic, and doubting. They may require excessive amounts of information to make a decision, only to distrust their choice. They may also blame themselves more for experiencing certain "shameful" or "aggressive" thoughts and feelings, and seek magical solutions to such uncontrollable ideas. These observations from the literature must be interpreted with some caution, however, since several of the studies by Reed (see Reed, 1985) included individuals who seemed to have an obsessive compulsive *personality* style, rather than OCD. Furthermore, the research by Sher et al. (1983, 1984) was not conducted with clients seeking treatment for their checking symptoms. In fact, very few studies of the specific beliefs and assumptions of those with OCD have been conducted. The research by Freeston and colleagues appears to hold much promise for identifying actual problematic thought and belief patterns among clinical OCD subjects (Freeston et al., 1992). Their development of the Belief Inventory (Freeston et al., 1993; see Appendix F) to assess these areas in nonclinical and clinical subjects is in the preliminary stages. In view of the inherent cognitive components in OCD (obsessive ideas, thoughts, images, and impulses), the paucity of research on cognitions, similar to that already conducted for depressive clients, seems surprising.

Cognitive Models for OCD

In accordance with the relative scarcity of research on cognitions specific to OCD, cognitive theoretical models for this disorder are also underdeveloped and have not been generally adopted. Foa and Kozak (1986) have conceptualized anxiety disorders in general as specific impairments in affective memory networks. Neurotic fears, they propose, are characterized by (1) the presence of erroneously high estimates of threat; (2) unusually high negative valence for the threatening event; and (3) excessive responding to such perceived threats (e.g., physiological, avoidance, etc.). These authors suggest that no single type of fear structure is common to all obsessive compulsives. With respect to the first characteristic, however, as noted earlier, most OCD sufferers base their beliefs about danger on the absence of evidence that guarantees safety. That is, they view situations as dangerous unless proven safe. Furthermore, they fail to assume *general* safety, in spite of specific experiences of exposure to feared situations in which no harm has occurred. Consequently, although rituals are performed to reduce the likelihood of harm, they can never really guarantee safety and therefore must be repeated.

Obsessive compulsives' overestimate of threat is partly supported by research. However, not enough of this research has been conducted on properly diagnosed OCD subjects, and the proposed negative valence for threat has not been adedquately documented. That is, we do not yet have clear evidence that OCD clients perceive negative events in a more unpleasant light than do most people. Nonetheless, these intriguing suggestions have considerable importance, since they bear directly on possible cognitive treatments that might enhance exposure outcome. With respect to the third characteristic of anxiety-disordered individuals, physiological and avoidance responses to threatening events, findings from a recent study do not support this contention: Obsessive compulsives were not more avoidant or more responsive on electrodermal measures than normals (Foa, McNally, Steketee, & McCarthy, 1991).

According to Foa and Kozak (1986), the persistence of fears in OCD clients may result from failure to access their fear network (all components associated with the specific feared situation). This could occur either because of active avoidance or because the content of the fear network precludes spontaneous encounters with situations that evoke anxiety in everyday life. In addition, anxiety may persist because of a specific impairment in mechanisms that influence change. For example, cognitive defenses, excessive arousal, faulty premises underlying beliefs, and erroneous rules of inference may hinder the processing of information that would alter the problematic fear structure. Again, these propositions require further testing to validate the theoretical model.

Salkovskis (1985) has also formulated a cognitive model of OCD. This model suggests that normal intrusive thoughts, images, and impulses lead to disturbance when they are particularly salient for the individual and are associated with negative automatic thoughts. Discomfort arises not from the possible harm itself, but from thoughts and basic assumptions about being *responsible* for danger or harm to others or self. These in turn lead to self-condemnation, requiring OCD sufferers to take precautions to exonerate themselves from blame (and shame). The problem, Salkovskis has suggested, is not the intrusions themselves, but the *processing* of them in relation to automatic thoughts and beliefs about them. Negative mood exacerbates OCD symptoms.

Efforts at neutralization (overt/behavioral and covert/mental rituals), according to Salkovskis (1985), are used to reduce discomfort, responsibility, and possible feared consequences of having a thought. Since the initial effort to engage in rituals is minimal compared to tolerance of the discomfort, it becomes the adopted mode of coping. Such neutralizing efforts actually maintain the obsessive thoughts via negative reinforcement (see Chapter 3 for a discussion of the two-factor theory and negative reinforcement). Supporting this model is the finding that individuals with OCD showed more sensitivity about responsibility for harm, but not for threat or loss, which lacks a component of responsibility (Salkovskis, 1989).

Another explanation for OCD traits and symptoms is provided by Guidano and Liotti (1983), who have suggested that OCD clients may devalue or underestimate their ability to deal adequately with threatening situations, resulting in pervasive uncertainty, discomfort, and feelings of helplessness. Consequently, clients with OCD are likely to view rituals (and avoidance) as the only available coping method, since other more appropriate ones are lacking. In line with this conceptualization, Beech and Liddell (1974) have proposed that ritualistic behaviors are maintained not only to reduce immediate discomfort, but also to address the obsessive compulsive's need for certainty before terminating an activity. The above-mentioned experimental findings lend some support to these assertions, particularly with respect to the overspecification and need for certainty evident in OCD.

Warren and Zgourides (1991) have proposed a rational–emotive therapy (RET) model for OCD, emphasizing the role of irrational beliefs. They hypothesize a general biological vulnerability, influenced by developmental and learning experiences that determine what thoughts are considered unacceptable and what meaning is attached to particular thoughts and general beliefs about the self, others, and the world. Stressful events that lead to negative emotional states foster intrusive thoughts, which become salient if they are associated with irrational beliefs and thinking styles that generate even more negative affect. Attention narrows on these intrusive thoughts, and hypervigilance for them is exacerbated. Associated depression occurs when additional irrational beliefs are directed at the unacceptability of and intolerance for the restrictions of the disorder. Warren and Zgourides (1991) identify three basic irrational beliefs shared by those with OCD: "1. I must make the correct decision. . . . 2. I must have perfect certainty that I won't be the cause of harm to anyone. . . . 3. I must not have bizarre or unacceptable thoughts or impulses" (p. 122). Again, evidence for their theoretical assertions has not yet been provided.

Pitman (1987) has proposed a cybernetic model of OCD, suggesting that various pathological symptoms (perfectionism, doubt, indecision, omnipotence, overspecification, and obsessions and compulsions themselves) derive from persistent high error signals, which are experienced internally and cannot be corrected through behavioral actions. He argues that there may be several explanations for the high error signals, such as intrapsychic conflict that leads to displacement activities (e.g., rituals). Another explanation may be a faulty "internal comparator mechanism," which registers a mismatch in the brain no matter what perceptual input it receives. This might explain why one Orthodox Jewish woman I saw, who feared violating religious laws regarding sex, reported that an obviously cream-colored vaginal discharge looked "bloody." Alternatively, Pittman has suggested, some obsessives may suffer from a reduced capacity to withdraw attention from salient perceptual signals. That is, they cannot effectively distract themselves from intrusive ideas, images, and so on. Pittman has tied each of these possible explanations for OCD symptoms to neuroanatomical underpinnings.

A theoretical discussion of cognitions in OCD would not be complete without mention of the extensive work by Wegner (1989) on thought suppression in nonpsychiatric populations. A series of studies by Wegner indicated that efforts to suppress particular thoughts resulted in a rebound effect: Suppressed thoughts actually recurred *more* frequently after subjects tried to block them. According to analogue studies, conditioning may play a role in this process. The process of trying not to think about something in a particular situation may become associated with that context, which then serves as a reminder of the unwanted thought. Mood state may also influence this process. Depressed individuals are less successful in suppressing negative than positive thoughts, and the more negative the tone of distractor thoughts, the more effective they are in suppressing negative thoughts. These findings imply that obsessive thoughts, which are invariably unpleasant, may be more easily suppressed by using other unpleasant distractor thoughts.

Wegner (1989) suggests that obsessive thinking may arise because initial efforts to control thoughts fail, leading to escalated efforts at suppression, which in turn highlight the thinking itself. Even greater efforts at control are sought, and the cycle escalates still further. Self-distraction works only temporarily and interferes with habituation of the unwanted thoughts. Wegner proposes that a return to thinking about the unwanted thought (exposure, paradoxical intention) will be needed to actually reduce it, though he notes that this may not be *all* that is needed.

It is clear that although several theorists have attempted to provide a cognitive model for OCD, there is as yet no coherent effort to explain all of the tentative experimental findings pertaining to perception, attitude, memory, and other mental processes in this disorder. Often therapeutic methods are attempted before theoretical models are well developed, and this is certainly the case for cognitive treatments of OCD. The few studies of the effects of cognitive therapies on this disorder have applied existing methods, such as RET or self-instructional training (SIT), without adequate research evidence of the relevance of these strategies for cognitive treatment of OCD. The few studies that have examined these treatments are discussed below.

Cognitive Treatments

Before discussing cognitive treatments, I should note that several writers have observed the ability of exposure-based therapies to modify thoughts and beliefs, merely by requiring clients to remain in anxiety-provoking situations until their fear has subsided. It is quite apparent that thoughts or beliefs about the dangerousness of the situation do change following such an experience. We (Foa & Steketee, 1979) have suggested that exposure treatment does not actually correct cognitive deficits, but that it does result in reclassification of some circumstances as non-dangerous. Whether exposure also modifies other types of cognitions common in those with OCD, as discussed earlier, has not been directly studied. Emmelkamp and colleagues' findings from two studies of the effect of cognitive treatment versus exposure suggest that irrational beliefs, as measured via a standardized instrument, change little overall following exposure therapy (Emmelkamp & Beens, 1991; Emmelkamp et al., 1988). Nonetheless, it is important to determine what specific effects exposure has on clients' attitudes.

In an early attempt to test the efficacy of one form of cognitive therapy, Emmelkamp et al. (1980) studied the contribution of SIT to combined exposure and response prevention by randomly assigning 15 OCD clients either to exposure with response prevention or to this combination preceded by SIT. Subjects from both groups benefited equally at posttest, showing clinically significant improvements on OCD measures (the average gains ranged from 41% to 78%). Thus this cognitive procedure did not add to the efficacy of gradual exposure and response prevention. However, as Emmelkamp and Beens (1991) have acknowledged, it is highly questionable whether SIT is the most appropriate cognitive technique to address obsessive compulsive complaints.

Emmelkamp (1982) reported results of an unpublished study by Bleijenberg (1981), in which exposure therapy and rational therapy were compared in a crossover design for 10 obsessional volunteers. Cognitive therapy, which consisted of disputing irrational beliefs and making rational analyses of obsessional situations, neither altered cognitions nor improved OCD symptoms. In another study using a similar design with "real" clients, Emmelkamp et al. (1988) assigned 18 OCD clients to either RET or self-controlled exposure *in vivo*. Both treatments produced significant changes in most measures of OCD symptoms (average improvement 78%), with continued gains 6 months later (average improvement 94%). However, the follow-up data should be interpreted conservatively, since several clients received additional treatment as needed. Subjective ratings of anxiety and depression also improved with both methods, though RET demonstrated some superiority over exposure for the latter.

In a second study of RET, Emmelkamp and Beens (1991) replicated the above-described findings in 21 clients randomly allocated to RET or to self-controlled exposure and response prevention treatment, followed by the addition of exposure treatment for both groups. Both groups improved substantially on all measures of outcome, but did not differ significantly from each other. There was no evidence that RET was even slightly less effective than exposure and response prevention, or that exposure and cognitive therapy produced an additive effect. Irrational beliefs did appear to decline more following RET; interestingly, this significant difference was not evident until 4 weeks following the end of the treatment period. Thus, not surprisingly, change in beliefs seems to require a longer period of time than change in obsessions and compulsions. These studies are the first to show that a cognitive treatment alone was clinically beneficial for OCD. The use of RET appears to have been more appropriate for some of the cognitive dysfunctions found in OCD, such as perfectionism and erroneous beliefs about risk.

Case studies have also demonstrated benefits from employing cognitive therapy strategies for OCD. Kearney and Silverman (1990) reported that alternating between cognitive therapy and response prevention was effective in treating a suicidal adolescent with OCD who found *in vivo* exposure too distressing to tolerate. Salkovskis and Warwick (1986) used cognitive therapy to alter unrealistic beliefs when exposure therapy failed to resolve the contamination fears of a client worried about skin cancer. Though the attribution of the successful outcome to the cognitive therapy has been disputed (e.g., Gurnani & Wang, 1987), its addition appeared to enable the client to benefit from exposure treatment, and may have implications for treatment of those with fixed, unreasonable obsessive beliefs (overvalued ideas).

Summary and Discussion

As evident from the research findings presented in Chapter 3, the combination of exposure and response prevention therapy has produced improvement in 75–80% of those with obsessions *and rituals* who undertake this treatment. In view of this high degree of success, it seems unlikely that any added treatment could produce gains that statistically exceed those already achieved by this form of therapy. It is therefore not surprising that cognitive methods added to exposure and ritual prevention have not improved upon the benefits conferred by the latter combination.

Nonetheless, a treatment tailored specifically to correct cognitive distortions common in OCD clients may enhance immediate outcome or (perhaps more probably) reduce relapse. Furthermore, clients with obsessions only or with obsessions accompanied by cognitive compulsions may demonstrate more benefit from the addition of efforts to correct cognitive errors in the obsessional aspect of this disorder. Longer trials with larger sample sizes comparing combined exposure and response prevention to this combination plus specialized cognitive correction are needed at this point. However, as Reed (1985) has proposed, it is not at all clear that cognitive procedures commonly used in other disorders (such as RET and Beckian cognitive therapy) are appropriate for obsessive compulsives, who generally recognize their obsessions as irrational and are characteristically overcontrolled. Treatment, Reed suggests, should include the "de-emphasis of the thought and the reduction of attention paid to it" (1985, p. 213).

Regardless of the correctness of Reed's suggestion, it seems only logical that to be effective, cognitive therapy for OCD must be tailored to the cognitive difficulties evidenced by this population. For example, overvalued ideation (conviction that the obsessive fears are correct) has predicted a poor outcome following behavioral treatment (e.g., Foa, 1979). Cognitive treatment involving logical discussion of the actual probability of a negative outcome or of its potential impact (its valence) seems to produce little change in firmly held beliefs. Efforts to correct misconceptions may be useful in cases where there is genuine inaccuracy in assumptions, but this is rarely the problem in most instances. Instead, OCD clients may have *exaggerated* the perceived danger of a potentially harmful situation. Beck's model (Beck et al., 1985) recommends deliberate testing of the accuracy of such automatic beliefs. But this may not in fact be feasible, since testing requires direct exposure, which overvalued clients often refuse to engage in (they sometimes refuse exposure therapy altogether), or they may carry out the exposure convinced that the apparent absence of catastrophe can be explained by other circumstances (such as luck).

It may be that cognitive treatments will have more validity for OCD clients if they are focused on very basic assumptions about oneself, the world, and the future. Indeed, there is both research evidence and clinical conviction that OCD clients often hold unrealistic assumptions. For example, beliefs may include the following: "I must do everything perfectly," "People will reject me if I make mistakes," "Taking even small risks is unnecessary and dangerous," and/or "I am responsible and should be held accountable for every action I take." Clinical impression suggests that many failures and relapses occur among those who hold such unchanging beliefs, particularly when guilt and excessive responsibility are involved. So far, Emmelkamp and colleagues' two studies of RET provide the only empirical evidence that such a strategy may be effective.

Further study of this issue is essential. However, research must first establish which cognitions are important in the development or maintenance of OCD symptoms. Only then can we begin to determine whether needed cognitive changes are best achieved via cognitive treatments or by other (e.g., behavioral, biochemical) methods. Since there is currently inadequate evidence regarding the efficacy of cognitive treatments for OCD symptoms, it is not routinely included in standard behavioral treatment programs. Informally, however, many clinicians engage in dialogue with clients regarding their beliefs and assumptions when these surface during exposure sessions and appear to interfere with habituation of anxiety or discomfort (especially guilt).

5

Biological Models and Treatments for OCD

This chapter presents research findings and clinical conclusions regarding biological characteristics of OCD and etiological models derived from these findings, along with pharmacological treatments for this disorder. Since the focus of this volume is on behavioral treatments, findings from studies of biological treatments alone (pharmacotherapy and psychosurgery) are presented only briefly. More attention is given to the few studies investigating the outcome of combinations of medications and behavioral treatments.

Genetic Factors

The number of reports in the literature of monozygotic twins concordant for OCD points to probable genetic factors in the etiology of OCD (Black, 1974; Carey & Gottesman, 1981; Marks, 1986). Concordance rates are considerably higher among monozygotic twins (averaging 65%) than dizygotic twins (15% average), though the concordance rates for the former are far from perfect, indicating that nongenetic factors must come into play (for reviews, see Pauls, Raymond, & Robertson, 1991; Turner, Beidel, & Nathan, 1985). Since studies of twins raised apart are extremely rare and have not been reported for OCD, the influence of environmental factors on OCD cannot be extracted from these reports. Turner et al. (1985) suggest that a genetic vulnerability model, in conjunction with life stress and environmental factors, may explain the findings.

Parents and siblings of clients with OCD show a higher incidence of this disorder than relatives of psychiatric controls, though only a relatively small percentage (0–25%) appear to be affected (see Chapter 2, Table 2.4). Table 2.4 indicates that obsessive and compulsive traits and features are more often present among parents than are actual diagnoses of OCD. Obsessions and compulsions appear to occur on a continuum from mild to severe, and may be linked to particular personality traits in families, as discussed in Chapters 2 and 11.

A genetic connection between Gilles de la Tourette's syndrome and OCD has been clearly supported in recent investigations, though only 5% of clients diagnosed with OCD are also diagnosed with Tourette's (Pauls, Towbin, Leckman, Zahner, & Cohen, 1986; Pitman, Green, Jenike, & Mesulam, 1987). It has been suggested that the same genetic factor underlying these disorders may be manifested differently, depending upon other biological (e.g., gender, disease processes) and environmental factors. Genetic transmission, then, accounts for a small but significant portion of the variance in the development of OCD.

Other Biological Characteristics

History of Physical Trauma and Disease

With regard to physical causes, several organic manifestations exhibited by OCD patients have been documented. Higher rates of birth abnormalities, history of head trauma, epilepsy, encephalitis, meningitis, and Sydenham's chorea for OCD sufferers than for normals suggest a possible etiological role of early physical trauma or disease processes (for a review, see Hollander, Liebowitz, & Rosen, 1991). In addition, compared to normal subjects, those with OCD show a high frequency of neurological "soft signs" (e.g., Denckla, 1988); difficulties in fine motor coordination are evident, as well as a tendency to be hypervigilant and highly reactive to novel stimuli. On neuropsychological testing, no common cognitive deficits for OCDs are evident across a series of studies, though there appear to be distinct subgroups of clients who demonstrate impairment in several areas (for a review, see Hollander et al., 1991). The tendency of OCD subjects to be slower in completing tests is consistent with several of the cognitive patterns summarized in Chapter 4 (difficulties in decision making, and overconcern about risk taking and making errors).

Brain Wave Activity

Abnormal electroencephalographic responses have been observed in OCD subjects in several investigations. In studies of brain wave patterns in response to evocative stimuli (evoked potentials), obsessional clients differed from controls during cognitive activity (Ceiseilski, Beech, & Gordon, 1981), and these differences increased with the complexity of the task (Beech, Ceiseilski,

& Gordon, 1983). In addition, OCD subjects showed specific evoked potential responses that appeared to constitute a specific biological marker for this
disorder (Shagass, Roemer, Straumanis, & Josiassen, 1984), and may point to
frontal lobe dysfunction during cognitive processing efforts of OCDs (McCarthy & Foa, 1990).

Brain Structure and Function

Brain imaging studies of OCD have examined brain structures (via X-ray
computed tomography [CT] and magnetic resonance imagery [MRI]) and
functions (via xenon-measured blood flow and positron emission tomography
[PET]); this research has yielded interesting and in some cases conflicting
findings. A summary of findings from CT studies by Baxter, Schwartz, and
Guze (1991) indicated that although one study did not differentiate OCDs
from normal controls, two showed differences. Inconsistencies in the use of
controls and different methods of calculating brain structures were noted.
One study using MRI technology in OCD patients did not provide significant
findings (for a review, see Insel & Winslow, 1991).

An examination of brain function was conducted by Zohar et al. (1991),
who used xenon measurement to examine cerebral blood flow in 10 OCD
clients under relaxation, imaginal flooding, and direct exposure conditions.
Findings indicated greater peripheral physiological reactions, but not more
cerebral blood flow, under increasing exposure conditions. In fact, blood flow
actually decreased during *in vivo* exposure, perhaps because blood was
shunted from the observable cortical regions (higher-order information-
processing areas) to other parts of the brain (lower-order centers) that were not
"visible" to investigators using this method.

PET scan technology clearly differentiated OCD patients from depressed
patients and from normals in several studies (reviewed by Baxter et al., 1991).
However, the observed loci of differences in brain function (metabolic rates)
varied considerably across studies, probably as a result of very substantial
differences in methodologies. Several studies implicated the left and right
orbital gyrus as sites of greater metabolic activity for OCD subjects, with one
study showing hemispheric differences for males and females (Baxter et al.,
1988). Since orbital areas are thought to be involved in habituation and
extinction of responses in animals, and thus in efforts to suppress pain-
ful feelings and associated thoughts, investigators have speculated that
OCDs may have abnormalities in mechanisms that cope with unpleasant
internal stimuli. Brain metabolic reactions have also been studied via
PET scan in responders and nonresponders to medication treatment.
However, the inconsistent findings shed little light thus far on specific
mechanisms of action.

Biochemical Markers

The search for biological markers for OCD has led to several studies of variables identified as distinctive for depressed subjects. OCDs resemble depressed patients in nonsuppression on the dexamethasone suppression test, decreased rapid-eye-movement latency, and decreased platelet imipramine, though differences in the specific results for these last two potential markers suggest that these may denote phenotypic differences. By contrast with depressed patients, OCD subjects show elevated cerebrospinal fluid levels of 5-hydroxyindoleacetic acid, a serotonin metabolite. Weizman, Zohar, and Insel (1991) conclude that, taken together, the studies comparing major depression and OCD do not support a direct biological linkage between these disorders, despite their frequent co-occurrence.

Extensive research efforts to determine whether serotonin is a marker for OCD have met with limited success. Improvement in OCD symptoms has not been consistently linked to plasma levels of serotonergic drugs, and studies of serotonin in the blood and uptake of serotonin in platelets have not shown differences from normals in several studies. Efforts to demonstrate abnormalities in serotonergic function in OCD patients relative to controls have yielded inconsistent findings (Jenike, 1991). Drugs that provoke the symptomatic responses of a disorder (e.g., obsessive thinking and ritualistic behaviors) can help identify biochemical substrates for the disorder. Goodman, Price, Woods, and Charney (1991) conclude that challenge studies of the serotonin system partly support its role in pathogenesis and/or drug effects on OCD. For example, the serotonin receptor agonist m-chlorophenylpiperazine (m-CPP) induced obsessive symptoms in OCD patients but not in controls (Zohar et al., 1989). Furthermore, a serotonergic antagonist, metergoline, induced partial relapse in patients successfully treated with a serotonin reuptake inhibitor clomipramine (CMI) (Benkelfat et al., 1989). Despite these very interesting findings, the major evidence for serotonin as playing a key role in OCD lies in the effectiveness of drugs that block serotonin reuptake.

The role of noradrenergic function in OCD is uncertain, since results for two noradrenergic challenge drugs, clonidine (an adrenergic agonist) and yohimbine (an adrenergic antagonist), have not yielded consisted findings. Perhaps the most compelling argument against a major adrenergic role in OCD is the surprising inefficacy of noradrenergic antidepressants like desipramine for this disorder. Data for dopamine and endogenous opiate systems are too sparse to permit investigators to draw any firm conclusions at this point. Studies of these compounds using brain imaging procedures as further assessment strategies may yet yield more useful information, but at present the specific biochemical markers for OCD remain unavailable.

Biological Models for OCD

Baxter et al. (1991) conclude that evidence supports OCD dysfunctions in the frontal lobe–anterior cingulate–basal ganglia loop, though considerably more research using consistent methodologies is needed. These and other authors (e.g., Insel & Winslow, 1991) suggest that the primary pathology in OCD may be in the striatum, interfering in turn with the cortex, which must increase its activity to compensate. Thus, the orbital cortex, and perhaps limbic structures (e.g., cingulate), may serve compensatory functions for the impaired striatum. In this model, the inability of the striatum to screen what usually are easily inhibited sensations (impulses), thoughts, and motor behaviors may result in their intrusion into consciousness. Tics and obsessions may result, accounting for OCD symptoms and Tourette's syndrome (see also Pitman, 1987). Conscious, rather than automatic, efforts to combat intrusions from instinctive drives (aggressive, sexual, etc.) would be needed. Different affected areas of the striatum may account for manifestations of OCD, Tourette's, and tic disorders.

The findings regarding brain wave activity presented above indicate clearly that OCD clients differ from other populations. Whether such differences indicate biological causality or are consequences of the disorder cannot be inferred from the data. Regardless of the etiological pathway, treatment outcome (via drugs or psychological methods) may not necessarily depend upon the mode of acquisition of the OCD symptoms (Kettl & Marks, 1986). Unfortunately, few efforts have been made to determine whether treatment effects vary with the client's medical history or biological characteristics.

Pharmacotherapy

Serotonin Reuptake Inhibitors

Although this book is intended to instruct clinicians in the application of behavioral treatment for OCD, some knowledge of the effects of medications is essential. Clients invariably ask for such information or are already receiving drugs before seeking a behavioral consultation. The relative efficacy of drugs and behavior therapy for OCD is an important concern for many clients. The most effective drugs for OCD symptoms appear to be the serotonin reuptake inhibitors clomipramine (Anafranil), fluoxetine (Prozac), fluvoxamine, and possibly sertraline (Zoloft) and paroxetine (Paxil) (for a review, see Jenike, 1990). The effects of these medications do not appear to depend on their antidepressant properties, suggesting that they have specific antiobsessional effects (see Steketee & Shapiro, 1992).

TABLE 5.1. Effects of Pharmacological Treatments

Study	n	% symptom reduction	% subjects improved (VMI[a])
Clomipramine (Anafranil)			
Thoren et al. (1980)	24	33–42	50
Ananth et al. (1981)	10	31–65	60
Mavissakalian et al. (1985)	7	35	43
Volavka et al. (1985)	8	32	100 (38)
Zohar & Insel (1986)	10	20–22	70 (10)
Marks et al. (1988)	12	22	25
Jenike, Baer, et al. (1989)	13	37–40	78 (47)
Greist et al. (1990)	13	28–35	73 (33)
Katz et al. (1990)	134	38	61
Mavissakalian, Jones, & Olson (1990)	33	31–47	74 (35)
Pato et al. (1988)	18	43–53	[b]
Fluoxetine (Prozac)			
Fontaine & Chouinard (1985)	8	17–59	71
Turner et al. (1988)	8	10–37	63 (50)
Lipinski et al. (1988)	34	17–23	77
Jenike, Buttolph, et al. (1989)	61	17–37	—
Markovitz et al. (1990)	11	30–37	82 (27)
Fluvoxamine (Luvox)			
Perse et al. (1987)	16	15–38	56 (0)
Price et al. (1987)	10	23–39	60 (0)
Cottraux et al. (1989)	13	34–49	54
Goodman, Price, Rasmussen, Delgado, et al. (1989)	21	13–22	43 (43)
Jenike et al. (1990)	18	15–22	—
Goodman et al. (1990)	21	29	52 (52)

[a]VMI, very much improved.
[b]In this study, 89% of subjects relapsed after clomipramine withdrawal.

As Table 5.1 demonstrates, although all of these drugs have been found to be significantly more effective than placebo, the *average amount of improvement* in OCD symptoms appears to be consistently below that produced by behavior therapy, though measurement differences make comparisons somewhat more difficult (Greist, 1990). Studies of clomipramine show average improvement rates ranging from 20% to 45% after 4–12 weeks; only 1 of 15 studies gives figures as high as 65%. Seven investigations of fluoxetine and six of fluvoxamine showed average benefits of about 20–40%, slightly below those of clomipramine. These figures contrast with substantially greater average improvement rates of 50–70% following behavioral treatment, according to various measures, with the greatest gains evident on target symptom ratings. Comparisons of outcomes of studies using identical measures (i.e., the Compulsive Activity Checklist and the Maudsley Obsessional–Compulsive Inventory) have shown greater mean benefits for exposure treatment. Unfortunately, no behavioral studies have yet employed the Yale–Brown Obsessive Compulsive Scale (YBOCS), commonly used in recent drug studies.

With respect to the number of subjects considered "improved," again, medication was somewhat less effective than behavior therapy. For clomipramine, about 60% of subjects were considered "improved" or "responders"; for fluoxetine, the rate was about 65%; and for fluvoxamine, 55%. By contrast, at least 75% were "improved" with behavior therapy. Again, measurement differences do confound comparisons to some extent. Very few studies allowed examination of drug effects at follow-up, but it appears that gains were consistently maintained or increased for both medications and behavioral treatment. However, 89% of clomipramine responders relapsed when the drug was replaced by placebo in a double-blind design, and duration of clomipramine treatment did not decrease the relapse response, which occurred even after 27 months on the drug (Pato, Zohar-Kadouch, Zohar, & Murphy, 1988).

Other Drug Treatments for OCD

Numerous drugs have been reported effective for OCD patients in case studies, but either have not been tested in controlled trials or have shown little usefulness in such trials. Tricyclic antidepressants other than clomipramine (imipramine, amitriptyline, nortriptyline, doxepin) have rarely proved consistently effective for OCD symptoms, except in individual case studies. An exception was a multicenter trial of clomipramine and imipramine, which showed no differences in efficacy between these medications (e.g., Mavissakalian, Turner, Michelson, & Jacob, 1985). The monoamine oxidase inhibitors (MAOIs) have not been effective for OCD in group trials, though case reports have indicated efficacy. Anxiolytic medications such as buspirone (Buspar) and alprazolam (Xanax) have shown inconsistent effects, which do not support their use except in isolated cases (see Jenike, 1991, for a review).

Although not generally effective alone for OCD, several drugs have shown promise in boosting the effects of serotonergic drugs. Buspirone has demonstrated efficacy in combination with fluoxetine (e.g., Markovitz, Stagno, & Calabrese, 1990), and lithium, clonazepam, tryptophan, trazodone, and alprazolam have been used effectively as augmenting drugs for various serotonergic medications in several case studies (for reviews, see DeVeaugh-Geiss, 1991; Jenike, 1991).

Comparisons of Behavioral and Pharmacological Treatment and Their Combination

The present chapter is focused on the phenomenology of and behavioral treatments for OCD. However, because mental health care providers are focusing increasingly on the effects of biological treatments on OCD, a brief discussion of recent developments in medications combined with behavior therapy is presented here. All but one of these studies have utilized antidepressant drugs that block the reuptake of serotonin, including clomipramine, fluvoxamine and fluoxetine.

Clomipramine and Behavior Therapy

In an uncontrolled study, Neziroglu (1979) treated 10 patients with clomipramine, followed by clomipramine and behavioral treatment. Clomipramine decreased symptoms over baseline levels by 60%, with a further improvement of 19.7% observed following behavioral treatment, suggesting an additive effect. Two large controlled trials in which the effects of clomipramine and behavioral treatment (exposure *in vivo* and response prevention) were compared have been conducted by Marks and his colleagues. Both studies employed complicated research designs, comparing behavioral treatment to relaxation or to instructions *not* to expose oneself.

In the first study, 40 obsessive compulsive patients were assigned to four treatment groups: (1) clomipramine followed by the addition of behavioral treatment; (2) clomipramine followed by the addition of placebo psychotherapy (relaxation) and then by behavioral treatment; (3) placebo drug followed by behavioral treatment; and (4) placebo drug followed by placebo psychotherapy and then by behavioral treatment (Marks, Stern, Mawson, Cobb, & McDonald, 1980). Clomipramine alone produced significant improvement in rituals, mood, and social adjustment, but only in those who were initially depressed. Maximum benefit from the drug was not achieved until week 10, indicating that a trial of only 4 weeks was insufficient to determine the full effect of clomipramine. As in other studies (e.g., Pato et al., 1988), relapse tended to follow drug withdrawal. Exposure led to substantial improvement (more in rituals than in mood state), and relaxation was ineffective. Gains were maintained 1 year later. The combination of clomipramine and exposure had a slight additive effect at week 10 and appeared to improve compliance with behavioral treatment—a finding that has direct clinical implications. Follow-up interviews conducted after 2 and 6 years indicated that results were essentially maintained, except for general anxiety, which returned to mild to moderate pretreatment levels (Mawson, Marks, & Ramm, 1982; O'Sullivan et al., 1991). Patients who were no longer on medications tended to relapse, and duration of drug treatment did not appear to moderate this loss of gains (O'Sullivan et al., 1991).

A second study used a complex randomized design for 49 OCD in-patients to compare clomipramine with placebo under conditions of self-controlled exposure (and ritual prevention) versus "antiexposure" instructions (Marks et al., 1988). A combination of therapist-assisted exposure and response prevention was then added after 8 weeks for half the subjects to test its effects relative to self-exposure. At the 7-week assessment, clomipramine added to the benefits derived from self-exposure for rituals and depression, although not for obsessions, anxiety, or general adjustment. However, this advantage of adding clomipramine disappeared after 15 weeks with further exposure therapy. Clomipramine without exposure was generally equivalent to exposure-only treatment. Not surprisingly, self-exposure was much more effective for OCD symptoms than were antiexposure instructions, and this benefit generalized to some extent to social adjustment, but not to mood state. Therapist-assisted exposure and response prevention added marginal benefit over self-exposure. The earlier finding that only depressed OCD patients responded to clomipramine was not replicated here.

Both studies by Marks et al. (1980, 1988) indicated greater average improvement for exposure over clomipramine at posttest; the later study found that many more patients improved with exposure (75–80%) than with clomipramine (22–33%). Combined treatment led to more subjects who were "much improved" after 1 year (73%, vs. 50% for exposure alone), although not to more average improvement across all subjects.

Fluvoxamine and Behavior Therapy

A study conducted in France compared fluvoxamine and behavior therapy (Cottraux et al., 1989). Three groups were contrasted: (1) fluvoxamine plus relaxation and instructions to *avoid* exposure; (2) placebo drug and behavioral treatment (imaginal and direct exposure plus ritual prevention); and (3) fluvoxamine and the same behavioral treatment. All three groups improved significantly and approximately equally after treatment, with only a slight advantage for combined drug and behavioral treatment at 6 months. This advantage disappeared by 11 months. Fluvoxamine led to more improvement in depression than either placebo or the combination of exposure and ritual prevention, and initial depression was associated with somewhat better outcome for the drug-treated patients only. This last finding may indicate that fluvoxamine may affect OCD symptoms partly through its antidepressant action—a finding that does not appear to be true for clomipramine. In contrast to findings with clomipramine, fluvoxamine alone showed better average improvement than exposure in two of three measures and produced more successes (54% vs. 40%) at posttest (Cottraux et al., 1989). After 11 months, however, mean improvement was nearly equivalent across treatments, and slightly more behaviorally treated patients were improved (50% vs. 45%).

Thus, the combination of fluvoxamine with exposure and ritual prevention showed some additive effect at 6 months, but this was minimal at 11 months. These findings contrast with those of Marks et al. (1988), who found that clomipramine conferred no advantage over exposure alone. The antidepressant action of fluvoxamine appears to be independent of its antiobsessive effects.

Fluoxetine and Behavior Therapy

In a study of fluoxetine, Turner, Beidel, Stanley, and Jacob (1988) compared 14 weeks of fluoxetine to 10 weeks of exposure and response prevention, which always followed drug therapy. Treatments were applied sequentially in a small sample of five outpatient OCD ritualizers. Fluoxetine improved depression and anxiety but not OCD symptoms, particularly obsessions. In contrast, behavioral treatment led to substantial clinical improvement in OCD symptoms, and to some extent in depression. As in the first study by Marks et al. (1980), medication had an effect primarily for patients with greater initial depression and anxiety. By contrast, the effect of behavior therapy was independent of mood state.

Imipramine and Behavior Therapy

To examine the impact of depression level, antidepressant drug treatment, and behavior therapy on mood and on OCD symptoms, we (Foa, Kozak, Steketee, & McCarthy, 1992) compared imipramine (a nonserotonergic antidepressant) with placebo in depressed and nondepressed OCD patients, followed by exposure and response prevention and by supportive therapy. Although imipramine improved depressed mood, it had little effect on OCD symptoms and did not enhance the effects of behavioral treatment. The combination of exposure and response prevention, with or without the drug, was highly effective after treatment and at follow-up.

Serotonergic Drugs and Behavior Therapy: Long-Term Effects and Effect Sizes

Long-term effects of behavior therapy, serotonergic drugs (clomipramine and fluvoxamine), and their combination were examined in an uncontrolled study of 62 OCD patients (Hembree et al., 1991). After 6–43 months, there was no differential effect of treatment on outcome. However, approximately 60% of those who received medications were still taking them, whereas only 4% of behaviorally treated patients had been prescribed drugs. In addition, over 70% of patients treated with exposure and ritual prevention were categorized as responders, compared to approximately 50% of drug-only patients.

To study further the relative efficacy of behavioral intervention and drug treatment for OCD, Christensen, Dadzi-Pavlovic, Andrews, and Mattick (1987) conducted a meta-analysis of effect sizes for tricyclic antidepressant drugs and behavioral treatments. According to their findings, drug and exposure therapies did not differ significantly, and both were superior to nonspecific treatments. Behavioral treatment effects appeared stable at follow-up, but this information was not available for drug treatments. Unfortunately, the criteria for the selection of studies for their comparison were quite broad, resulting in the inclusion of treatment methods that are not adequately representative of either the pharmacological or the behavioral treatments of choice for OCD. A more appropriate meta-analysis would require a comparison of serotonergic antidepressants with demonstrated efficacy for OCD (clomipramine, fluvoxamine, fluoxetine) to behavioral treatments combining exposure and ritual prevention.

Comment

According to most studies described earlier, serotonergic drugs (clomipramine, fluoxetine, and fluvoxamine) displayed both antidepressant and antiobsessive effects, compared with nonserotonergic antidepressants (e.g., imipramine), which exhibited only the former action. Behavior therapy also improved both depressive and OCD symptoms; it improved the latter to a somewhat greater degree and more lastingly than did either clomipramine or fluoxetine.

Thus, the combination of drugs and behavior therapy has shown little advantage over behavior therapy alone. In general, it should be noted that most studies indicated that both clomipramine and behavior therapy had a greater impact on ritualistic behavior than on obsessions, which responded more slowly and less completely. It seems probable that residual obsessional fears may be at least partly responsible for eventual relapses in some behaviorally treated clients. Relapses on drug withdrawal are likely to derive from other sources, including physiological and attributional factors.

Clearly, more trials will be needed to adequately examine the separate and combined effects of these serotonergic drugs and behavioral treatment. As Towbin, Leckman, and Cohen (1987) urge, such studies should attempt to utilize similar measures that separate OCD symptoms from depressive ones and that do not rely exclusively on self-report scales. Consistent use of the YBOCS (Goodman, Price, Rasmussen, Mazure, Fleischman, et al., 1989) by trained interviewers would help increase comparability across studies, and thus confidence in the validity of the findings.

Psychosurgery

On the basis of models for involvement of brain structures in the pathogenesis of OCD, a few studies have sought to determine whether psychosurgical procedures can effectively reduce severe obsessions and compulsions with few side effects. Chiocca and Martuza (1990) summarize findings for four types of surgical procedures. Cingulotomy is perhaps the best-studied procedure. Recently, Jenike, Baer, Ballantine, et al. (1991) reported on patients with OCD who received one or more cingulotomies over the past 25 years. At least 25–30% benefited substantially with very minimal adverse side effects, though the authors noted that 4 of 33 OCD patients treated with cingulotomy committed suicide. Another recent study of 32 patients placed the improvement rate at 25% for "functionally well" and an additional 31% "markedly improved" (Ballantine, Bouckoms, Thomas, & Giriunas, 1987). Comparisons with other anxious patients, however, suggested that cingulotomy is up to twice as effective for anxiety as for OCD.

Subcaudate tractotomies were conducted on 28 OCD patients, leading to substantial benefit in 50%, again with few side effects. However, the latest of these reports was in 1975, and all were retrospectively reported from the same institution in England (e.g., Goktepe, Young, & Bridges, 1975). Limbic leukotomy, also used in England, led to a much higher rate of clinical improvement in 84% of 49 OCD patients in a study by Kelly (1980). No long-term side effects were noted, but two patients committed suicide within 1 year. No further studies of this seemingly effective method have been published.

Anterior capsulotomy, developed and used in Sweden, led to considerable improvement in about 75% of patients in three studies (for a review, see Chiocca & Martuza, 1990). Two studies found capsulotomy much more effective than cingulotomy (e.g., Kullberg, 1977).

It is apparent that psychosurgery has led to substantial improvement for many patients with severe OCD; the best results have been provided by leukotomy and capsulotomy. Because psychosurgery is a radical treatment, it is reserved for those who who do not respond either to behavioral treatments or to serotonergic drugs or their combination. In the United States, however, only cingulotomy is currently being performed at the present time, and it is done at very few centers (e.g., Massachusetts General Hospital in Boston, University of Iowa Hospital).

Clinical Implications

Clomipramine, fluoxetine, fluvoxamine, and perhaps also sertraline and paroxetine are effective antiobsessive drugs, but are less potent than exposure and response prevention in eliminating OCD symptoms. Clomipramine appears to have a slight advantage over fluoxetine and fluvoxamine. The side effects (much less problematic with fluoxetine than clomipramine), and the tendency of patients to relapse on drug withdrawal (at least on clomipramine), suggest that medications are not the first treatment of choice. However, for clients who are very apprehensive about or not highly motivated for behavioral treatment, and for those who experience high levels of arousal, commencing treatment with drugs may enable them to engage in exposure and response prevention later on.

Many clients are likely to be taking a serotonergic drug already when they seek behavioral treatment. It is advisable to stabilize medications for at least 2 months prior to beginning exposure sessions, to better enable clients to distinguish the separate benefits of these two treatments. This time period is suggested because benefits from drug trials did not stabilize for 6–10 weeks. As evident from the Pato et al. (1988) study, patients who wish to discontinue drug therapy face a high risk of relapse. Behavioral treatment may protect against relapse, though this has not yet been tested. As medications are very slowly withdrawn, the therapist is advised to carefully monitor the client's symptoms, to consult regularly with the pharmacologist regarding dosage adjustment, and to use booster exposure sessions in order to consolidate gains in the nondrugged state.

Only in the case of failure to achieve benefit from medications or from behavioral treatment, or inability to tolerate either, should referral for surgery be contemplated.

6

Assessing OCD Symptoms

Preliminary Comments

In this and the next chapter, specific steps for assessing clients with OCD are described in considerable detail. The division of this information between two chapters has been determined somewhat arbitrarily and implies no required order for information collection. Usually 3–4 hours are needed to collect information and plan therapy, as well as to allow clients to ask questions and express concerns. Because of the quantity of information to be gathered, 90-minute sessions may be preferable to 60-minute ones, if this is clinically feasible. More time will undoubtedly be needed by therapists new to behavioral treatment of OCD and by those assessing complex cases with multiple symptoms or comorbid conditions. In addition, new information acquired during actual exposure treatment sessions may modify the course of therapy somewhat.

The present chapter outlines procedures for diagnosis and collection of information about clients' current OCD symptoms (obsessions, avoidance, and compulsions), the history of their symptoms, and their prior treatment history; it also gives guidelines for providing a brief description of upcoming treatment and introducing self-monitoring. The next chapter addresses the use of standardized instruments for assessing OCD symptoms, comorbid conditions, personality traits, functioning difficulties, familial relationships, social support, and general history. Answers to questions about etiology of OCD and about treatment plans, as well as suggestions for contracting for exposure and prevention of rituals, are also given in Chapter 7. Later chapters cover the implementation of behavioral treatment, including exposure in practice, exposure in imagery, and prevention of avoidance and rituals. The clinician is advised to read through all the assessment and treatment chapters (Chapters 6 through 10) before embarking on actual treatment with an OCD client.

Suggested scripts for the therapist are provided periodically, in order to illustrate various methods for introducing therapy material (e.g., giving a rationale, urging a reluctant client to engage in exposure). These scripts are merely suggestions and should not be repeated verbatim to every client. Different clients have differing needs; clinical judgment and flexibility are required for appropriately allaying fears, increasing motivation, addressing specific concerns or disturbing ideas, and so forth. Providing specific words cannot substitute for active listening and sensitive analysis of individual needs in assessing symptoms and delivering effective exposure and response prevention. Throughout the assessment process the therapist maintains an interested and concerned attitude, taking the role of a detective/collaborator who seeks to understand clients' behaviors, feelings, thoughts, and motivations.

Goals of Assessment

Three response systems have been linked to anxiety symptoms: behavioral (observable actions, such as rituals and avoidance), subjective (cognitive and affective responses), and physiological or somatic manifestations. With respect to the first two of these, the goal of assessment is for the practitioner to carefully observe, measure, and analyze clients' thoughts, feelings, and behaviors in various situations, in order to understand OCD symptoms in context and to devise appropriate treatment strategies. Somatic reactions may be examined via physiological recording of various responses (heart rate, skin conductance, respiration, temperature, etc.) during feared situations. Typically, these measures have been used only in research contexts. Because the symptoms of OCD are not strongly associated with particular somatic manifestations (in contrast, e.g., to symptoms of panic disorder), measurement of physiology seems less critical for an adequate behavioral analysis of symptom patterns and treatment planning. Note, however, that in some cases involving possible organicity or obsessive fears associated with physical behaviors (e.g., obsessions about choking to death, ritualistic breathing patterns to prevent suffocation), physiological measures may be very important in assessing and treating symptoms. Measures of physiology are discussed briefly in Chapter 7.

Because of its widely varying symptom manifestations, assessment of OCD can be more difficult than assessment of some other anxiety disorders. It requires several methods of gathering information. Clinical interviews serve as the primary source of information, with behavioral observations and questionnaires complementing clients' and family members' descriptions of the problem. The approximate content of the assessment sessions is given in Table 6.1. Whenever possible, the recommended interview, observation, and questionnaire instruments are included in the text or in appendices at the end of this volume. As noted in Chapter 7, although most standardized instruments for OCD were originally developed for research purposes, several

TABLE 6.1. Content of OCD Assessment Sessions

Session	Procedure

1–2	Orient client to behavior therapy
	Inquire about OCD symptoms and verify diagnosis (ADIS-R)
	Gather detailed information about OCD symptoms:
	    Complete YBOCS Symptom Checklist and YBOCS
	    Identify cues for obsessions (external and internal), fears of disasters
	    Begin list of obsessive situations
	    Assess insight into obsessive beliefs
	    Identify avoidance behaviors
	    Identify behavioral and mental rituals
	    Assess relatives' or others' involvement in OCD symptoms
	    Collect history of symptoms: onset, course, treatment history
	    Request self-monitoring and questionnaire completion at home

3–4	Review self-monitoring forms and questionnaires Assess comorbidity (e.g., anxiety, depression, personality disorders) Take a general history Assess social support Verify motivation for treatment Describe treatment program and rationale in detail Develop detailed hierarchy for exposure *in vivo* Determine need for imaginal exposure; identify content of exposure scenes Interview relative(s) and determine therapy role Contract with client for treatment Plan schedule of sessions Plan content of treatment sessions Plan homework

inquire about specific symptoms and thus provide very useful information for the practitioner.

Assessment of obsessions should include information about external sources of fear (tangible objects), internal triggers for fear (thoughts, images, or impulses), and worries about the consequences of not performing compulsions. The amount of passive avoidance behavior associated with obsessional thoughts is also closely examined, as are all forms of active behavioral and/or cognitive compulsions. Strategies for collecting this information are outlined in detail below.

Orienting the Client to Behavior Therapy

The first 1–2 hours of assessment have the multiple purposes of verifying the diagnosis of OCD, collecting information about the symptoms, and describing a plan of treatment to determine the client's motivation in continuing. The therapist commences with an explanation of the assessment plan, in order to orient the client to the therapist's expectations. This might take the following form:

As we discussed by phone, I'd like to get some information today about your symptoms and your history. Then we can discuss possible treatment strategies, and you can let me know if you'd like to continue working with me in this way. If we agree to work together on these problems, I'll be asking you to complete some forms at home before our next session. This will give me more information about your problems as they occur on a daily basis. We'll need to continue our discussion of your symptoms and other aspects of your life for two or three more sessions, in order to plan your treatment in some detail. Do you have any questions before we begin?

This sets the stage for information gathering, and also allows clients to inquire about any aspects of the therapist or therapy that immediately concern them before they commit themselves to therapy. Very general questions about treatment can be answered, but inquiries about specific aspects of exposure or ritual prevention should be postponed until the therapist has enough information to be able to provide examples from a client's own situation. Questions about the therapist's orientation, experience with OCD, and treatment success should be addressed immediately and as honestly and directly as possible. Clinicians can provide factual information about success rates from several studies of exposure and ritual prevention. Table 3.1 and Figure 3.1 can be used to illustrate.

Establishing the Diagnosis

The therapist begins the first session by inquiring about the client's presenting symptoms or the reason for referral:

We spoke briefly on the phone about your problems with checking. Can you tell me more about this?

Or,

You said that Dr. Johnson suggested you see me because of obsessive compulsive problems. What led her to make this diagnosis?

Solicitation of clients' descriptions of troublesome symptoms should be directed toward their actual internal experiences or behaviors under various circumstances. This is particularly important for those who have had extensive analytic psychotherapy, who often reply to questions about their experiences with interpretive explanations about the putative causes for their symptoms. For such a client, the therapist can interrupt and repeat questions as follows:

That's quite interesting. Right now, though, I'd like to understand exactly what you *do* and how you feel and think in these situations when your obsessive fears and compulsive rituals are occurring. Could you describe the most recent occasion when this happened? When was this?

The therapist then asks detailed questions about the experience, encouraging the client to describe symptoms without attempting to interpret their meaning.

There are several standardized interview methods available to help clinicians reliably diagnose OCD according to DSM criteria. Probably the most common are the Structured Clinical Interview for DSM-III-R (SCID; Spitzer, Williams, & Gibbon, 1987) and the Anxiety Disorders Interview Schedule—Revised (ADIS-R; DiNardo & Barlow, 1988). Both will be revised to incorporate DSM-IV criteria. Since the ADIS-R is specifically focused on anxiety disorders, it is somewhat more thorough in detailing and quantifying the symptoms associated with this disorder. It may be used formally or informally during the initial interview to identify the major obsessive, compulsive, and avoidant aspects of the client's symptoms. Questions from the ADIS-R are provided in Figure 6.1. These questions can be asked in any order that flows easily during the interview.

It is sometimes easier to ask about compulsive actions first, since many are observable events, and then to ask about the obsessive fears and avoidance behaviors on which they are based. During the first interview, these questions can be relatively brief, since the therapist is seeking to establish or verify the diagnosis of OCD and to identify the types of external and internal situations that provoke fears of disastrous consequences and resultant rituals. Very detailed questions about the exact content of rituals and obsessions are usually reserved for the second or later information-gathering interviews. For convenience, all information to be solicited regarding OCD symptoms is included together below. The practitioner can determine how much detail to collect in any given session as the assessment progresses.

Assessing Obsessions and Associated Discomfort

The clinician first inquires about the most bothersome obsessions spontaneously reported by clients, followed by questions about any other disturbing thoughts, images, or impulses. Clients usually readily report their main

1.a. Are you bothered by thoughts or images that keep recurring to you and that are unreasonable or nonsensical, but that you can't stop from coming into your mind? This is not the same as worrying about things that might happen. I mean things like repetitive thoughts about hurting or poisoning someone, or shouting obscenities in public; or horrible images such as your family being involved in a car accident.

        Yes ___ No ___

If yes:

Content: Thought _____

        Image _____

        Urge _____

How often do you experience _____? ___ times per day

How long does the _____ last? ___ minutes

While you are being bothered by the _____, how strongly do you believe that it is true (e.g., you have actually hit someone while driving, you will actually carry out the act, you have really given someone incorrect information that will harm them)?

        0 (Not at all)–100 (Completely) ___

At times when the _____ is not intruding (perhaps now), how strongly do you believe that it is true?

        0 (Not at all)–100 (Completely) ___

How does the _____ come into your mind? (Check for beliefs about thought insertion, externally imposed urges.) _____

---

b. *Resistance.* Do you try to get rid of the _____, or tell yourself things or use certain images in order to neutralize the _____?

        Yes ___ No ___

If Yes, specify: _____

c. *Avoidance.* Do you avoid certain situations or objects because they might trigger the _____?

        Yes ___ No ___

If Yes, specify: _____

Do you have other people do things for you so that you won't have to be in contact with certain situations or objects?

        Yes ___ No ___

If Yes, specify: _____

d. *Distress/Social Problems, Work Problems.* How much are you bothered by these thoughts/how do they affect your life? _____

(continued)

FIGURE 6.1. Diagnostic questions for OCD from the Anxiety Disorders Interview Schedule—Revised (ADIS-R). Adapted from DiNardo and Barlow (1988). Copyright 1988 by Graywind Publications. Adapted by permission.

2.a. Have you had to repeat some act over and over again that doesn't seem to make sense and that you don't want to do—for example, washing something over and over again, or counting things, or checking something repeatedly (such as locked doors or important papers), or retracing driving routes? Do you take an excessively long time to do things?

        Yes __ No __

If yes:

Content: _____

How often do you do this _____? __ times per day

How much time do you spend? __ minutes per day

b. *Resistance.* Do you try to resist doing _____ or did you resist initially?

        Yes __ No __

If Yes: How often/how much do you resist? _____

c. *Avoidance.* Do you avoid certain situations or objects because they might make you feel that you have to do _____?

        Yes __ No __

If Yes, specify: _____

Do you have other people do things for you so that you won't have to be in contact with these situations or objects?

        Yes __ No __

How anxious do you feel if you can't or don't carry out these acts? _____

What do you think might happen if you don't carry out these acts? _____

d. *Distress/Social Problems, Work Problems.* How much are you bothered/what problems does this create at work, home, socially? _____

FIGURE 6.1. *(continued)*

obsessive ideas and rituals, but often omit mention of more minor concerns or of ones experienced in the past that currently are not bothersome. A good strategy for soliciting more complete information is the Yale–Brown Obsessive Scale (YBOCS) Symptom Checklist, described below and provided in Appendix A.

Yale–Brown Obsessive Compulsive Scale and Symptom Checklist

The YBOCS Symptom Checklist (Appendix A) was developed as a research instrument, but also has excellent clinical utility (Goodman, Price, Rasmussen, Mazure, Delgado, et al., 1989; Goodman, Price, Rasmussen, Mazure, Fleischman, et al., 1989). The interviewer begins by defining the terms "obsessions" and "compulsions"—a very useful prelude to further assessment and treatment, since the technical terminology is often confusing to clients as well as therapists. The clinician then inquires about current or past experiences of 39 obsessive concerns and 25 compulsive rituals. The following types of obsessive symptoms are included: aggressive (fears of harming), contamination, sexual, hoarding/saving, religious, symmetry/exactness, somatic, and miscellaneous (which includes concerns about knowing, saying, or recalling correctly and superstitious fears). Although the list is not exhaustive of all possible obsessions, it is more comprehensive than any other available instrument and is very useful clinically. The interviewer is wise, however, to be prepared for new and unusual versions of obsessions. Some examples are fears of contamination by chocolate and by New York City; obsessions of not having enough beer on hand to relieve unexpected discomfort (and consequent hoarding of cases of beer); and one man's irrationally jealous fears that his girlfriend dropped papers with another man's phone number on it, leading to his collecting of all trash papers by the roadside.

After completing the YBOCS Symptom Checklist, the therapist and client select the three main target obsessions, compulsions, and avoidance behaviors that will be the focus of treatment. To quantify the degree of difficulty with these symptoms, the interviewer then uses the 10-item YBOCS[1] (Appendix B) to rate obsessions and compulsions separately on 0-to-4 scales according to time spent, interference, distress, resistance, and controllability. The obsessions subscore and compulsions subscore are summed to yield a total YBOCS score, which can range from 0 to 40. A cutoff score of 17 and above has been used recently in some drug studies to identify individuals whose symptoms are severe enough to qualify for treatment. The YBOCS has demonstrated good reliability and validity in assessing symptom severity, and has rapidly become the standard method for assessing outcome in drug trials of OCD (Goodman, Price, Rasmussen, Mazure, Delgado, et al., 1989; Goodman, Price, Rasmussen, Mazure, Fleischman, et al., 1989), as well as in behavioral treatment trials.

At present, the YBOCS is the only measure that assesses severity of OCD in a standardized fashion without regard to particular types of obsessions or compulsions (e.g., washing, checking, etc.). Together, the YBOCS Symptom Checklist and the YBOCS require about 30–45 minutes to complete. Although this may seem excessive for clinical session time, the clinical information gained, particularly from the Symptom Checklist, is well worth

[1]This terminology can be confusing. The acronym "YBOCS" by itself always refers to the scale that measures severity of OCD symptoms. The "YBOCS Symptom Checklist" refers to the list of symptoms used by an interviewer to determine the presence or absence of particular obsessions or compulsions.

the effort by the clinician and the cost for the patient. Also, for clinicians who wish to quantify how well their clients fare with specific treatments, the YBOCS stands out as the most comprehensive method for doing so.

External Fear Cues

Once the clinician has identified all the obsessive fears that a client can recall, it is important to solicit information about the specific environmental triggers for discomfort that will require direct exposure during treatment. The vast majority of obsessive compulsives experience obsessive fears in response to concrete situations, such as touching "contaminated" objects, closing and locking doors, or hearing a report of an auto accident on the radio. For those with contamination fears, the process of generalization of fear to similar or related objects or situations is extremely common. A feared contamination can "travel," because people who touch the feared object then touch other nearby things that come into contact with still more things, and so forth.

A very common example of generalization is fear of germs associated with urine or feces in public toilets, which spreads to fears of faucets used in restrooms, to doorknobs, to objects on the desks of those near the restrooms, and so forth. A less common, but still very "logical," example is illustrated by a woman who felt "contaminated" by a particular person in Hershey, Pennsylvania, and then became fearful of Hershey chocolate products and eventually of chocolate of all types. Similarly, one man present at the site of a radioactive spill in a laboratory of a large urban hospital began to fear and avoid the people present at the spill, the places they frequented, the subway stations they used, and finally all parts of the city where they lived (Foa & Steketee, 1977). For those with other types of obsessions, similar processes of generalization operate. One woman obsessed about being responsible for damage to others by fire; she eventually feared passing any operating appliance at home, at work, or in public places, in case she had inadvertently moved or damaged it. Particularly problematic were electrical heaters, since in her mind these were more strongly associated with fire.

As these examples indicate, it is essential to identify all situations that provoke discomfort and to ascertain the underlying source(s) of obsessive fear that logically connect the feared contexts (e.g., pesticides, causing fire, physically hurting someone, etc.). Although in most cases clients are well aware of the source of their fears, a few are fearful and avoidant without professed knowledge of the actual cause of concern. It is not uncommon to encounter clients who will not touch certain objects but who can no longer recall exactly how they began to fear contamination by these objects in the first place. It is apparent that the interviewer must play the role of detective, assembling all the "clues" and making sure that the "evidence" fits together logically; feared and avoided situations must be sensibly connected to one or more obsessive themes. In fact, with a thorough understanding of a client's obsessions, the clinician should be able to accurately predict the client's behavior in response to particular situations.

Internal Cues

All individuals with OCD have at least *some* internally experienced cues that trigger obsessive fear or another negative emotion, such as guilt, shame, disgust, or horror. Such cues take the form of ideas/thoughts, images, or impulses, and they may be the predominant triggers for obsessions and rituals in some cases without external cues. Examples include unwanted impulses to behave inappropriately or to harm others (e.g., to expose oneself in public, strangle a loved one, or sexually assault a child), intrusive sexual and/or religious images (e.g., images of Christ's penis or the Devil raping the Virgin Mary), or ideas of harm coming to others (e.g., ideas that one's spouse has died in a car accident on the way home, or that one's mother is lying terminally ill in the hospital). More benign but still intrusive forms of internal cues are sequences of numbers, sounds, or music in one's mind, and internal visual geometric patterns. Some clients respond obsessively to internal bodily sensations, which are interpreted with dread as possible signals of physical danger. Examples include difficulty swallowing for fear of choking, and overfocus on breathing for fear of suffocating or damaging oneself with inadequate oxygen. These bodily obsessions strongly resemble hypochondriacal fears and are typically followed by extensive checking or reassurance seeking to decrease discomfort.

As is apparent from the examples given above, many of the internal triggers for obsessive fears are shameful, and some clients may be reluctant to disclose their images or impulses to the interviewer. Direct questions with a matter-of-fact attitude and examples from other OCD sufferers are usually reassuring to reticent clients. Again, the YBOCS Symptom Checklist can be useful here, since it asks directly about such fears. Clients must be encouraged to disclose the specific content of obsessions, since deliberate direct or imaginal exposure is essential to successful behavioral treatment. Furthermore, guilt-inducing obsessive ideas are rendered a little less disturbing by the knowledge that others experience equally shameful thoughts and that the therapist is neither alarmed nor horrified by them. It is often very helpful to comment on the fact that research studies have found that approximately 90% of "ordinary" people experience intrusive ideas, thoughts, images, and impulses, and that the content is very similar to the types of fears reported by those with OCD (Rachman & DeSilva, 1978; Salkovskis & Harrison, 1984; refer to Table 2.2).

Nonetheless, some clients fear that by giving voice to their concerns, they will cause the very thing they seek to prevent. Usually such assessment problems can be worked with effectively. For example, a man who fears that saying aloud that his wife might develop cancer will "magically" cause her to become ill may be induced to write down his fears or report them indirectly. Or the therapist may be forced to guess, so that the client can nod assent without directly verbalizing his obsession. It is best not to be frustrated by such maneuvers, since this client does not seek to make assessment difficult, but only to prevent harm to his wife and manage his own discomfort.

Fears of Disasters

As some of the examples above suggest, fears of particular disastrous consequences following internal or external cues serve as the primary source of obsessive discomfort for many clients. Details vary from person to person. Most who fear contamination worry that they will cause themselves or loved ones to become ill or die from disease. Impulses are feared to be uncontrollable, leading to despicable acts such as killing or maiming someone. Images of accidents are believed to increase the likelihood of a loved one's death, as well as one's personal responsibility for it. Most who check repeatedly seek to avoid responsibility for mistakes that cause fire, break-in, damage, loss of important information, or embarrassment. Those who repeat actions compulsively invariably seek to prevent serious harm, such as accidents or punishment from God.

Questioning about such feared consequences might begin as follows:

So you worry about the heater catching on fire. What could happen then? Is there anything further that you think could happen? What else?

The therapist should continue this questioning until the client states that no other fears occur to him or her. If any obvious likely feared consequences have been omitted, the clinician can suggest these directly, asking whether the client has ever worried about them.

Some clients report that they are only vaguely fearful that something terrible will happen, but they have no idea exactly what, and no amount of questioning produces clear feared consequences. Others seem far more sensitive to internal or external obsessive cues and are relatively unmoved by what may follow. The main purpose of their rituals and avoidance is to reduce their internal discomfort rather than to prevent other harm. Some of these individuals do express concern that if high obsessive anxiety is not reduced by rituals it may lead to permanent psychological damage, such as going crazy. One woman with fears of stabbing small children worried less that she would actually do so than about the possibility that these thoughts meant that she was becoming psychotic. Such concerns can be viewed as a special version of a feared disaster.

Insight into Obsessive Fears

Foa (1979) noted that clients who had "overvalued ideas" about the probability of harm did not habituate across repeated exposures to obsessive situations and did not benefit from behavior therapy. Thus, it is also important to assess the strength of clients' beliefs in the feared disasters they report. Most obsessives spontaneously report that they know that their fears and rituals are ridiculous or nonsensical, and that they perform compulsions to reduce discomfort. If questioned when highly anxious during exposure to obsessive fears, these individuals often lose the rational perspective they can maintain under calmer circumstances. However, a small percentage of those with OCD are always convinced that their fears and rituals are valid, and that those who are not fearful in such circumstances are in error.

To assess this issue, both the ADIS-R and the YBOCS include questions about a client's degree of insight into his or her symptoms. This allows the interviewer to inquire about how logical clients perceive their own actions to be, and whether they genuinely believe that the rituals are necessary to prevent real harm or damage from occurring. The therapist may prefer to ask such questions at the point at which fears of disastrous consequences are initially described. Once the therapist is satisfied that all feared harm has been identified (see the suggested therapist script above), he or she can ask about the client's belief in the rationality or perceived likelihood of these fears. Even when a client has already volunteered that his or her fears are unreasonable, it is still wise to assess the degree of belief in harm, since the desire to be viewed in a positive light may motivate such statements.

To assess the degree of belief in feared consequences, the therapist may ask:

How likely do you think it really is that if you don't check the heater, the drapes will catch on fire and the house will burn down? Let's use a scale from 0 to 100, where 0 means that your fear is completely illogical and it could never happen, and 100 means that your fears are very justified and will always happen if you don't check. How would you rate the actual probability of fire if you leave for work and don't check?

The interviewer needs to be sure that clients are not rating their fears or emotions, but their actual *beliefs*. If a client gives a number greater than 1 or 2, the therapist should question further as follows:

Um, 40 out of 100. That means that you believe that 4 times out of every 10 that you leave home, the house will definitely catch on fire during the day because you didn't check the heater. Or, to put it another way, you think that if 10 people left their homes without checking, 4 would find fires burning when they returned. Is that what you mean?

In the case of one client who feared causing the death of her family or friends at dinner by not cleaning a can carefully and spreading botulism, I commented:

O.K., 20 out of 100. So you are convinced that 2 out of every 10 people who eat dinner at your home will become seriously ill and die if you stop washing each can 10 times as you do now. That would also mean that if I came to eat at your house five times, I'd probably be dead before I could come the sixth time. Is that right?

Generalizing the experience to other people also helps to clarify the extent of the belief. For example, the therapist in this case might have asked whether the client thought that if other people (the therapist, a relative, a friend) did not check or wash under the same circumstances, they too would have the same odds. This line of questioning is meant to introduce an alternative vantage point from which to test the actual belief system.

In the face of such questioning, most clients disavow their original stated belief, revising their ratings downward to a much smaller number that better matches reality. However, some are unreasonably convinced that the disaster will happen and insist on their overrated estimate of probability, providing some explanation for why their beliefs do not match those of most people. They may presume that they are unusually vulnerable to disease because of a weak constitution, or may believe that they are deficient in some characteristic that allows others to behave more cavalierly. For example, one client believed that her fear of running over pedestrians in her car was quite justified by her "poor driving" (questionably substantiated by her husband) and by her inability to concentrate her attention, since her mind wandered during driving, as well as during other tasks she considered less dangerous.

Listing Obsessive Fears

To organize information about obsessions for use in planning exposure treatment, it is usually helpful to develop a chart such as that given in Figure 6.2, with categories for obsessively feared situations and the degree of discomfort evoked. Eventually this list will be used to schedule exposures on

Obsessive theme _____

External feared situations

(specific situations or objects that provoke anxiety or are avoided)	Discomfort (0–100)	Session #
1.		
2.		
3.		
4.		
5.		
6.		
7.		
8.		
9.		
10.		
11.		
12.		
13.		
14.		
15.		

Internal feared cues

(thoughts, images, or impulses or bodily sensations that cause fear)	Discomfort (0–100)	Session #
1.		
2.		
3.		
4.		
5.		
6.		

(continued)

FIGURE 6.2. List of obsessive situations for exposure.

7.

8.

9.

10.

Feared consequences

(feared harm from external or internal source—e.g.,   Discomfort   Session #
becoming ill, going crazy, etc.)   (0–100)

1.

2.

3.

4.

5.

FIGURE 6.2. *(continued)*

specific days during treatment. To provide greater clarity in communicating about the patient's degree of discomfort (anxiety, guilt, shame), the therapist should teach the patient the "Subjective units of discomfort" (SUD) scale, ranging from 0 (no discomfort at all) to 100 (the most uncomfortable/fearful ever felt). It is often helpful to facilitate use of this scale by asking how clients would rate themselves "at this very moment" and in a few other nonobsessive situations, before asking about specific obsessive ones.

Using the SUD scale, clients can rate the degree of anxiety provoked by each internal or external trigger for obsessions and rituals. Occasionally, clients find it difficult to quantify their discomfort, and may refuse to use the scale or may need to reduce the numbers to 0 to 10, or even 0 to 5. In some cases the SUD scale may prove unhelpful, and instead clients can be asked to rank-order the list of obsessive situations according to degree of difficulty—that is, which ones would be easier to do than others.

Obsessive fears can be organized into themes, with specific cues for fears and rituals grouped under the appropriate hierarchy. The themes listed in the YBOCS Symptom Checklist are probably too general to be useful. Examples of more specific ones might include "fears of pesticides," "fears of physically harming loved ones," "contamination by sticky substances," and "fears of being responsible for fire."

In some cases, these themes reflect tangible fears (and avoidances); in others, they refer to disastrous consequences. Each thematic heading subsumes several sources of obsessive fear. For example, "fears of pesticides" might entail fear and avoidance of Raid, D-Con, boric acid, touching grass in a treated lawn, or the like. "Fears of being responsible for fire" could involve worries about using or being near objects such as stoves, electrical appliances of many types, heaters, or matches, as well as reading newspaper articles about fires.

Many of those with OCD have more than one type of obsession, though they may use the same ritual to reduce discomfort. For example, one woman who feared pesticides of almost any type also avoided situations associated with AIDS, such as red marks that reminded her of blood, restaurants with waiters who might be gay, and discarded Band-Aids. Washing and wiping served as rituals to relieve discomfort from both sources, sometimes making it difficult to determine why she was washing.

Identifying as many elements as possible for each hierarchy is important in planning exposures. It is impossible, however, to identify every possible cue requiring exposure. No matter how thorough the questioning, the patient invariably omits some aspect of his or her very habitual behavior that goes unnoticed. Additional situations in need of exposure will be identified during exposure sessions, when both patient and therapist are in a better position to observe behavior, thoughts, and feelings more closely.

Assessing Avoidance and Rituals

Avoidance

Knowing which cues provoke discomfort (anxiety or guilt) also allows the interviewer to anticipate and inquire about situations that the client unwittingly avoids. Some forms of avoidance are obvious, such as refusing to use public toilets, shake hands, use the stove, eat in restaurants, or drive. But more subtle forms of avoidance are common and require careful questioning (sometimes of relatives), and often actual observation of clients' actions in a variety of settings. Whenever the therapist observes odd behavior that may be avoidant, he or she should inquire about it.

Examples of avoidance include walking a circuitous route to avoid stepping on brown spots (possible dog feces) or to avoid seeing glass, nails, or trash that the person feels compelled to collect; sitting forward on chairs to avoid "contaminated" areas; and not reading newspapers or magazines or watching TV to prevent learning about accidents one might have caused or diseases one might acquire. Inquiries about presymptomatic functioning may help solicit information about prior activities that are currently avoided. For example, one client had given up parallel parking to avoid backing up, lest she run over a child.

Rituals

In addition to obsessions and avoidance, the practitioner should ask about all behaviors or thoughts that the client employs to *reduce* discomfort provoked by obsessive ideas. As noted earlier, it is sometimes easier to begin the assessment of symptoms with questions about rituals, since these are often the most obvious and functionally troublesome manifestations of the disorder. Clients may have more than one ritual for a single source of obsessive fear, or, as in the case of the woman who feared both pesticides and AIDS (described above), they may use the same ritual to relieve discomfort from more than one obsessional theme. For those with chronic symptoms, discomfort may be relieved by abbreviated versions of more complex rituals, such as wiping, rinsing, spraying with alcohol, or even using a mental image or word (e.g., "Palmolive") to replace washing with soap and water.

Many clients have developed cognitive compulsions to relieve discomfort from intrusive images. Mental or cognitive rituals often go unreported as compulsions because clients have come to think of mental phenomena as "obsessive" and behaviors as "compulsive"—a distinction that does not necessarily match the discomfort-increasing or discomfort-reducing function of the symptom. Questions such as "Do you ever try to reduce your obsessive worries by thinking particular thoughts or picturing certain images?" may prompt reports of mental rituals. Examples include praying, thinking "good" thoughts or images to neutralize "bad" ones, mentally listing events, and making repeated efforts to remember particular information or remind oneself of prior reassurances.

The YBOCS Symptom Checklist is useful in soliciting information about compulsions the client has not already mentioned. Included in the Symptom Checklist are the following types of rituals: cleaning/washing, checking, repeating, counting, ordering/arranging, hoarding/collecting, and miscellaneous (e.g., mental rituals, list making, measures to prevent harm). Since rituals serve to maintain obsessive fears, identification of all discomfort-reducing compulsions is essential to the success of behavioral treatment. The following questions, using washing as an example, may be helpful:

So you find yourself washing too much. How many times a day do you wash your hands? How long does each washing take to complete on average? Can you tell me exactly what you are doing that takes you that long? Do you wash any other parts of your body in a compulsive way? What about showers? How long do they take? What are you doing during the shower? Do you wash parts of your body in a particular order—for example, your genitals or the soles of your feet? [These are often sensitive areas for clients who are fearful of germs.] What about rinsing? Does that take a long time? How about the process of drying and using a towel? Any problem there?

Involvement of Family Members in Symptoms

Family members often become involved in helping those with OCD to avoid feared situations and complete rituals. For example, a spouse may take responsibility for chores the afflicted partner is too uncomfortable to perform, such as taking out the trash, washing dishes, doing laundry, or checking the house before leaving. Some family members actually carry out rituals for their relatives, as in the cases of a wife who checked the house ritualistically at her husband's request before retiring each evening, and a husband who showered immediately upon arriving home from work to remove contamination his wife feared. Usually, spouses or parents carry out these activities willingly to help relieve clients' obvious suffering. Less commonly, they do so reluctantly to comply with orders from autocratic OCD sufferers.

Information about relatives' specific involvement in avoidance and rituals, its history, and its rationale is essential for treatment planning. In addition, the clinician should inquire about involvement of any other persons (friends, neighbors, coworkers) in such patterns, knowingly or unwittingly.

Description of a Typical Day

Extremely helpful in soliciting information about feared and avoided cues is the client's description of a typical day in minute detail from the moment of waking until falling asleep. The therapist can lead the client through the remembered day, stopping to inquire about obsessions and compulsions in considerable detail. Particularly important is information about how obsessions are triggered, what situations are avoided, and how rituals are carried out. For example, washers should be asked how long each ritual usually takes and what exactly they are doing during the process (such as scrubbing fingernails carefully, washing between fingers six times, beginning a shower by washing "clean" parts first and then doing genitals and soles of feet last, or omitting washing legs and feet altogether because they are too contaminated). Those with repeating rituals should be asked when rituals occur, how often they repeat an action or mental procedure, how they decide it is safe to terminate the process, whether they count, whether they always use the same ritual for a particular obsessive thought, and so forth.

This degree of detail provides a window into the client's experience, permitting the therapist to see how each incident of obsessive discomfort is handled and to identify the logical connections among the discomfort, avoidance, and rituals. The interview process should leave the therapist with a clear understanding of the interrelationship between rituals and obsessions. If information seems conflicting, the therapist should inquire further until the relationship between the two seems consistent and logical.

History of OCD Symptoms

A detailed account of the onset of current and previous obsessions and compulsions is likely to help the clinician identify factors pertinent to the present OCD symptoms. In particular, many clients report having had similar or different obsessions and compulsions earlier in life, with periods of full or partial remission. Examination of historical precipitants may indicate a broader thematic underpinning for the current seemingly circumscribed fears, and may suggest needed interventions or maintenance strategies after therapy. Onset and exacerbation of symptoms following stressors of various types (e.g., childbirth, marriage, death of a loved one) is common, requiring evaluation of the potential impact of such events on the client's current situation. In addition to behavioral treatment for current symptoms, some direct focus on stressors and/or developmental issues may be needed to reduce the overall discomfort level. Exploration of general history (e.g., religious upbringing, parental rules, unusual traumas or experiences, and sexual teachings and experiences) may also shed light on attitudes and beliefs that play an important role in maintaining obsessive worries and rituals.

Exploration of prior efforts to seek treatment for OCD symptoms is useful in determining the client's current motivation and expectations of therapy efficacy. Most clients have a lengthy history of treatment by other methods, most commonly psychodynamic psychotherapy and medications. For some these therapies have been unhelpful, whereas for others they have led to partial or transient gains. A few describe prior applications of behavioral methods (e.g., relaxation, desensitization, thought stopping) that were usually inappropriate for OCD and therefore unhelpful. Such clients will require a careful explanation of the planned treatment strategies (see Chapter 7) to allay concerns about failure. For clients who have received some prior exposure and ritual prevention, the clinician must carefully investigate the content of treatment sessions and homework assignments to determine why the therapy was unsuccessful. Consultation with previous therapists is highly desirable to obtain details about the intervention and their impressions of a client's response.

Behavioral Observation

Self-Monitoring

Since it is often not possible for the therapist to observe clients' avoidance and compulsions (as in the case of one client whose worst compulsions occurred just before going to bed at night), client self-monitoring is an essential source of information. Only OCD sufferers themselves have immediate access to their internal cues for obsessions, subjective experience of discomfort, mental compulsions, and compulsions that occur in private contexts (e.g., bathroom rituals). Daily diaries of such events are therefore critical in providing information for treatment planning and generating hypotheses about external influences on compulsive behavior. In addition, they can be used to assess clients' willingness to complete homework assignments between sessions (a critical factor in the efficacy of exposure therapy) and to monitor ongoing progress during behavioral treatment.

Generally, the first or second interview ends with the clinician's request for self-monitoring of specific obsessions and compulsions during the coming week. The therapist gives the client a week's worth of forms, deciding with the client which symptoms should be recorded and how. An example of such a form is given in Figure 6.3. This diary can include information about the frequency and duration of particular obsessions and compulsions of interest. If needed, significant others (e.g., spouse, parents, siblings, roommates, nursing staff) may be asked to keep records of the client's behavior to supplement incomplete information from the client, unless this will present interpersonal difficulties. In some cases, clients are reluctant to comply with the therapist's request because of shame or merely the unpleasantness associated with closely observing their unwanted symptoms. Some clients' routines have become so habitual that they are unaware of actions that seem repetitive, unnecessary, or unreasonable to others. In the case mentioned above, the client's husband provided forgotten details about the bedtime ritual. Obviously, monitoring by a relative should not be requested if it might exacerbate an already conflictual relationship.

Therapist Observation

Observation of clients in situations where obsessions and rituals typically occur is invaluable in providing informative details about symptomatology. Although observations can sometimes be postponed until actual exposure sessions have begun, a clinician is strongly advised to accompany a client to at least two locations (especially the client's home) to observe avoidance, discomfort, and/or rituals. Such observations almost invariably lead to new information that the client did not think to mention during the interview.

For example, one client of mine forgot to note that her kitchen contents were carefully arranged in "clean" and "dirty" segments that could not be intermingled. In another case, a foot-deep pile of dirty underwear and towels covering the entire bedroom floor provided a new understanding of the severity of one man's symptoms and of his reluctance to invite others to his home. Observing one woman's effort to prepare to take a shower indicated that she carried her towel above her head from the hall closet to the bath-

Please record the actual *number of minutes* or *number of times* you perform the two rituals specified on this form. Please note the situation that led to your need to do the ritual, as well as the amount of discomfort or anxiety on a scale from 0 to 100, where 0 means completely calm and 100 means extremely upset or disturbed.

Please note the following suggestions from your therapist for keeping records of rituals: _____

_____

_____

Example:

Ritual A: Washing   Ritual B: Checking for harm
            _____   _____

			Minutes ritualizing	
Time of day	*Situation that led to ritual*	*Discomfort*	*Ritual A*	*Ritual B*
9:30 A.M.	Took out the garbage	70	4 min.	
11:30 A.M.	Bathroom—urination	80	5 min.	
1:00 P.M.	Drove car to center of town	85		10 min.
4:00 P.M.	Used iron	60		2 min.
6:30 P.M.	Cleaning up after dinner: checking stove, oven, faucet	55		15 min.

Please record your rituals below:

			Minutes ritualizing	
Time of day	*Situation that led to ritual*	*Discomfort*	*Ritual A*	*Ritual B*

_____

_____

_____

_____

_____

_____

_____

_____

_____

_____

_____

_____

_____

_____

_____

FIGURE 6.3. Self-monitoring form.

room. She could not keep "clean" towels in the bathroom linen closet and feared that as she traversed the hall, the towel would brush against her "dirty" body or "contaminated" walls and door frames. Observation of actual ritualistic behavior can help identify problem behaviors that will require attention during response prevention.

Behavioral Avoidance Test

Clinicians might also consider conducting a "behavioral avoidance test" (BAT) of the degree of passive avoidance and subjective anxiety experienced in specific feared situations. Such measures have been utilized in some research studies (e.g., Marks, et al., 1975; Steketee & Foa, 1985). Examples of situations in which a BAT may be used include physical proximity to a selected contaminated object, duration of hand washing after touching a contaminated object, or time spent observing an asymmetrical arrangement of objects before beginning an ordering ritual. In its strict form, the BAT is less well suited to checking or repeating rituals, unless assessment of subjective anxiety and of self-reported mental phenomena (images, impulses, mental rituals) is permitted. Although such assessments are usually confined to research contexts, the BAT is merely a formalized version of therapist observations of the client in a natural context identified as very problematic by the client. A hallmark of behavioral treatment is the therapist's careful measurement of behavior and of progress following treatment. To document gains, the clinician is well advised to consider formalizing his or her behavioral observations for later demonstration (both to the client and to fellow therapists) of the successful outcome of treatment.

Summary

It is apparent that interviews are the main vehicle by which much of the essential information about OCD symptoms is gathered, including the external and internal triggers for obsessions, as well as feared consequences. The ADIS-R clarifies diagnostic questions, and the YBOCS Symptom Checklist can be used to collect information about all variants of obsessions and compulsions. Assessment of insight into beliefs is important, since they may have considerable relevance for treatment. A list of all obsessive feared situations will be used later to develop a complete hierarchy for treatment. Family involvement in OCD symptoms is questioned, and a full discussion of avoidance and of rituals serves to help plan treatment. In addition to informal information obtained via interview, a formal interview measure, the YBOCS, serves as an excellent way to quantify the severity of current symptoms. Self-monitoring of obsessions, discomfort evoked, and compulsions is essential for accurate assessment of daily experiences. Although a formal BAT is probably not essential for clinical treatment, some direct observation of the client in obsessive and compulsive contexts is extremely useful in identifying specific issues to be targeted during therapy.

7

Continued Assessment and Treatment Planning

Chapter 6 has provided strategies for assessing OCD symptoms in considerable detail, including listing obsessive situations and associated discomfort levels, as well as determining when and how rituals are executed. A history of OCD symptoms is taken, and self-monitoring of these OCD symptoms via daily report forms and appropriate questionnaires is requested. The present chapter begins with a brief discussion of the optional use of standardized self-report instruments and monitoring of physiology. It then focuses on responses to commonly asked questions and assessment of comorbid conditions, personality traits, functioning difficulties, familial relationships, and social support, as well as the taking of a general history. Interviewing of one or more close relatives who are well aware of the OCD symptoms, in order to obtain their observations and potential assistance in a treatment program, is proposed. After the treatment program and rationale are described in detail, the therapist can verify the client's motivation for treatment and establish the contract for therapy. The need for imaginal exposure must be determined and the content of exposure scenes planned, along with exposure *in vivo* and ritual prevention. As noted earlier, the clinician should not feel constrained to follow the order in which assessment information is presented here.

Collecting More Details

At the beginning of the second or third session, after exchanging greetings, the therapist requests the daily self-monitoring forms and the questionnaires. These are reviewed with the client to allow discussion of aspects of symptoms that were not evident in the previous session. Note that in asking immediately for this material, the therapist establishes the expectation that homework will be completed as requested. If the client has not done so, the importance of the requested material should be emphasized, and the task should be reassigned. The therapist may also consider asking whether the client understood the reasons for the requested homework, since perhaps a lack of understanding led to poor compliance. This homework information, along with further conversation about daily details of obsessions and compulsions (described below), will allow the specific planning of the next 10 or more treatment sessions. The therapist may wish at this point to request that the client complete some additional standardized instruments.

Standardized Questionnaires

In addition to careful interviewing of clients and relevant family members, several questionnaires are available to quantify the severity of OCD symptoms, and in some cases to identify specific manifestations of the disorder. Questionnaires are listed in the order of their likely usefulness from a clinical standpoint. There are several possible uses of such standardized measures. For instruments for which normative data are available, clinicians can compare clients' scores to determine relative severity (and in some cases severity of subtypes) of OCD symptoms. Quantifying clients' degree of impairment before treatment enables clinicians to readminister the measure later as a means to demonstrate benefits to clients who fail to see their progress. Measuring symptoms in a standardized manner also allows clinicians to publish results in cases of particular interest.

Maudsley Obsessional–Compulsive Inventory

Available in Appendix C, the Maudsley Obsessional–Compulsive Inventory (MOC) is composed of 30 true–false questions concerned exclusively with symptom dimensions (Hodgson & Rachman, 1977). In addition to a total obsessional score, the MOC yields five subscales (checking, washing, slowness–repetition, doubting–conscientious, and ruminating) and has been found to be sensitive to treatment effects and to have adequate validity and test–retest reliability (Rachman & Hodgson, 1980; Sternberger & Burns, 1990a, 1990b). Its subscales render this instrument useful for assessing changes in particular symptoms, and its focus on OCD symptoms to the exclusion of personality traits has rendered this instrument useful in the assessment of treatments directed at obsessional and compulsive symptoms. Responses on the MOC permit normative comparisons with other OCD subjects studied in prior research, but the validity of the numerical score depends to a large extent on whether clients have the common types of compulsions assessed by this instrument. Clients with atypical symptoms (especially mental rituals) may not score in the pathological range on this measure, despite incapacitating symptoms.

Compulsive Activity Checklist

Philpott (1975) developed the Compulsive Activity Checklist (CAC), a checklist administered by an assessor to evaluate the degree of obsessive compulsives' impairment in 62 daily activities. Somewhat briefer assessor-rated and self-rated versions of 39 items (Cottraux, Bouvard, Defayolle, & Messy, 1988; Marks, Hallam, Connolly, & Philpott, 1977) and 38 items (Freund, Steketee, & Foa, 1987; Steketee & Freund, 1993) have also been used. This questionnaire allows identification of specific problem situations not necessarily covered in a clinical interview, though it is not as comprehensive as the YBOCS Symptom Checklist, described in Chapter 6. The CAC has been found to detect changes following treatment (Foa et al., 1984; Freund et al., 1987; Marks et al., 1980), and to meet acceptable validity and interrater but not test–retest reliability criteria (Cottraux et al., 1988; Freund et al., 1987). Two shortened versions proposed by Cottraux et al. (1988) and by Steketee and Freund (1993) (the latter, the CAC-R, is provided in Appendix D) are intended largely to remove items that appear more symptomatic of agoraphobics than of obsessive compulsives. These have not been adequately tested as yet.

Obsessive Thoughts Checklist

The Obsessive Thoughts Checklist (OTC), a 29-item inventory (Appendix E) assessing obsessional thinking, has demonstrated good internal consistency, test–retest reliability, and discriminant validity in a preliminary study on a small cohort of OCD, depressed, and phobic patients and controls (Bouvard, Mollard, Cottraux, & Guerin, 1989). This instrument has not been widely adopted at this time.

Belief Inventory

Freeston and colleagues have begun preliminary investigations of a method to assess cognitions that appear to be common among individuals with OCD (Freeston, Ladouceur, Thibodeau, & Gagnon, 1991; Freeston et al., 1993). This is a long-overdue endeavor that is likely to assist researchers in identifying common faulty thinking processes in OCD, and eventually to develop effective cognitive treatment strategies. For clinicians who wish to obtain further information about their clients' thoughts and beliefs (apart from the interview context), the Belief Inventory (Appendix F) lists 20 attitudes, requesting a response on a 6-point scale ranging from "strongly true" to "strongly false." Preliminary evidence shows good reliability and validity in nonclinical populations.

Target Symptoms Rating Scales

Likert-like scales adapted from phobia research have been used by independent assessors, clients, and therapists to measure the severity of clients' main obsessive fears, avoidance, and compulsions (for a review, see Kozak et al., 1987). These instruments are particularly useful for rating change following treatment, since they assess the particular symptoms targeted during behavioral treatment. Such measures are somewhat more suitable for washers (whose main fear component is contact with discrete external contaminants) than for checkers (whose obsessive thoughts are centered primarily on fears of potential catastrophes that occur in many contexts). Target symptoms derived from the CAC can be rated on scales of severity in this way, though often the items rated are more specific than targets selected for the YBOCS Symptom Checklist. An example of a rating scale for target symptoms is provided in Appendix G.

Leyton Obsessional Inventory

Of standardized instruments devised to measure severity of OCD symptoms, the 69-item Leyton Obsessional Inventory (LOI; Cooper, 1970) was undoubtedly the most widely used until recently. A true–false card-sorting procedure measuring symptoms, traits, resistance, and interference, this instrument has shown adequate discriminant validity and test–retest reliability (Emmelkamp, 1982). It has been criticized for its inadequacy in assessing intrusive thoughts and washing rituals and for the interdependence of its four scales, requiring a lengthy and repetitive administrative procedure. A shortened 10-item paper-and-pencil version of this inventory, the Lynfield Obsessional Compulsive Questionnaire, was developed to circumvent the cumbersome administration procedure required by the LOI and to better assess obsessional ruminations (Allen & Tune, 1975). Evidence for reliability and validity has been demonstrated on a small sample of only 19 OCD subjects, and thus far this latter instrument has not been widely adopted.

Other Questionnaires for OCD Symptoms

The Sandler–Hazari Obsessional Compulsive Inventory (Sandler & Hazari, 1960) assesses both obsessional traits and symptoms, but has failed to discriminate clients from controls and has questionable validity (see Emmelkamp, 1982, for a review). Similarly, the obsessive–compulsive subscale of the Hopkins Symptom Checklist has been found inadequate with regard to some aspects of its reliability and validity (Steketee & Doppelt, 1986). The newer obsessive–compulsive subscale of the Symptom Checklist–90 may provide a better brief assessment of OCD symptoms, but it has not been adequately tested on an appropriate sample.

The Minnesota Multiphasic Personality Inventory (MMPI) yields what has been labeled an obsessive compulsive profile, but its validity, too, has been questioned. Doppelt (1983) found that neither scale elevation nor code (personality) types of the MMPI predicted outcome for obsessive compulsives. In addition, clinical impression suggests that many OCD subjects tend to score in the schizophrenic range on the MMPI despite the absence of true symptoms of this disorder, perhaps because of the bizarreness of their obsessions.

The newly developed Padua Inventory is a 60-item measure of common obsessive and compulsive symptoms (Sanavio, 1988) that has been tested on normal Italian, American, and Dutch samples and on an obsessional Italian group (Sternberger & Burns, 1990c; van Oppen, 1992). Item consistency and reliability have been found to be satisfactory, and convergent and discriminant validity have been demonstrated. Factor analyses have shown four factors, which are similar across studies. This measure includes items about obsessions and urges to ritualize that are not contained in other instruments.

Physiological Measures

Physiological responses such as heart rate, skin conductance, and respiration tend to covary with the intensity of anxiety (e.g., Lang, 1979). Although agreement between subjective and psychophysiological measures is far from perfect, elevations in one sphere in response to exposure to feared obsessive situations tend to be accompanied by increases in the other. Physiological measurement can be expensive and inconvenient unless an existing laboratory facility or portable equipment is readily available. Even with ready equipment and expertise, such assessment may not be useful for many clients, since relatively few obsessive situations can be reproduced accurately in the lab. For these reasons, physiological measures are rarely used in nonresearch settings and are not considered essential to successful assessment and treatment. Interested readers are referred to Kozak et al. (1987) for further information regarding assessment of physiology of fear.

In addition to the above-mentioned measures of physiology, some investigators have studied biochemical responses of OCD clients (including dexamethasone suppression test responses, cortisol, and cerebral blood flow), as well as neurological activity using MRI and PET scan technology (see Chapter 5 for a brief review). The clinical utility of these assessments in providing information about obsessive discomfort and compulsive behavior is not yet clear.

Responding to Clients' Questions about Their Symptoms

Etiology of OCD Symptoms

At some point during assessment, most clients inquire about the therapist's beliefs about why they developed their symptoms and have been unable to control them. Many are convinced that there is a biological explanation for both etiology and maintenance, because of substantial mass media coverage of biological issues and of the positive effects of serotonergic medications. By this point, the therapist has considerable information about a client and can provide a general explanation of etiology such as the following:

At this time, most clinicians and researchers believe that there are multiple causes for OCD. Unfortunately, we have limited information about the contributions of various factors. I can only give you guesses as to why people in general or you in particular might have acquired these symptoms.

For some people, particular traumatic experiences seem to be important factors. They felt strong fear or other unpleasant feelings during this trauma, and naturally began to try to avoid situations or even thoughts associated with things that reminded them of the traumatic event. As we said earlier, when avoidance fails, rituals are developed to reduce discomfort. [If the client's history of symptoms included a traumatic experience, this can be discussed here.]

In some cases, we believe that early teachings, either from parents or at school or someplace else, may have set the stage for obsessive fears and efforts to avoid particular thoughts or ideas or situations. [Again, examples should be drawn from the client's personal experiences. These might include parental injunctions such as "If you can't do it right, don't do it at all!", or parochial school teachings such as "Thinking is the same as doing" in reference to common sexual or aggressive images or thoughts that were considered sinful.] Such teachings are often impossible to follow, and so serve as a trap from which there is no good escape except avoidance and rituals. Children are particularly vulnerable to these kinds of injunctions because they usually accept what adults say, without being able to use their own judgment about the reasonableness of these rules.

This is a very important topic for discussion later in therapy, since many clients hold irrational beliefs and attitudes adopted from childhood injunctions or unspoken rules or expectations. Such beliefs may interfere with these clients' willingness to engage in exposure (e.g., in the case of exposure to obsessive sexual or religious images that the individual believes are sacrilegious and therefore forbidden by the church) or with their ability to maintain gains after intensive treatment is completed. At this point in the session, however, the therapist only mentions this as one of several possible contributing factors to the development of the disorder. Depending on the client's response, discussion of this topic is likely to recur during exposure sessions (see Chapter 11 for further comment on this issue). The therapist continues:

Another possibility is that obsessions and compulsions are biologically based. This might occur through genetic transmission or through some other biochemical or physical source. In the case of genetic inheritance, it seems that somewhere between 20% and 25% of immediate relatives of people with OCD will show signs of OCD itself. It is actually more likely that they will have other anxiety or depressive symptoms that are not OCD-related. Interestingly, even when there are relatives who have OCD symptoms, often they have different ones than the OCD person has. So for some people there may be an inherited tendency to develop OCD symptoms, but how it manifests itself probably depends on other factors in each person's experience and upbringing. There is some information to suggest that at least one part of the brain (probably the frontal lobe) may be involved in OCD symptoms, but we have a long way to go before researchers understand how this works. Similarly, we know that, so far, drugs that affect the way the body processes serotonin are more effective in reducing OCD than other types of drugs. But, again, we don't yet know why this is true.

We need to be aware that biology and experience influence each other, so that our learning experiences produce biochemical reactions in our bodies and our body chemistry produces emotional reactions. These are only some possible explanations for why certain people develop obsessions and compulsions. It's quite likely that some combination of factors is involved in most cases, and at this point you and I can only guess at why you developed OCD.

In all cases, the clinician will want to leave time for clients to respond to this explanation and to voice their own theories about this issue. Regardless of the explanation preferred, it is important to emphasize that learning plays an important role in decision making about how to respond to obsessive fears and compulsive urges. Individual responses can either maintain or enhance fears, or reduce them. Treatment will focus on providing skills and experiences that will enable clients to feel less anxious, to tolerate the discomfort better, and to make different decisions so that they can better control their OCD symptoms, especially when they are under stress in the future.

Explanations for Maintenance of Symptoms

To address questions about maintenance of obsessions and compulsions in spite of their ego-dystonic nature, the following explanation may be used:

It is hard to figure out why these symptoms have become so habitual, despite the fact that they are obviously maladaptive and very unpleasant for you. It is often hard for others, as well as yourself, to understand why you have such unreasonable fears (or guilty feelings) and why you go through rituals that seem unnecessary to others. But there are logical reasons why people do such things.

When we were going through the list of obsessions and compulsions earlier, we saw that obsessions are ideas, thoughts, images, or impulses that provoke discomfort and cause fear or guilt. Compulsions or rituals do just the opposite: They are behaviors or thoughts that you engage in to relieve this discomfort. This becomes quite a trap for even the most reasonable of people. None of us like to feel afraid or upset or uncomfortable. We try first to avoid the unpleasant situation, and if that's impossible, we do whatever makes us feel better at the moment—sometimes even when it is not in our best interests in the long run.

Now, in many ways it would be nice if you could just avoid the situations or ideas that upset you, like phobic people who are afraid of heights and just don't climb ladders or look out of windows in high buildings. But obsessions are not so easily avoided, because they are often internally generated by just thinking certain thoughts, and many external situations that trigger your fears cannot be avoided. [Here the therapist should provide specific examples from the client's own experiences. Fear of contamination by pesticides is used here as an illustration.] For example, you can't always avoid contact with an area that may have been sprayed with pesticides, much as I'm sure you'd like to in order to avoid contamination.

When we can't avoid, we try to escape the unpleasant sensations as soon as possible and in whatever way makes us feel better. So when an obsessive idea occurs—for example, when you're walking down the grocery store aisle and you realize you're right next to the pesticides—you become upset and search for some way to relieve this feeling. If at some time in the past, escaping from this kind of situation and/or washing calmed your fears, your automatic impulse is to run away and/or find a bathroom so you can wash. As soon as you do this, you feel better—or at least you're convinced that if you hadn't done so, you'd certainly feel much worse than you do now. So overall, the effect of escaping and washing is to reduce your discomfort. Every time you do this, you solidify your conviction that to manage obsessive fears you need to ritualize, and you get caught in a vicious cycle.

Does this explanation make sense to you?

At this point the therapist should evaluate how clearly the client understands this theoretical explanation, since it forms the basis for the treatment strategy of exposure and prevention of avoidance, escape, and rituals. Asking the client to describe how this model applies to him or her, using a different set of examples than the therapist has used, will indicate the degree of understanding and acceptance of these ideas. As evident from the manner of the explanation, the therapist seeks in all cases to normalize clients' experiences as much as possible, rather than encourage them further to view their symptoms as bizarre and "crazy," as many clients have done up to this point.

Rationale for Behavior Therapy

At this point the therapist must move on to explaining the treatment format and assessing the client's motivation to engage in exposure and response prevention, as well as his or her social support for doing so. Explanation of the therapy could continue as follows (the example of fear of contamination by pesticides is again used):

Let's go back to how we believe OCD symptoms are maintained for you and most people, so you can understand how treatment works. Right now, to reduce your obsessive fears of being contaminated by pesticides, you avoid many situations or you ritualize by washing. This only works temporarily until the next time you are exposed to possible contact with pesticides. You've probably noticed that over time it takes longer and longer to complete a ritual because it is only effective in a limited way. The obsessive fears are still there, waiting to re-emerge.

To treat OCD successfully, we must drastically reduce your obsessive fears themselves, so that you are not so easily upset by these ideas [thoughts, images, impulses, situations]. An effective way to accomplish this is to expose you deliberately and gradually to the very situations you try to avoid until your fear eventually subsides. It "habituates," probably in the same way that we all grow accustomed to unpleasant noises on the street after a time. Exposure is done in a gradual manner, with both of us deciding on the order in which to do the exposures so that they are manageable for you. Exposure should also be continued for long periods, to give your mind and body a chance to get used to the situation so it seems less upsetting.

In addition, we must block your automatic tendency to ritualize, because these would just interfere with the exposures, giving you less opportunity to become accustomed to the problematic obsessions. We can also eliminate rituals at the same gradual pace that we do exposure, so when we're working on a particular area, like handling a can of Raid, you would be asked not to wash at all afterward or in the future. But you would still be allowed to wash *briefly* after touching the trash outside if this bothers you even more. Eventually, we will do exposures to all your obsessive fears, so that in the end you are much less uncomfortable in such situations and your urge to ritualize is much reduced.

Assessing Motivation for Treatment

Finally, the strength of the client's motivation for engaging fully in treatment at this time is an important indicator of likely success. The combination of exposure and response prevention is a very anxiety-provoking therapy, and its demands on OCD sufferers must not be underestimated. Clients will need substantial willingness to tolerate the discomfort provoked by behavioral therapy, and it is often helpful if clients are thoroughly upset by their symptoms and the resultant functional impairment and unpleasant emotions. Motivation is best assessed by describing treatment in sufficient detail to give each client a clear picture of the daily treatment activities that will be expected, without minimizing or exaggerating the requirements. Clients' reactions to this description will usually clarify whether they are willing to proceed. Clarification and encouragement about the gradual nature of exposure may be needed to address questions and unreasonable fears, but accuracy is best to minimize argument, noncompliance, and later dropout.

Describing Treatment Effectiveness

Each client will need an opportunity to ask questions about how treatment would be applied for himself or herself and about how effective it is likely to be. Questions about the specific application cannot be completely answered until information gathering is completed; therefore, the therapist may have to postpone specific explanations of the process for another session or two. Treatment efficacy should be addressed by providing a very brief summary of the research literature (see Chapter 3), perhaps as follows:

Many studies have examined the effects of this behavioral treatment for OCD using exposure and ritual prevention. These studies are very consistent in showing that about two-thirds to three-quarters of clients benefit substantially, and most are able to maintain their gains for years afterward. The odds, then, are very much in your favor, particularly if you are very serious in your efforts to follow the treatment program carefully.

It is important to be aware, though, that treatment will not completely remove all your fears or urges to ritualize. But it should enable you to feel much less upset, and therefore to be able to easily resist urges to avoid situations or behave in a compulsive manner. It may be useful for you to know that more than 90% of the population has unpleasant intrusive thoughts, images, or impulses from time to time. Two research studies have established that this is extremely common among ordinary people. The difference between ordinary obsessions and those of people who develop OCD is that ordinary disturbing ideas provoke less discomfort and are more easily dismissed. So if 90% of people have unwanted ideas intruding in their heads, it would be unrealistic to expect that after treatment you will never experience any obsessions or urges to ritualize. Our treatment goal, then, is for you to feel less upset by your obsessive ideas and to be able to dismiss them more easily, without resorting to avoidance and rituals, which only increase the probability that the obsessive ideas will persist and be disturbing.

If you like, I can recommend some books about OCD symptoms and behavioral treatment and its effects. Would this be useful to you?

Several books describing behavioral and pharmacological treatments for OCD have been specifically written for clients and their relatives. A list of these references is given in Appendix H. The Steketee and White (1990) book contains a detailed explanation of all aspects of treatment, and is intended as a self-help book or as a companion volume for clients who are in behavioral treatment.

Scheduling Therapy

The therapist will need to schedule subsequent sessions to begin the intensive phase of treatment involving exposure and response prevention. Since this program requires sessions more than once a week, some advance planning—taking into consideration the client's and therapist's schedules—is needed at this point. Major gaps for holidays or vacations should be avoided during the first 6 weeks of treatment, to allow the client to make substantial progress in therapy. Interruptions early in treatment are likely to interfere with the client's strong motivation to withstand the sometimes intense discomfort that comes with exposure to very upsetting situations.

Deciding on the Use of Imaginal Exposure

By this point, the therapist has sufficient information to determine whether exposure can be accomplished easily in a direct (in vivo) manner, or whether imaginal exposure is likely to be needed. As noted in Chapter 6, this decision is based on the presence of feared disastrous consequences, which may not easily be provoked during *in vivo* exposure. If the assessment indicates that many of the client's obsessive fears are focused on future harm, the therapist is well advised to develop scenes that allow for processing of this imaginal material.

Clients who fear their own disease or death from contamination rarely require imaginal exposure, since contaminating themselves through direct contact automatically provokes these fears, which can then habituate. However, in the case (for instance) of a mother who fears killing or harming her daughter by contaminating her, direct exposure may not adequately provoke the images of the child's death that so frighten her. Of course, harm to the child may be feared to occur through other routes, such as failure to check adequately, failure to counteract an aggressive impulse by repeated actions, or failure to neutralize an image of the dead child with a corrective image of the child alive and well. In all of these cases, prolonged imagining of the very disaster the client fears leads typically to habituation of this fear.

To plan scenes for imaginal exposure (or "flooding," as many behaviorists label this method), the therapist and client first identify all of the disasters that occur to the client as a consequence of failure to ritualize. These feared outcomes can be rank-ordered by degree of anxiety provoked, with each outcome put in a separate scene. These scenes include exposure to external and internal cues without doing rituals, followed by complete descriptions of the consequences feared by the client. For example, a woman who feared running over pedestrians, especially small children, was first asked to imagine driving in a crowded place and hitting an adult who was injured but not killed. Once she habituated to this image, she imagined injuring a child, then hitting and killing an adult, and finally hitting and killing a child. These images provoked incremental amounts of discomfort and thus formed a hierarchy of feared disasters. Some clients may also fear being arrested for these actions and going to jail. If so, such images can be included in later scenes. Examples of scripts for imaginal exposure are given in Chapter 9.

Assessing Comorbidity

Additional symptoms that the client finds problematic can be assessed via a diagnostic interview and standardized questionnaire in some cases. With some exceptions (discussed in Chapter 11), there is little information about whether and how such comorbid conditions may interfere with therapy. However, clinical experience suggests that if other concurrent Axis I disorders or symptoms are connected to the OCD symptoms, the therapist must investigate this closely to determine the relationship and how it might affect exposure and response prevention. Identification of comorbid conditions is essential, since they may require additional treatment strategies or modification of the planned behavioral treatment. The reader is referred to Chapter 11 for a more detailed discussion of complicating conditions.

As mentioned in earlier chapters, the most common comorbid conditions are other anxiety disorders and depression. Although panic attacks are not common occurrences in OCD clients, they may impede treatment. For example, one woman experienced panic attacks and agoraphobic avoidance in response to situations that triggered her obsessive fears. This client was taught coping skills and cognitive interventions to control panic symptoms. Concurrent marked social phobia usually indicates the need for additional treatments aimed at this difficulty to return the client to a reasonably functional lifestyle. Some clients with symptoms of Post-Traumatic Stress Disorder (PTSD) may require therapeutic intervention for these symptoms. For example, one woman's PTSD symptoms coexisted with washing rituals, which appeared to have developed as a direct consequence of a sexual assault. Treatment required that the traumatic memories be addressed directly prior to and during exposures to feared contaminants. In some cases of comorbid anxiety disorders, antianxiety medications may be considered; however, the therapist should use caution about the amount of such medication, since benefits from exposure treatment depend upon clients' experiencing at least some obsessive fear.

Concurrent diagnosis of a psychotic disorder or schizotypal personality disorder appears to render many clients unsuitable for behavioral treatment of OCD (Baer & Minichiello, 1990; Minichiello et al., 1987). Awareness of other Axis II personality traits (e.g., avoidant, dependent, or obsessive compulsive ones, such as perfectionism or rigid moral beliefs) may lead the therapist to include cognitive treatment strategies to alter dysfunctional beliefs and attitudes underlying some of the obsessive fears. Personality traits need not be assessed formally, particularly if the clinician feels a need to commence therapy soon. Most likely, many of these traits can be identified simply through regular contact during the assessment and treatment sessions, and can be discussed as needed.

Direct assessment of alcohol and drug (prescription and nonprescription) use is needed prior to therapy. If substances are abused to relieve discomfort, specific measures to reduce consumption may be needed, so that obsessive fear can habituate during exposure without interference from chemical agents.

Depression has been identified as a poor prognostic factor for behavioral treatment by some investigators (e.g., Foa, Grayson, et al., 1983; Marks et al., 1980), though not by others (e.g., Mawson et al., 1982; Steketee et al., 1985). In one study (Steketee, 1987), I found that although pretreatment depression was not a predictor, high levels of depression and anxiety at the end of therapy were associated with relapse. In cases of severely debilitating depression, especially with suicidal ideation, the clinician should consider the use of antidepressant medications prior to beginning behavioral treatment. This issue is considered further in Chapter 11.

Since most OCD clients also exhibit depressed and anxious moods, some assessment of the severity of these conditions and of the likelihood of their interfering with treatment progress will be helpful. For this purpose, the Beck Depression Inventory (Beck, Ward, Mendelson, Mock, & Erbaugh, 1961) and the Beck Anxiety Inventory (Beck, Epstein, Brown, & Steer, 1988) are very useful, as well as relatively brief. If other comorbid problems have been identified (e.g., social anxiety, panic symptoms, PTSD symptoms, personality disorders), the therapist may wish to include appropriate questionnaires for further assessment of these areas.

Many comorbid conditions, such as those mentioned above, do not necessarily require concurrent or prior therapy before OCD symptoms can be directly addressed. If there is doubt about their relationship to the OCD symptoms, the therapist, in consultation with the client, can forge ahead with therapy on the understanding that the treatment plan may require modification if other symptoms interfere with the client's ability to carry out or benefit from exposure, blocking of rituals, and homework.

General History and Functioning

The "typical day" scenario discussed in Chapter 6 is also likely to shed light on the individual's general functioning. A general history is needed to enable the therapist to know the client well and to take into account his or her general functioning and present situation in conducting treatment. Identification of important experiences and their potential association with the client's current symptoms may help during planning and execution of exposure and blocking of rituals. Further information can be obtained by asking specific questions about medical history, education, work history, current employment, financial situation, past and present social and family relationships (including dating, sexual, and marital history), traumatic experiences, and previous treatment for OCD or other conditions.

Assessing Family Support

The therapist can inquire about the reaction of the client's family members or friends to his or her symptoms and efforts to seek therapy. This will begin a discussion of the nature of these interpersonal relationships, with an eye toward identifying individuals who may be of assistance to the client and therapist during behavioral treatment. If the client agrees, an interested spouse or other family member(s) can be invited to attend the last assessment session prior to the beginning of therapy. The stated purpose of this invitation is to enable significant others to meet the therapist, to provide their perspective on the client's symptoms, and to ask questions about the planned therapy and their potential role in this process. This interview, then, takes place in the presence of the client (unless there are compelling reasons for a private interview, as in the case of parents of young adolescent or child clients).

Often relatives have observed avoidance and ritualistic behaviors that a client has not mentioned, usually because they are so habitual that the client no longer thinks of them as "symptomatic" of OCD. Relatives' information about symptoms is often very useful to the clinician. Also, assessment of the interpersonal interaction between the client and a relative provides information about how supportive and helpful the relative is likely to be during therapy. Behavioral treatment is sufficiently anxiety-provoking that assistance from relatives as supporters and supervisors can be extremely helpful, unless such assistance would be conflictual and actually increase tension. In some cases, in fact, clients are encouraged to undergo behavior therapy while living away from problematic relatives. In one case, treatment led to the client's precipitous departure from her parental home—an event considered by both client and therapist to be very therapeutic.

The therapist might begin the interview as follows:

I suggested that [the client] ask you to come today because it is often very helpful to have a family member's perspective on the obsessive and compulsive problems. This also gives you a chance to ask me any questions about what we are planning to do during the therapy. First, I'd like to ask about your thoughts about [the client]'s problems.

The therapist can then observe whether the relative appears to be supportive of the client. Next, the relative is invited to ask any questions about OCD or treatments for it, as well as about the specific therapy planned. If genuine concern and caring are evident without excessive criticism or hostility, and the client has already expressed a willingness to involve the relative in helping in the recovery process, the relative may be invited to assist with homework assignments. The therapist can explain the relative's role as follows:

During treatment, [the client] will have daily assignments to expose himself [herself] to gradually more difficult obsessive situations, and to block or prevent compulsive behaviors. [Examples are usually needed here.] You can help by sympathizing and encouraging [the client] whenever he [she] seems upset during the course of exposure homework. Sometimes it can be helpful to distract [the client] when he [she] is obsessing about an exposure situation. Anything that would make it easier to resist an urge to go through a ritual would also be helpful. It is very important not to be critical at such times, since any negative comments from you at these times are only likely to make the struggle seem harder. Positive comments to [the client] for trying to complete homework or for making even small progress can be very helpful. [To the client:] What could [the relative] do that you would find helpful during treatment?

A discussion of tentative roles during therapy ensues, with the knowledge that modifications may be needed during treatment.

Inpatient versus Outpatient Treatment

Research suggests that there are no clear advantages for either inpatient or outpatient treatment, since neither has proved superior in a controlled trial (van den Hout, Emmelkamp, Kraaykamp, & Griez, 1988). In practice, outpatient treatment is generally more advantageous, since clients usually have better access to situations that disturb them. For some clients, hospitalization removes them entirely from cues that provoke their fears. For example, one woman with extensive checking of locks and fire hazards in her home declared that the hospital would be a haven for her, since she would feel no sense of responsibility in this context. From her point of view, it was the hospital staff's responsibility to ensure safety, not hers. In such cases as this one, hospitalization would obviously make behavioral treatment unusually difficult.

Generally, hospitalization is arranged only only if unusual circumstances are present: (1) The client believes that he or she cannot carry out exposure and ritual prevention without constant supervision; (2) the client is very depressed and considered potentially suicidal, necessitating medications and close supervision prior to and during treatment; and (3) the client has no supportive family members to assist at home and wishes for help from the nursing staff. Therapists who intend to conduct exposure and response prevention treatment in hospital settings are urged to spend considerable time discussing and monitoring the treatment plan with all staff members who will be in contact with their clients. A successful outcome requires considerable time and energy to ensure that the treatment plan is carried out appropriately.

The Therapeutic Contract

The assessment ends with the therapist's commenting encouragingly about the client's ability to benefit substantially from the treatment program. The therapist should neither minimize the discomfort and difficulty involved in completing this treatment, nor scare the client unnecessarily. Confidence and encouragement, along with a firm and realistic attitude, will be most helpful at this point.

Prior to starting exposure and ritual prevention, a formal written or oral contract should be negotiated regarding the roles of the client, therapist, and family members or friends, as well as the specific tasks to be undertaken. The purpose of the contract is to solidify the client's commitment to the therapy program and to make it easier for the clinician to be firm when hesitation occurs. Because treatment is of necessity anxiety-provoking, clients' motivation must be fairly high to enable them to engage in the exposure process essential for improvement. Clients who have agreed to a planned series of sessions with expected content often feel more compelled to hold up their end of the bargain. In the face of balking, the therapist can merely remind clients of the agreement and of the reasons for it, avoiding argument and confrontation. Clients who feel that they can no longer abide by their original contract can then be advised that treatment can be delayed until they feel better able to proceed, or the contract can be revised to focus on different problems.

The contract is not intended to confine a client rigidly, such that specific exposures *must* be conducted on particular days or in a prescribed manner. Rather, treatment should proceed flexibly, taking into account unexpected stressors, problems during the exposure, unusually high anxiety levels, and external factors beyond the therapist's or client's control. The contract serves as a reminder to both clinician and client that certain procedures and behaviors are expected on a routine basis.

Summary

In addition to the YBOCS and its accompanying Symptom Checklist, described in Chapter 6, some standardized assessment instruments may be helpful in quantifying and clarifying symptoms, including the MOC and the CAC. Suggestions are given for addressing common questions asked early in treatment. Assessment should continue to acquire information about comorbid conditions, personality traits, difficulties in general functioning and in familial relationships, and the degree of social support available to clients. A general history is needed for a better understanding of the context in which symptoms developed and continued, as well as the consequences of the OCD symptoms for sufferers. Interviews with close relatives or friends who are aware of the OCD symptoms can be helpful in treatment planning and in developing awareness of potential difficulties after exposure treatment has ended. After providing a clear rationale for exposure and response prevention, the therapist can ascertain the degree of the client's commitment to treatment. At this point, decisions about including imaginal exposure are made, and the content of imaginal and direct exposure is planned. A contract for therapy can then be established. As noted earlier, the clinician should not feel constrained to follow the order of assessment procedures presented here.

8

Implementing Direct Exposure Sessions

Refining the Hierarchy

During information gathering, a treatment hierarchy is developed that lists in order of difficulty all situations requiring direct exposure (see Chapter 6, Figure 6.2). A client assigns ratings ranging from 0 (no discomfort) to 100 (maximum discomfort) to each situation, according to the degree of anxiety or discomfort that exposure is expected to provoke. Depending upon the rating of difficulty, therapist and client together decide to which treatment session each situation should be assigned. This is also recorded on the list of obsessive situations (Figure 6.2).

Planned hierarchies constitute rough contracts between clients and therapists for what will be done during each session. Of course, contracts are subject to modification, depending on clients' experiences as exposures are undertaken. Misestimates of expected discomfort must be accommodated to enable clients to progress at a consistent pace that matches their ability to manage anxiety. These hierarchies also allow therapists to remind reluctant clients of their earlier commitment to engage in specific exposures. When the going gets difficult, especially after the first few exposure sessions, it is sometimes essential to remind clients of their goals, of the progress they have already made on their hierarchies, and of the advantages to them of continuing the exposures.

General Format for Exposure Sessions

Except for the first one, treatment sessions begin with a review of the homework recorded on an appropriate form (see Figure 8.2, below, for an example). The therapist compliments the client on progress made, inquires about difficulties and anxiety levels, and briefly discusses other related events during the week. Next, therapist and client review the planned exposures for that session, agreeing on their order, format, and location. Exposure is then initiated, with the therapist modeling whenever useful and instructing the client in technique. As noted previously, exposure sessions will require clinicians to balance firmness and encouragement with empathy and respect, particularly when clients are required to confront very uncomfortable situations.

Often, the therapist may need to modify the manner in which clients carry out particular aspects of a task, to encourage more contact or more normal behaviors. For example, those with contamination fears are encouraged to touch objects or places completely, gradually spreading a supposed contaminant from fingers to entire hands, rubbing it on their arms, faces, hair, and other body parts they consider sensitive to contamination. The goal is to feel covered by the contaminant so that no "clean" places remain on the body. In addition, contaminants must be spread completely to other "clean" areas of the environment during treatment sessions, if possible, as well as for homework assignments. For those with other types of obsessions, thorough exposure, whatever that may entail, is encouraged.

Clients are encouraged to concentrate on, rather than distract their attention from, exposure situations. Individual hierarchy items are confronted for as long as needed to enable clients to become noticeably more comfortable with them (though they rarely become completely at ease) before the next situation is added. The therapist should neither go too slowly nor rush clients through their experiences. Duration of exposure should be adjusted to the needs of clients, as determined by their self-reported anxiety levels, the therapist's observation of manifest discomfort, and clients' willingness to proceed to the next situation.

Throughout the process, the therapist inquires about anxiety levels every 5–10 minutes and whenever a change in the exposure situation is initiated. A therapy session recording form for this purpose is given in Figure 8.1 and is very useful for later reference regarding clients' typical reactions during treatment. Thoughts and feelings about the situation should be requested regularly, to help clients focus on the exposure situation and process all aspects as fully as possible. Particularly for those whose fears include ideas of disastrous consequences, the therapist should encourage discussion of possible harm that clients envision. Imaginal exposure may be needed for those whose feared consequences do not appear to be fully expressed during *in vivo* exposure (see Chapter 9 for details of exposure in imagery).

At the end of the session, the therapist and client agree on the homework to be completed prior to the next formal exposure session. Specific in-

---

Client name: Date:

Session number:

Review of homework assignment:
    Time spent on homework:
    Exposures accomplished:
    Pattern of anxiety responses during exposure:
    Comments:

Response prevention:
    Were there any violations?
    If yes, describe:

Description of today's exposure in vivo:

Anxiety levels (0–100):
Beginning: 50 minutes:
10 minutes: 60 minutes:
20 minutes: 70 minutes:
30 minutes: 80 minutes:
40 minutes: 90 minutes:
    Comments:

Homework assignment:

FIGURE 8.1. Therapist form for exposure sessions.

structions are given concerning the amount and method of contact with the situation. Writing out homework assignments and providing a form such as that given in Figure 8.2 for recording practice and outcome (e.g., discomfort reduction) facilitates clients' cooperation and accurate following of instructions. Only if a client cannot carry out a particular homework assignment should the therapist accompany him or her to that situation.

Name: Date:

Assignment number:

#1 Situation to practice:

Time to practice:

Anxiety levels:
Beginning: 40 minutes:
10 minutes: 50 minutes:
20 minutes: 60 minutes:
30 minutes:
  Comments:

#2 Situation to practice:

Time to practice:

Anxiety levels:
Beginning: 40 minutes:
10 minutes: 50 minutes:
20 minutes: 60 minutes:
30 minutes:
  Comments:

FIGURE 8.2. Homework form.

Beginning the Treatment

At the beginning of the first treatment session, the therapist might proceed as follows:

Let me first ask you how your week went and how you feel about starting the exposures today.

Discussion about the client's experiences and probable apprehensions ensues. The therapist agrees that exposure even to the first few feared situations on the hierarchy will probably be uncomfortable, but notes that hundreds of others with OCD have undertaken this treatment and that anxiety usually lessens after a relatively brief period of an hour or more. Some reminders of the agreement and plan are usually helpful:

If I were in your shoes, I'm sure I'd be worried about what we'll do and how it will feel, too. Let's just go over how we'll proceed today and for the next several sessions. We've agreed to plan for about 15 sessions and add more if we need them. I'd like to have you go over the list again briefly, to make sure that you agree with the order of the situations and that we haven't left out something important out that you remembered during the week. Here's our list. [The therapist waits for confirmation of their plan, discussing changes as needed.] O.K., we'll start with the first couple of items on the list, the ones you rated at a 35 and 40 discomfort level. My role is to encourage you to do the exposures as fully as possible, so you are really paying attention to all aspects of the situation that usually bother you. Your job is to confront each circumstance actively and deliberately, to stick with it, and to keep me informed about how you're feeling and what you're thinking. We can't really know exactly what it will be like for you until we start, but I'll support your efforts and help you manage the discomfort as we go along. In the end, though, it is you who will have done the very hard work.

Research findings suggest that clients who attribute gains to their own efforts (willpower) during therapy are more likely to have a better outcome following behavioral treatment (Steketee et al., 1985). It is important, therefore, to emphasize the client's decision-making role throughout the exposure process. Before the exposure treatment is begun, the exposure hierarchy is reviewed and desired changes are made. The therapist is advised to be alert for delay tactics from clients who are understandably reluctant to begin an anxiety-provoking experience. Such tactics may take the form of extra questions (especially those already answered in prior sessions) or pressing unrelated problems clients wish to discuss. Limiting the length and topics of conversation at the beginning of the first actual exposure session is likely to facilitate progress.

Hierarchies are given below for two different types of OCD symptoms, along with beginning treatment scenarios for each hierarchy.

Typical Treatment of Clients with Contamination Fears

One client, whom I will call Amy, suffered from extreme fears of contamination by pesticides. She agreed that her fears were out of proportion to the actual danger inherent in using such chemicals, and recalled that several years earlier she had not been concerned about this problem. Amy's hierarchy, constructed during the second and third assessment sessions, is given below.

Hierarchy: Fear of Contamination from Pesticides

Exposure situation	Discomfort (0–100)	Session #
Walk down grocery store aisle where pesticides are kept	35	1
Touch inside of grocery store carts that might have held pesticide containers	40	1
Touch unopened D-Con, Raid, etc., in grocery	45	2
Purchase groceries placed on checkout counter that had pesticide containers on it	45	2
Touch cleaning products in kitchen cupboard where pesticides used to be kept	45	3
Touch corners of kitchen floor and baseboards where pesticides might have been used	50	3
Touch surfaces in basement where pesticides used to be stored	55	3
Pet a dog who was dipped for fleas last summer	55	3
Bring unopened pesticides home to kitchen counters and put in cupboard	60	4
Handle unopened containers and touch other objects in kitchen, bathroom, etc.	60	4
Handle unopened containers and touch objects in baby's room	65	5
Touch opened container of D-Con, Raid, etc.	70	5
Spray Raid outside the house	80	6
Walk on neighbor's lawn with pesticide sign; return home and walk around, touch floors	80	6
Spray Raid in corner of the kitchen	90	7
Set out D-Con traps or ant traps under cabinets in kitchen	90	7
Pet dog with recent flea/tick collar	95	8
Allow baby to pet dog and play on kitchen floor	100	8

Realistic Concerns about Danger

As is apparent from Amy's hierarchy, many situations feared by those with OCD do have some element of risk or danger involved, but clients have lost their ability to make rational judgments about the actual dangerousness of feared situations. In Amy's hierarchy, the most difficult situations were selected to be as "risky" as possible within the confines both of her willingness to expose herself and of experts' knowledge about acceptable exposure. It is obvious that some individuals without OCD would not allow pesticides to be used in their homes except in extreme situations, such as infestation. However, most people consider some use of pesticides reasonable and allowable, in accordance with public health guidelines. Where to draw the line for a given client depends upon the person's attitudes prior to onset of obsessions, as well as current scientific knowledge about acceptable risk. For example, current knowledge linking small amounts of asbestos with cancer indicates that it would be quite inappropriate to ask a client fearful of asbestos actually to touch it.

Nonetheless, in general it is better to err on the side of risk taking than of caution, since those with OCD often develop their debilitating symptoms precisely because they misestimate risk and avoid it excessively. In addition, the therapist needs to be aware that many clients will not agree to expose themselves to high items on a hierarchy early in treatment, because their fears color their rational judgment. Often, they can proceed with these "dangerous" situations as lower ones are successfully negotiated.

Use of the Hierarchy

The review of the hierarchy at the outset is intended to remind clients of the planned sequence of situations and of their commitment to the exposure and response prevention treatment. Though a client may add an item or two to the list at this point, it is very likely that additional fearful situations will be discovered during treatment. These can be incorporated into ongoing or later exposure sessions as appropriate. Individual exposure sessions often include several hierarchy items of approximately the same level of difficulty or discomfort. Since situations rarely occur all in the same location, the therapist must be prepared to accompany a client to different places. For convenience, items can be grouped and assigned to treatment sessions according to their location, as long as they are roughly equivalent in degree of difficulty.

To get Amy started on her hierarchy, the clinician accompanied Amy to her local grocery store, reminding her on the way of exactly what they would do:

So today we'll start by just walking down the aisle where the pesticides are kept. I'd like you to pay close attention to the items on the shelf that especially bother you. We'll probably want to touch some things near them, so you can actually handle things that feel a little "contaminated." After we've done that, we can go on to touching the inside of carts that you believe might have held pesticide containers, and any other objects that seem to fall into this category. I'll be asking you to tell me your anxiety level every few minutes. Please let me know if the discomfort level changes suddenly at any point, so I can keep in touch with how you are feeling. How anxious are you right now, thinking about what we'll be doing?

In view of the potentially awkward public situations encountered by therapists and clients during exposure sessions, some comments on how to handle exposure sessions conducted in such contexts are warranted here. Generally, it is not necessary to notify store managers, security personnel, or other staff about the activities planned. In fact, it is doubtful whether most employees would understand without lengthy explanation, or whether they would give permission. Furthermore, clients may be very uncomfortable with public disclosure of their psychiatric difficulties. Instead, exposure sessions in grocery stores, shops, train stations, or any public place can almost always be carried out without calling attention to the therapeutic activities. Conversation should be kept to a minimum to convey essential information, and carried on in low tones. Actions such as touching objects to contaminate them or oneself should be carried out in as "normal" a fashion as possible. Exposure can be prolonged by having a client examine an object closely (as if deciding about a purchase), holding it while looking at other things in the store, putting it in the cart and fingering it periodically, returning to re-examine other identical objects and picking one of a different color (brand, style), and so forth.

If adequate exposure requires spending 30 minutes in a small shop under the watchful eye of a sole proprietor, to avoid suspicion it is wise to plan to purchase something small or to engage the shopkeeper in some discussion about an item of interest. Problematic experiences (unexpectedly high anxiety, a client's noticing a friend in the shop) can be dealt with by exiting the scene temporarily and returning later that session or another time. Occasionally a client or therapist will encounter a friend or acquaintance during such exposure sessions. It is advisable to have a plan for how to introduce the other and terminate the contact quickly.

Obtaining Discomfort Levels

The therapist's last question to Amy above enabled her to provide some estimate of her anticipatory anxiety about the upcoming exposure. For many, this expectant fear is considerably higher than the fear actually experienced in the real situation. If this proves true during the first few exposures, it is likely that obsessions are partly maintained by this mechanism of high anticipatory anxiety followed by avoidance before there is any chance of actually encountering the feared contaminant. The therapist can remind these individuals to disregard their fearful expectations, and remember that these feelings do not really represent how they are likely to feel during actual exposure. Some clients, however, underestimate their expected degree of discomfort and must be encouraged to continue with exposure situations that are more difficult than they thought they would have to manage. Fortunately, most fairly accurately assess their probable level of discomfort, and exposure sessions can proceed as planned.

At the beginning of the first session, the therapist encouraged Amy to comment on any internal thoughts or ideas that occurred to her during exposure. This allowed the therapist a window into her internal dialogue, so that corrective action could be taken for problematic reactions or assumptions. For example, to minimize discomfort, clients may try to convince themselves that the feared object or situation is not actually present or is present in small amounts. Some may try to distract themselves by thinking about other things or by comparing the present situation to a worse one and minimizing its difficulty. Others plan to perform rituals "inadvertently" (e.g., by washing for other rational reasons, thereby removing the supposed contaminant) soon after the therapist has ended the session. Clients inclined toward perfectionism and rigid rules may put extra pressure on themselves to make rapid progress or to do the exposure thoroughly, thereby pushing themselves too quickly into more difficult exposure situations. Still others may feel overwhelmed by the degree of struggle required and wish to quit. No matter what the internal dialogue, it is important to gain clients' trust so that they are willing to share disquieting thoughts about treatment. To Amy, upon their arrival at the grocery store, the therapist said:

O.K., here we are. Let's start with the aisle that the pesticides are on. Where is it? [Therapists can count on clients to know exactly where the avoided objects are located!] Let's walk by and look closely at all the brands. What's your discomfort right now on the 0-to-100 scale? [Amy gave a level close to the expected one.] Now, which type shall we work on first?

Encouraging Self-Controlled Exposure

Whenever possible, clients should choose exposure situations themselves from within the range of contracted exposures, to maximize their self-control. As researchers have noted, self-controlled exposures enhance clients' abilities to maintain gains after formal treatment has ended (Emmelkamp & Kraanen, 1977). Amy's therapist continued:

Tell me why you picked this one. What are the levels you associate with the various pesticide brands you see here?

Clients who choose to face more difficult situations can be applauded for their efforts to confront their fears courageously. Those who select less fearful ones will probably require special encouragement to struggle against anxiety. Amy's therapist then asked her:

What are you thinking right now? What's your level of discomfort right now?

Again, the therapist can follow clients' leads to address potential problems as they arise. Nonetheless, the therapist should not become too distracted by their responses, but should move on to the next situation as soon as they grow more comfortable with the present one. Reported thoughts are appropriate for discussion during the exposure session as long as their content is related to the situation at hand. That is, clients may discuss their reactions to the stimuli, fears about consequences of exposure, their associations to earlier experiences with them, or redollections of the onset of this particular concern (in Amy's case, pesticides). Distraction via conversation about other topics should be avoided, since it appears to hinder habituation.

Like many clients, Amy asked the therapist, "Doesn't this bother you?" A direct response was called for, without taking the focus from her reactions:

No, this doesn't upset me. But you probably already know that it doesn't upset most people who come to shop here. Here, would it help if I touch it too?

The therapist picked up a can identical to the one Amy was holding that was next to the pesticides, and kept the discussion focused on thoughts and feelings about the items, Amy's fearful reactions to them, and how other people view pesticides.

Clients are well aware that their reactions are very different from those of other people around them, though they may express surprise that others approach their feared situations with equanimity. It is difficult for many to imagine not experiencing obsessive discomfort, since this is all they have known in recent years. Only continued exposure is likely to reduce clients' fear and increase their understanding of a different viewpoint.

Habituation and Managing Anxiety

Clients who report discomfort ratings of 35 to 40 out of the possible 100 may not habituate substantially to these relatively low-ranking hierarchy items, partly because of their anticipation of upcoming more difficult ones. If discomfort does not reduce after 20 minutes or so, it is probably most useful to continue with other planned or relevant exposures, checking with the clients at each addition. New exposures added during a session need not always be planned and listed in the hierarchy. Once in the situation, new ideas about appropriate exposure items or situations often present themselves to both therapists and clients. Amy's therapist asked her:

O.K., what's your level now? [Amy responded with a 35.] How will you feel if we hold these things right next to the pesticides? [A level of 60 was given.] O.K., that's a bit more than we planned. Here, what about a couple of these houseware things? Here's a can opener and a corkscrew. How much will these bother you? [Amy responded with a 40.] O.K., here you go. [Amy accepted the new objects gingerly.] Good for you. How do you feel?

Now, whenever you do an exposure, be sure you really touch it completely. Rub it all over your hands. Good. Now rub it on your face and hair and any other part of you that you usually protect from contamination. Your job is to cover yourself in contamination from that can opener. Here, watch me. Like this. Fine! It's pretty obvious that you don't like it, but you're doing fine. Now the corkscrew. Good! What are your reactions?

After several minutes of Amy's holding these items, with her anxiety levels remaining stable or declining, the therapist inquired:

Are you ready to add anything new from what you see here, or shall we move on to the grocery carts?

A fairly typical habituation of subjective anxiety responses during an *in vivo* exposure is depicted in Figure 8.3. This client was a 69-year-old man who was extremely fearful of forgetting things or losing important objects. This obsessive fear had worsened considerably as he grew older, and it appeared that his fears stemmed partly from his fears of aging. He reported that nearly all feared situations produced high levels of anxiety, and thus the first exposure session depicted in the figure shows an unusually high peak anxiety rating of 90, which declined rapidly during the session. Therapists should be aware, however, that many clients' obsessive fears do not decline so rapidly nor so completely as did this man's. Slower rates of habituation do not necessarily indicate poorer prognosis.

Changing Clients' Attitudes toward Risk

Throughout the treatment, the therapist encourages clients to take some responsibility for identifying items that should be included in the exposure

Anxiety Levels during Exposure Treatment

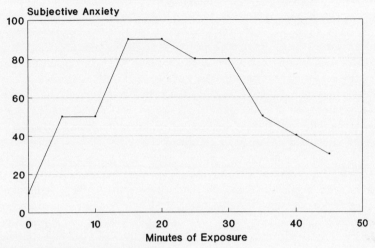

Exposure to throwing out cigar wrappers
in 69-year-old man fearful of losing
important objects

FIGURE 8.3. Habituation of subjective anxiety responses during the first exposure session in a 69-year-old man fearful of forgetting things or losing important objects.

situations. Whenever possible, clients should take charge of planning the treatment exposures, as well as homework assignments. Strong reinforcement of such efforts is warranted whenever it occurs, until the seeking out of situations that provoke obsessional discomfort is an established habit. The therapist can encourage clients to view this as a sort of detective game of "search and destroy" in regard to unreasonable fears. To Amy, who pointed to a shoe polish container, the therapist suggested:

Fine. Why don't you go ahead and hold the shoe polish if that bothers you too? Is it worse than these other things we're holding? What's your level? [She reported a 50.] I'm impressed by your willingness to let me know what's even harder to do and to try it. That approach will serve you very well during this treatment.

Use of Humor

Humor is often a helpful coping strategy for managing anxiety. Exposures that put clients and therapists in awkward situations observed by others can be used as opportunities for humorous comments about the oddity of the circumstance they are in. Humor should always pertain to the exposure context rather than distracting from it. Amy's therapist continued:

So here we are, hanging out at the pesticides, holding onto can openers and corkscrews. I wonder what the store manager will tell his wife about us tonight? "There were these really odd birds just hanging out around the pesticides. I can't figure out what the heck they were up to. I was afraid they were never gonna leave." Maybe it's time we moved on to touching the insides of grocery carts. That really ought to confuse him! Ready? Let's take these corkscrews with us for now. I've always wanted my very own contaminated corkscrew anyway!

Such use of humor is only appropriate if clients appear able to join in the amusement. It often serves to help reduce discomfort, particularly later on during treatment when higher-ranking items are encountered. However, if clients seem very distressed, humor is probably out of place and should be avoided in favor of expressions of empathy for their struggle and confidence that, with continued work, the clients will eventually find exposure tasks easier.

Adding New Exposure Items

During Amy's grocery store visit, retaining contact with the contaminated objects continued the previous exposure while adding a new planned item to the hierarchy. To Amy, the therapist proposed:

Let's both take a cart, and how about a little carrying basket too for each of us? That way we can accomplish exposure to several of these at once. You pick the carts and baskets that would bother you the most. Which ones do you want?

After Amy had chosen, the therapist questioned her about which characteristics of the cart led her to do so. Most clients will cooperate and select the more contaminated items, but a few will avoid doing so. Detailed questioning during early exposure sessions enables the therapist to gain a thorough understanding of what clients consider "contaminated," as well as of their level of motivation and the degree of encouragement and support required for engagement in and benefit from the exposure. Such detail is not required in later sessions, when the therapist has learned how to view contaminants from the clients' point of view. Amy was asked:

Why did you pick these two? [Amy pointed to dark marks on the metal, indicating that these made her think of pesticides, even though she knew that this made no sense.

Still, these carts bothered her more.] Anything else about them, or is that the main thing? [Amy noted that the bottom was worse than the sides, because pesticides might leak or fall over in the cart.] All right, that's the part you need to touch most. How anxious will that make you?

If a client reports a number consistent with earlier expectations when the hierarchy was planned, both parties proceed with the exposure to the new item and discuss the client's reactions. If, however, the new item provokes substantially stronger anxiety reactions, the therapist may postpone contact with the worst parts until some habituation has occurred during this session or until a later session in treatment. In this case, Amy indicated an expected anxiety of 60. The therapist replied:

Sixty? That's a bit higher than we were planning for this session. Do you think you can do this now or do we need to wait until the next session? [Amy shook her head no.] No? Now, why am I not surprised? O.K., if you touch this shiny metal part here on the side of the cart, how much will that be? 40? I bet you can do that now. Am I right?

Encouragement to follow through on new exposures conveys an assumption that clients should not be rigid in following the planned hierarchy and should challenge themselves to progress further whenever possible. Amy's therapist continued:

Go ahead, touch it with both hands, not just the finger. Like this. [Therapist modeled.] That's right, the whole palm. Fine. I can tell this is hard for you. You're doing a great job of tolerating the fear. Just hang in there. We can walk around the store and put a few things in the carts to keep touching them.

After the exposure was complete, therapist and client put some of the items from the cart back on the shelves, purchasing others (including some of the contaminated ones) to avoid suspicion from store personnel.

Observing Closely

If Amy had chosen a shiny, clean-looking cart over a dirtier one, the suspicious therapist would have asked:

I'd have thought that this cart here would upset you more. It looks dirtier. How much would touching the bottom of this one be?

Most clients will admit when questioned directly in such a situation that they chose the easier task, and will usually say why. Often they do not feel able to manage the more difficult one and are reluctant to push themselves further at that moment, though they may do so on another occasion. If Amy had given such an explanation, the therapist would have said:

I understand your reluctance to pick the harder one, but it is better for us if you just tell me that it's too hard for you right now. You are the best judge of what you can manage, and I'll respect your judgment. My job is to encourage you to do exposures while being as supportive as possible. I need your help in letting me know exactly how you feel.

The timing of movement from one item to another during any given exposure session is dictated by clients' discomfort levels and willingness to proceed. With Amy, the therapist remained for at least 15–20 minutes in each situation until she reported both some decrement in discomfort (though not usually to baseline levels) and an ability to move on to a new planned situation. It is important to allow some time for clients to accustom themselves to new exposures prior to the end of the session. The therapist can judge the time needed on the basis of the initial reaction to earlier similar situations or on clients' reports of probable anxiety. Usually, it is unwise to introduce entirely new items with less than 20 minutes to go, and often 30 or more minutes are needed for more disturbing ones.

Common Issues during Exposure to Contaminants

Before I continue to describe exposure procedures for clients with other types of obsessive fears, a few comments are in order regarding commonly encountered issues during exposure for contamination fears.

Compartmentalizing

Over many years of coping with their fears, many clients have developed strategies for compartmentalizing "clean" (uncontaminated) and "dirty" (contaminated) places or objects. One man's closet was divided into one section that contained clothes untouched by objects or places associated with his feared contaminant, and another section where he put contaminated clothes. Because washing the contaminated clothes was upsetting for him, this "dirty" section of the closet grew much larger than the "clean" part. He also maintained separate kitchen drawers with uncontaminated utensils and contaminated ones, selecting one or the other depending on whether he was already "clean" or "dirty" himself. During exposure treatment, the deliberate and complete mixing of the "clean" and "dirty" objects should be scheduled according to the expected level of discomfort.

Idiosyncratic Client Behaviors

During exposure treatment, the therapist should keep a sharp eye out for behaviors that appear even slightly odd (i.e., not what most people would do under the same circumstances), since these "idiosyncracies" often represent subtle avoidance behaviors. Examples include carrying "clean" towels clutched to one's chest to prevent possible contact with doorways that are perceived as contaminated, and putting hands in pockets to avoid inadvertent contact with contamination. Many variations of opening doors are used to minimize contamination: turning the less contaminated base of the doorknob with thumb and forefinger; backing through doorways or using elbows rather than pushing them open with the palm of the hand; and/or opening cupboards by the edge of the door rather than the handle. Examples are endless, and many clients have used these methods for so long that they are no longer aware of their accommodation to their fears. It is up to the therapist to help clients identify these "miniavoidances" and encourage them to stop using them during exposure treatment.

Typical Treatment of Clients with Fears of Harming

Below are given the hierarchies for a second client, Jim, who feared harming others by causing a fire or by driving over pedestrians, and also feared hurting his cat. Three hierarchies were developed and employed concurrently during treatment.

Hierarchy 1: Fears of Responsibility for Harm—Fire

Exposure situation	Discomfort (0–100)	Session #
Make coffee at home with electric pot	35	1
Use toaster and popcorn maker, without unplugging after use	40	1
Use and turn off faucets in upstairs bathroom; leave without checking them	40	1
Pass by coffee machine in convenience store without checking it	40	2
Use iron at home; unplug; leave without checking	45	2
Use stove at home; turn off; leave without checking	50	2
At work, use copy machine near coffee pot; no checking	45	3
At work, use computer, dictaphone, lights without checking	45	3
Stand near stove in friend's kitchen without checking	55	3
Get coffee at convenience store and exit via door near hot soup container	55	3

(*continued*)

Use iron; turn off; leave plugged in; leave room	60	4
Use utensils near stove without checking stove	65	4
Go to bed at night without checking stove	65	4
Go to bed without checking furnace	75	5
Sit at desk at work near electric heater	75	5
Use kitchen area (not appliances) at work	75	5
Use hot plate at work	75	5
Turn on electric heater at work; turn off; leave without checking	80	6
Use stove at home; no checking	80	6
Enter kitchen at night, no lights; leave without checking	85	6
Make coffee at work	90	7
Turn on heater at work	95	8

Hierarchy 2: Fears of Responsibility for Harm—Hitting Pedestrians

Exposure situation*	Discomfort (0–100)	Session #
Ride bicycle on bike path with pedestrians	40	1
Drive to end of block and return	45	1
Drive to grocery store (2 blocks), light traffic	60	2
Drive to mall (1 mile), light traffic	65	3
Drive to treatment session in daytime	65	4
Drive to grocery store, heavy traffic	70	5
Drive to mall at night	70	5
Drive to mall in daytime, heavy traffic	75	6
Drive to center of small town during lunch hour	75	7
Drive to friend's home at night	80	7
Drive into city downtown during lunch hour	80	8
Drive on highway, passing motorcycle	85	8

*Since Jim felt less anxiety when accompanied, because he assigned some responsibility to the passenger to notice whether anything had happened, all driving was to be done alone. Since he drove very slowly to reduce his fears, he was also required to drive at the posted speed limit, unless traffic did not permit this.

Hierarchy 3: Fears of Responsibility for Harm—Injury to Cat

Exposure situation	Discomfort (0–100)	Session #
Close front door with cat in kitchen	25	1
Close front door with cat nearby	35	2
Close back screen and door, cat in another room	40	2
Close back screen and door, cat nearby	50	3
Close front door, cat underfoot	50	3
Close back screen and door, cat underfoot	60	4

Exposure to Multiple Hierarchies

Jim's therapist decided to conduct exposure to all three hierarchies concurrently, planning sessions at home, in the grocery store, or at work to fit the general progression of the hierarchies. Some adjustment of the order of items was required to schedule the location of sessions conveniently. The therapist conducted the first session at home. In the first exposure session, after reviewing the hierarchies and checking on reactions or observations during the previous week, the therapist proceeded as follows with Jim:

O.K., for today we agreed to work on using appliances and the faucets without checking, as well as closing the front door with the cat in the kitchen. Now we need to think how to do this to prevent you from checking after we're done. Are you ready? [With Jim's assent, the therapist headed for the kitchen.] What's your discomfort level right now? [After the response:] Now, which appliance shall we start with? [Jim made his choice.] The coffee maker is fine—why, I've been wanting a cup of coffee all morning!

Again, humor can be helpful to ease the discomfort if clients react well to its use. The session continued with Jim making coffee and leaving the pot on "warm," and then making popcorn and toast and leaving both appliances plugged in after finishing. Jim was encouraged to leave the room without checking before going upstairs. He turned the faucets in the tub and sink on and off once, and then, at the urging of the therapist, left the room without a backward look. They both sat on the stairs, reviewing what was just done; the therapist inquired about anxiety, any other feelings, and thoughts. This allowed Jim to focus on the exposure situation for a while without checking. The therapist suggested that he think about the feared consequences, allowing himself to picture them if that was what came to mind spontaneously. Jim reported images of electrical sparks on the appliances, but noted that he didn't smell smoke yet. The therapist immediately suggested that they leave the house, so that Jim could not use his ability to smell to reassure himself about fires.

Now we need to leave the house by the front door, since we're also working on the cat problem. Then you can do a little driving. How uncomfortable are you now? [Jim reported mild to moderate discomfort.]

Pushing the Limits for Risk

Jim questioned the therapist about the need to leave the coffee pot on "warm," noting that most people probably don't do this.

Yes, I agree that most people would turn it off on leaving, but many people leave it on for hours while they are in another part of the house, and this certainly happens in many work settings. Right? So for you to become much less concerned about it, we need to have you behave on the riskier end of what we'd consider "normal." If you didn't have this checking problem, we wouldn't be restricting you at all, but it is important to be sure we do all the things that could happen under normal circumstances. What's the probability that leaving the coffee pot on "warm" now while we go out for an hour will cause a problem?

Most clients will agree that this is a common behavior and unlikely to cause a problem, and understand the argument that maximum exposures are needed in treatment to reduce fears completely. It is important to convey to clients that their former approach to minimize risk has not been helpful, and may indeed be responsible for many of their current difficulties. Thus, it is important to seek out riskier situations than may be manageable for them. However, if clients are highly anxious about such maneuvers, they can be postponed until later exposure sessions. To Jim, who reported an anxiety level of 50, the therapist said:

Your level is somewhat higher than we'd planned for today. Can you tolerate it? It's always best to tolerate as much as you're able to, but if this is too difficult we can have you go turn off the coffee pot now, but without checking it or the other appliances you used. [Jim strongly preferred to do this.] O.K., how would you turn it off without checking? [The two strategized about where to keep his eyes to avoid checking.] O.K., let's go.

Another brief discussion about how to exit the front door without checking ensued, and Jim and the therapist left the house. The therapist praised Jim:

Well done! What's your level now? What are you worried about most of what we've just done? [Jim responded to both questions.] I'd like you to keep worrying about that as much as possible, to keep it present in your mind and not avoid the thoughts or try to talk yourself out of the fears. If you find the fear subsiding by itself, that's fine, but don't do anything artificial to feel better. Let's go sit in the car for a bit and have you verbalize any thoughts that occur to you about what we just did.

Moving On to the Next Item

The therapist focused attention on the exposure actions, checking with Jim frequently about thoughts and feelings. Jim was given sufficient time to process the exposure experience without distraction and sometimes in silence before undertaking the next task. As he reported less discomfort, the therapist suggested proceeding with the first item from the second hierarchy—driving a block without checking for injured pedestrians. Jim agreed, and the therapist helped him plan the driving strategy, getting out of the car to allow him to drive alone. In a case like Jim's, the decision whether to have the client drive alone or accompanied depends on the degree of discomfort experienced in each situation. Often, clients with fears of harming others while driving have little difficulty with the therapist present in the car, since they assign him or her responsibility for knowing whether a pedestrian was hit. In such cases, the therapist must wait alone while the clients do the driving task. However, if some anxiety occurs with the therapist present, both client and therapist can go on the driving exposure task, the therapist absenting himself or herself later in the exposure process as the client is prepared to drive alone. Jim was encouraged to go alone:

Now, I'll wait here and I won't be watching you, since this is a time for you to learn to feel comfortable without anyone, including yourself, checking on you. We agreed that you'll turn the rear and side view mirrors so you really have to crane your neck to see behind you. You'll drive down to the stop sign, cross the intersection, turn around, and return. Ready? What's your level?

On his return, the therapist asked several questions:

How'd it go? What was the highest anxiety level? When was that? Were you able not to look in the mirror? Sounds like that was hard because of the kid and dog at the corner, but you did it, and I'm impressed. Let's wait and let you deliberately worry about it for a bit, without looking down the street. I want to be sure, though, that you're not checking in your mind about what happened. Do you understand the difference? It's important to let yourself feel the fear without trying to fix it. Then, after a bit, you can drive again for a block in the opposite direction.

Were Jim to repeat the task on the same route, he could have checked for injured pedestrians, further reinforcing his fears and checking behaviors. Thus, another route had to be chosen.

Duration of Exposure for Fears of Harming

The optimal duration of exposure sessions is unknown, and the question is particularly problematic for clients with checking or repeating rituals, for whom remaining too long in a situation allows repeated ritualizing. Clients with contamination fears can easily be exposed for prolonged periods, because contamination remains unless it is deliberately removed by washing, wiping, or the like. But for those with checking, repeating, or certain mental rituals, it is often impossible to continue exposure for prolonged periods because the circumstances do not allow it. Therefore, it is essential to continue to change exposure situations frequently, or else to remove clients from them soon after exposure, in order to maximize the benefits from therapy. In addition, for some clients for whom a particular feared situation produces anxiety that does not decline readily, it may be helpful to progress to the next higher item. The greater discomfort in this new situation may make the previous one seem less disturbing by contrast.

Homework

At the end of session 1, Jim was assigned to continue daily exposure to using appliances without checking and to driving alone for approximately one block. He was given the therapist's phone number, in case of difficulties with the homework assignments that required immediate consultation. The therapist should clearly define the rules for calling, thus enabling clients to respect the therapist's personal boundaries. In general, clients call infrequently (if at all), but report that knowing that they can reach the therapist if they need to reduces their worries. Sometimes clients do call, upset because of a situation that was much too high on the hierarchy and could not be adequately dealt with at the moment. In such cases, the therapist can provide assistance in managing discomfort and reassurance that this will eventually be addressed in therapy. Suggested strategies for managing discomfort are given later in the chapter.

Exposure Session 2

The second session is usually conducted in the same location as the first one, beginning with the therapist asking for a written report of homework (see Figure 8.2). After discussion of homework, the first session's exposures are repeated somewhat more rapidly; therapist and client then move on to subsequent situations on the list. Thus, Jim was encouraged to add using the iron and stove in a typical way. This required advance preparation for the session, such as having a shirt ready to be ironed and food ready to be cooked. Jim and the therapist then left the house by the front door with the cat nearby; after a discussion of his anxiety reactions, Jim drove a longer distance without checking.

Later Sessions

The format of conversation for later sessions is similar, with the therapist asking for anxiety levels frequently and inquiring about reactions, thoughts, directly related memories, and the like. Sessions last for 60–90 minutes, as required by the planned activities. Homework consonant with the expected discomfort level is again assigned, and may also include tasks for which the therapist cannot easily be present and that clients feel able to do unsupervised. In Jim's case, he agreed to go for a bike ride between sessions without checking to see whether he had run into a pedestrian. For homework after the third session, he agreed to visit a friend's home and stand near the friend's stove without checking.

Treatment in subsequent sessions proceeds in much the same way as outlined at the beginning of this chapter. Progress through the hierarchy is rarely exactly as planned; adjustments are nearly always made in the order of items, how long exposures continue, or how many times they are repeated. Often clients discover new items that need to be added to the list. Nonetheless, treatment proceeds gradually from easier to more difficult items as clients indicate their readiness. The therapist's task is to press clients to do as much as they seem able to manage without becoming overwhelmed, all the while expressing genuine pleasure at their progress and providing frequent support and encouragement. It often seems as if the therapist pushes with one hand and supports with the other. Management of motivational problems, evidenced by poor compliance with instructions and homework assignments, is discussed in Chapter 11.

For most clients, treatment does not become easier until they have endured exposure to their most feared item. For this reason it is desirable to progress as fast as feasible toward the highest-ranking situations on the hierarchy, perhaps by the seventh or eighth session. Not all clients can proceed at this pace, but many do with encouragement and regular homework practice. After this point, they become increasingly able to engage in exposures without the therapist present. After exposure to the most feared situations, patients continue with these and related situations in later sessions, until little increase in discomfort can be provoked by any previously feared situation. In later sessions, then, less session time is spent in deliberate exposure and more in discussion of the week's exposure, other experiences, and eventually planning for the future.

Generalization

Particularly for clients in inpatient settings, generalization of symptom reduction from the treatment site to natural situations requires special planning and assignments. Clients for whom most exposure is self-conducted in natural situations have little difficulty with generalization, since it is automatically programmed into the treatment format. But clients treated in the hospital, especially away from their hometown, will undoubtedly require one or more home visits or special arrangements with a "cotherapist," who may be a family member or another therapist in the hometown. Difficulties in doing exposure without the therapist's reassuring presence can be minimized by assigning daily homework and by increasingly requiring clients to engage in self-exposure and prevent rituals during the last half of the treatment program.

It is also possible that a lack of generalization of anxiety reduction to similar situations in other contexts indicates that the focus of exposure is off target. That is, the therapist has missed an important thematic focus of a client's obsessive fears, and therefore the exposure situations are not maximally relevant to the fear. The therapist and client should review possible fear themes to determine whether this is true. An example of this was the case of a woman who failed to habituate to exposure to situations of being observed by others (social anxiety), because her actual fear was of going insane. This fear merely manifested itself more often when others were observing her, though indeed it was present under other circumstances as well. Usually the missed fear theme is a more global one than previously thought, such as a fear of losing control of one's impulses and of being a truly "bad" person, rather than only a fear of stabbing one's daughter.

Managing Discomfort

There are several strategies for coping with high anxiety during exposure experiences during or after therapy sessions. The first group of methods is predominantly intended to alter beliefs and attitudes. Humor has already been mentioned as one method for managing uncomfortable feelings; indeed, most people spontaneously use humor from time to time in this way. Another cognitive strategy is to help clients remind themselves of the actual degree of danger present, in contrast to their own fears. Since many are fully aware of the unreasonable nature of their obsessions and compulsions, this strategy may have limited usefulness in actually reducing discomfort. However, for those who have acquired new insight into the irrationality of their worries, this reminder may be helpful in enabling them to cope with the discomfort and persist in exposure. Of course, they should not be encouraged to pretend that there is *no* danger at all, since this is rarely true. Risk taking is often what clients need to learn during the exposure sessions. The therapist may wish to encourage clients to recall that earlier in their lives, they were not uncomfortable with the situation that now confronts them. Such memories may encourage some. A reminder that anxiety has declined in earlier sessions and lower-ranking items are actually less bothersome now can also help clients' to stick out difficult exposure situations. This strategy can obviously only be used after clients have some experience with discomfort reduction during prior exposures.

A second method for coping with discomfort is relaxation training. Although relaxation training has been used successfully in exposure programs with other types of anxious clients, it has not usually been employed with OCD clients. This probably stems from the poor outcome produced both by relaxation alone (e.g., Rachman et al., 1971) and by systematic desensitization for OCD symptoms (e.g., Beech & Vaughn, 1978; Cooper et al., 1965). There is no particular reason why clients who wish to learn relaxation or meditation techniques should not be taught these procedures. However, the experience of many behavior therapists who treat OCD is that anxiety levels during exposures are frequently too high for relaxation to be effective. Usually, anxiety is at least moderate, and relaxation is too weak a procedure to produce much effect. It is therefore not ordinarily recommended as an anxiety management strategy. On the other hand, for clients with relatively mild discomfort, relaxation may be useful. It may also serve to enhance attention to the stimuli presented (Rachman, 1980), and may thus help clients to process anxiety-related information.

A third strategy is paradoxical intention, in which discomfort is deliberately exaggerated until clients report that their anxiety plateaus and declines. Often the decline appears related to the perceived improbability of the exaggerated obsessive fear carried to extremes. This method is another form of exposure, usually to feared disasters. For example, Jim, who was fearful of harming others by mistakenly turning on an appliance at work, might picture himself inadvertently turning on the coffee pot when he used the copy machine, leaving for lunch, and returning to find the entire building and indeed the entire city in flames. A coworker could be pointing at him, accusing him of leaving the coffee pot on and therefore of being entirely responsible for billions of dollars in damages and thousands of injured or dying. For many clients, such a scenario is both the logical extension of their fears and also quite ridiculous and unbelievable to them. The absurdity of the magnified disastrous consequence is often anxiety-reducing. Note that this type of scene, though in considerably less exaggerated proportions, can be used for imaginal exposure scenes (see Chapter 9). Generally, paradoxical intention is recommended for use with moderately rather than highly disturbing exposure situations, since clients may be unwilling to exaggerate already highly anxiety-provoking exposures.

Finally, another strategy for managing anxiety is to call the therapist, a family member, or a friend to talk over fears and help pass the time in a supportive environment until the fears seem more manageable. As noted in Chapter 7, identification of supportive people at the outset of treatment is helpful in providing opportunities for anxiety management during difficult exposure periods. Such helpers should be carefully selected for their noncritical attitude toward the clients' symptoms, and their willingness to consult the therapist to gain some knowledge about how to behave when called. Family and friends might use any or all of the following strategies: encourage clients to talk about their fears, ask for details to facilitate this, sympathize with anxiety, suggest waiting until they feel calmer before doing anything further, remind them of prior situations in which they eventually felt better, ask them what other options they might consider, inquire about the reality of the fears, and discourage rituals.

When to Terminate Direct Exposure

As noted earlier, the therapist should gradually decrease his or her involvement in deliberate exposures, encouraging clients to take over responsibility for such endeavors. Once clients' most feared situations provoke only mild discomfort, accompanied direct exposures can be eliminated altogether. At this point, clients should be encouraged to continue daily exposures to the most difficult situations on their own, reporting periodically to the therapist. Weekly or twice-monthly sessions can focus on additional problems (see Chapter 11), with the clinician inquiring at each session about struggles and triumphs related to obsessive fears. As the focus shifts to other problems and as sessions are decreased in frequency, some regular (e.g., weekly) "checkup" regarding previously feared and avoided situations is recommended.

9

Implementing Imaginal
Exposure Sessions

Indications for Imaginal Exposure

As discussed in Chapter 3, several research studies have shown that direct exposure *in vivo* to feared obsessive situations is more effective than imaginal exposure ("flooding in imagination") to the same circumstances. However, the combination of both methods has produced excellent outcomes (e.g., Foa & Goldstein, 1978). Exposure in fantasy has been particularly helpful in maintaining the gains of OCD clients who fear disastrous consequences of failing to ritualize (Foa, Steketee, & Grayson, 1985; Foa, Steketee, Turner, & Fisher, 1980). It appears that the addition of imaginal exposure allows such clients to be exposed more completely to the internal (mental) stimuli that trigger their fears, rather than only to the external ones.

The decision to include imaginal exposure in treatment depends upon three sequential questions. First, do clients' obsessive fears predominantly involve mental images, rather than external events? Second, do clients report that fears of disastrous outcomes of failing to ritualize are prominent features of their obsessive fears? Third, to what degree does direct exposure alone access (bring to mind) obsessions about these feared consequences?

Those who report no mental images associated with obsessions and no disastrous fears are unlikely to achieve any benefit from imaginal exposure that could not be better accomplished by *in vivo* exposure. Imaginal exposure should only be considered in such cases if exposure is difficult to implement in practice or if a vivid memory of a particular experience remains salient.

An example is the case of a woman who feared contamination by her mother and things her mother had touched. No potential consequences other than high anxiety were reported. Gradual exposure to objects from her mother's home was not difficult to accomplish, since these could be sent to her. However, direct contact with her mother, who lived at a considerable distance, was difficult to implement on a gradual basis in practice, and her mother was unable to travel to the client's home to "contaminate" it. Imaginal greeting and touching of her mother and touching of her mother's furnishings were employed for several sessions prior to an actual scheduled visit to her mother's home. Following this visit, the therapist also employed imaginal exposure of a visit by the mother to the client's home. Another example in which imaginal exposure was expedient was the case of a young woman whose main feared contaminant, dead animals at the roadside, was easily reproduced in imagery but difficult to locate in practice.

Imaginal exposure is essential for those whose fears are predominantly focused on harming others, because of their own unwanted thoughts and images about this very outcome. In such cases, a clear image appears in the person's mind and is experienced as horrifying and difficult to dispel. Images often appear spontaneously, without any apparent connection to external situations. For example, one Catholic woman who feared and ritualized in response to images of herself stabbing the baby Jesus required exposure in fantasy to reduce her anxiety to these images. Since concrete cues for the obsession are not always present, exposure *in vivo* may be inappropriate in such cases; imaginal exposure is therefore essential. An example is given later in this chapter.

Routine inclusion of imaginal exposure is appropriate for any client who reports obsessive fears of catastrophes, but it may not be essential for all such individuals. The therapist and client together can best determine whether exposure in fantasy is needed by having the client report on his or her mental experiences during the first few direct practice exposures. If direct exposure easily provokes obsessive worries about these consequences, and these fears habituate during *in vivo* treatment sessions or homework practice, imaginal exposure is probably unnecessary. However, since the potential benefits of imaginal treatment are not likely to be evident until after therapy has ended, it is important that the therapist err on the side of caution here. If there is any question about full access to feared consequences during *in vivo* exposure, imaginal exposure should be implemented.

Exposure in fantasy may also be indicated for clients whose severe avoidance and anxiety makes the prospect of *in vivo* exposure seem un-manageable. Examples of this application are contained in two cases with "bowel obsessions" reported in the literature: Imaginal exposure to fears of fecal incontinence, somatic sensations, distressing thoughts, and feared social consequences facilitated subsequent *in vivo* exposure (Beidel & Bulik, 1990). Some clients who are otherwise unwilling to undergo exposure and response prevention treatment may consent to imagining their feared situations. For example, a woman who fears being observed looking at women's breasts or men's genitals may be more easily treated imaginally, prior to engaging in more direct practice. In such cases, imaginal exposure may serve merely to enhance motivation to engage in direct contact with feared situations. The therapist is cautioned, however, to make such clients aware that *in vivo* practice must eventually follow the imagery for treatment to be lastingly effective.

Contraindications

Before the clinician spends substantial time and energy constructing scenes for imaginal exposure, it is wise first to test clients' abilities to picture scenes vividly. Though such individuals are relatively uncommon, some clients cannot form or retain a clear image, or else they do not experience physiological and subjective emotional responses to upsetting images, despite their best efforts. These individuals should be distinguished from those who deliberately struggle against the vivid emotional images for motivational reasons. Clients of the latter type may eventually decide voluntarily to allow themselves to experience the scenes fully and to react with expected discomfort. For them, motivational issues can be explored to enhance cooperation.

By contrast, clients of the first type report with frustration that no matter how hard they try, their images are not clear and/or their emotional arousal remains minimal. Before abandoning imaginal exposure, the therapist might first attempt to enhance imagery by having clients picture scenes that are neutral or even relaxing, with elements likely to evoke strong responses. One such scene might include picking up a bright yellow lemon, feeling the texture of the fruit, holding a knife and slicing open the lemon, feeling and hearing the sound of the knife on the cutting board, and eventually tasting the tart juice. The emphasis on sensory (stimulus) elements of sight, touch, sound, smell, and taste enhances the scene's vividness, and with practice such vividness may be transferred to imagery relevant to clients' obsessive fears. Similarly, to provoke emotional reactions, clients might be asked to picture scenes from memory of events that in the past produced strong pleasure, surprise, sadness, anger, physical pain, or fear. Failure to elicit substantial vividness or emotional responses to these images can be taken as a sign that clients are unlikely to benefit from treatment by imaginal exposure.

Therapist Reactions

Clinicians inexperienced in imaginal "flooding" may feel uncomfortable using this treatment, since it requires clients to give verbal and visual expression to their worst fears, which are invariably unpleasant. However, it is very clear that clients' efforts to *avoid* thinking about or imagining these unpleasant ideas have only led to their entrenchment as provocative cues for discomfort. A reasonable strategy to manage such ingrained cognitions is to stop avoiding and instead to allow free mental expression of unwanted thoughts, images, and impulses. Nonetheless, exposure in fantasy requires that the therapist follow clients' leads in encouraging reporting and imagery of the worst fears, regardless of their unpleasantness. Horrific components need not be added or exaggerated unless reported directly by clients, since these have not been demonstrated to enhance outcome. Therapists invariably become more comfortable with this procedure after they practice it and acquire evidence of its efficacy in reducing discomfort with upsetting images.

Developing the Hierarchy

Like scenes for exposure in practice, scenes for imaginal exposure should be arranged hierarchically to accommodate clients' differing levels of discomfort. Those who fear only a single consequence may have only one disaster image that disturbs them, although the degree of fear may still vary with the type of tangible obsessive cue or the stage of the disaster. For example, feared contamination from blood-associated objects may be associated only with fears of developing AIDS, but a client's probability estimate for acquiring the disease may vary considerably from situation to situation, moderating the degree of fear. Typically, once the client is asked to imagine the feared consequence (in this case, developing AIDS), the level of discomfort is dictated by this image, overriding the fluctuation due to the concrete source of the AIDS.

Clients' fear may fluctuate considerably with the progression through the imagined disaster scenario. That is, imagining hearing the diagnosis from the physician and discussing it with others is likely to be less disturbing than imagining hospitalization with the immediate prospect of dying. For some clients, however, proximity to death is actually less upsetting than earlier phases of uncertainty about the diagnosis. One of the advantages of imaginal exposure is that mistakes in exposure level can easily be adjusted by asking clients to erase an image and recreate it to produce the desired effect. As with *in vivo* exposure, clients' reported discomfort levels determine the sequencing of imagined scenes.

Hierarchies for clients with multiple feared consequences can be arranged by type of consequence. For example, driving fears accompanied by extensive checking of the rear view mirror and retracing of routes may be associated with the consequences of driving over animals, adults, children, and one's own child, in ascending order of fear level. In this case, the hierarchy can move from scene to scene according to who is run over, though the therapist will want to incorporate some change of external circumstance (location, time of day, description of person) to enhance generalization of fear reduction to different elements of the fear construct.

An example of a hierarchy of scenes for imaginal exposure is given here for a client, George, who feared that his thoughts of loved ones' being injured, becoming ill, or dying would actually come to pass unless he corrected the mental images. Scenes were assigned to appropriate sessions of therapy according to the discomfort evoked.

Hierarchy: Fears of Harming Others by Thoughts

Imaginal exposure situation	Discomfort (0–100)	Session #
An older coworker dying of a heart attack	50	1
Sister in the hospital for surgery	60	2
Son injured (not seriously) by a car	70	3
Wife with early diagnosis of breast cancer	85	4
Mother dying of complications of surgery	90	5
Wife dying of cancer	95	6
Son dying of leukemia	100	7

As is evident from George's list of situations, the nature of the imagined harm is less important than the degree of the client's debilitation that results. Note also that George's hierarchy is shorter than the hierarchies for *in vivo* exposure given in Chapter 8. This is typical of most clients, who report a limited number of catastrophic fears compared with the number of concrete cues that can trigger such fears.

As with exposure to concrete cues in practice, multiple hierarchies may be needed to address obsessions with different thematic content. George, for example, might also have had religious images of blasphemy and feared punishment from God that disturbed him independently of the illness/injury/ death fears. In this case a separate list of scenes would have been generated, and the decision about the order of sessions during treatment would have depended on either George's request or the therapist's understanding of any interdependence of the themes. Usually, less disturbing fears are presented first, unless it is expected that successful treatment of one type of obsession will result in reduction of discomfort to other obsessive images. It is probably wise to present only one hierarchy until reactivity to those scenes is greatly reduced, before beginning another group of feared scenes.

Constructing the Scenes

During imaginal exposure, the clinician guides clients through movie-like images generated by the clients and modified as needed by the therapist. The goal is to match as precisely as possible the images that clients generate spontaneously when in the feared obsessive situation. This requires that scenes be derived directly from clients' imaginations, be as vivid as possible, and provoke discomfort. The therapist's task is to help clients attend to their fear images so that they can be accurately reproduced for treatment sessions. It is generally not useful to write out entire scenes verbatim prior to exposure, since a client's immediate mental experiences must be followed in the images, and these are rarely entirely predictable or consistent across occasions. Still, it is helpful to outline images with the client in advance. In this way, both therapist and client are aware of the approximate content, expected level of anxiety, and necessary limitations to be imposed by the therapist to block rituals in the scene, and by the client to control his or her level of discomfort.

According to Lang's (1977) theory, scenes should contain both stimulus and response elements, as well as any meaning concepts that clients report as relevant. Thus, the therapist should take care to include sensory elements—those perceived by sight, sound, smell, taste, and touch. Emphasis on some of these cues over others will depend on the nature of the obsessive cues. For example, scenes associated with contamination obsessions are likely to focus heavily on touch. Clients' physical actions during the scene are also detailed, including walking, speaking, yelling, and so forth; obviously, such behaviors are closely associated with sensory reactions. Emotional reactions should be solicited, including fear, anxious worry, anger, frustration, sadness, embarrassment, surprise, shame, or guilt. The therapist also calls clients' attention to internal physiological reactions accompanying these emotions, including rapid heart rate, tense muscles, irregular breathing, lump in the throat, a flushed face, and so on. Finally, thoughts and mental associations are requested to ascertain the idiosyncratic meaning of the circumstances.

George's therapist proceeded to solicit information from him as follows (this is an abbreviated account):

O.K., now that we have a list of the scenes, let's flesh them out a bit so I have some idea of how the image should go. Start with the first one, about your coworker dying of a heart attack. How would that scene start? Where might you imagine him to be if this image popped into your head? [George suggested the workplace.] Um-hmm. Now describe him briefly to me so I have some idea what he looks like. [George obliged, and the therapist noted visual cues to include.]

Do you picture yourself in the image with your coworker? [When George said "Yes," the therapist inquired about his location and role, reserving further details for the actual session of exposure in fantasy.] Now, what exactly happens to him? How do you get the idea that he's having a heart attack? [Again, a few details were provided and noted by the therapist.] What else happens? Are there other people in the scene? Does an ambulance come? What's the worst part of the scene for you—when would you be most upset? Is it worse if you don't know the outcome or if you think he actually dies?

[Since George reported the latter response, the therapist asked:] Should we include a funeral that you attend?

A therapist continues to question a client in this manner until satisfied that the outlines of the image are fairly complete and can be used to prompt a very detailed scene during the session. Again, the actual narration during treatment should contain considerably more detail than this summary description, in order to prompt vivid imagining (see the example later in this chapter for such details). Scenes may move forward rapidly in time, if appropriate, or they may be quite static, concentrating repeatedly on the details of a particular image. The speed of the action is determined by a client's reactions. The therapist dwells at length on parts that produce substantial increases in discomfort, and moves more rapidly through parts that are less upsetting. In the scenario outlined above, the therapist would have focused at length on the coworker's initial attack and George's feelings of responsibility for this. Once George's anxiety had declined somewhat, the scene would have jumped rapidly to a hospital or a funeral scene. This flexibility is one of the distinct advantages of imaginal exposure.

Imaginal exposure is delivered without allowing clients to ritualize in the images. This requires a contract in advance whereby clients are enjoined not to carry out or picture themselves carrying out any compulsive acts or thoughts that artificially reduce fear, since these interfere with habituation of discomfort and hinder progress. Clients agree to report to the therapist any spontaneous additions to the scene that reduce discomfort suddenly. The therapist may have to construct imagined blocks for these rituals in the imagined scenario. For example, if George had tried to picture his coworker as his former healthy self, the therapist would have refocused on his falling to the floor. In a clearer example, a client sought to avoid feeling responsible for an imagined break-in by imagining calling the police; the therapist stated that the phone was out of order. Avoidance can be similarly blocked. One client who tried to avoid pedestrian areas in her driving imagery was forced by construction to travel the busy main street.

The therapist continues to obtain summary details of all the hierarchy scenes from a client until the content of scenes is clearly relevant to the client's obsessions. For George, the therapist's notes for presenting the final scene of his son dying of leukemia were outlined as follows. (Note that these were merely guides for the therapist, who actually presented the scene in greater detail and with appropriate grammar.)

Your son is lying on a bed in the hospital. The room contains another boy admitted for a broken leg. Note sound of hospital intercom, bustling of nurses; sight of bed, son's facial expression, wasted-looking body; medical smells; feel of chair under you, touch of boy's hand. You react with strong guilt about your image of son with leukemia now happening in reality; feelings of responsibility, sadness, sense of loss, fear, anger, frustration. Feel a lump in your throat, some tension. Any sensations associated with guilty feelings? Walk around the bed, sit in chair, touch son, speak to wife and daughter. Thoughts about your failure to erase the image when you had a chance; perception of blame from wife; sense of neglect as a parent; idea that God is punishing you for your sinful thoughts by having your son develop leukemia, just as you'd feared. You were right. It's your fault.

The above-described aspects of the scene were derived entirely from questioning George about the most feared elements. Although clients usually do not create this degree of detail in their own obsessive images, they will usually do so in response to the therapist's probing about what it would actually be like if their obsessive fears came to pass.

Implementing Imaginal Exposure

Before presenting a scene in fantasy, the therapist should be sure that a client can sit, or preferably recline, in a very comfortable chair. The external environment should impinge minimally on the client's comfort and attention; physical discomfort and loud noises can distract attention away from the image, reducing vividness, reactivity, and (with these) habituation of anxiety and efficacy. Sessions may have to be scheduled to avoid the sounds of rush-hour traffic, construction work, or interruptions by colleagues or phone calls. A client who is distracted by the idea that the therapist is watching him or her closely can turn the chair sideways to minimize these concerns. It is helpful, however, for the therapist to be able to see face or body movements, in order to gauge the degree of felt discomfort at specific points in the scene.

The room light should be dimmed but not darkened completely, to allow the client to concentrate more fully on the image with eyes closed. The scene can be taped for playback between sessions as homework. The scene is begun by the therapist with a description of the physical elements of the image and periodic questioning of the client for details. The client should be instructed to "be in the scene" like an actor in a play, seeing the details "as if you were there," rather than being a member of the audience observing from outside the action.

The therapist's task is to obtain sufficient feedback from the client to be able to accurately add details that are consistent with his or her images. It is quite distracting for a client to have the therapist suggest that he or she turn *left* to go into the next room, when the adjacent room in the image is to the *right*. To prevent such mistakes, the therapist must ask where the room is. Thus, the therapist inquires frequently what the client sees, hears, touches, smells, feels emotionally, feels physiologically, and thinks. Some clients report that if they speak too often while imagining, it interferes with the vividness of their images. In such a case, the clinician has little choice but to narrate the agreed-upon details, consulting the client only infrequently.

Brief reports of anxiety or discomfort levels are requested every 5–10 minutes during the fantasied exposure and can be recorded on the form in Chapter 8 for *in vivo* exposure (Figure 8.1). The client can merely give a number and return his or her attention immediately to the image. The number should reflect how the client actually feels sitting there in the chair imagining the scene, not an estimate of how the client would feel if the scene were really happening. This numerical report provides the therapist with important information about whether the client is reacting to the image (increase of discomfort over baseline levels prior to imagining) and habituating as the scene continues. Of course, habituation should not be expected until the most disturbing aspects of that particular image have been presented for some period of time. Clinicians should allow 60–90 minutes for habituation to occur for most clients, though less time may be required for scenes lower in the hierarchy and for second or third presentations of an image. In one study conducted by Foa et al. (1992), therapists generally felt that the 45 minutes allowed for imaginal exposure was insufficient in many cases.

Like *in vivo* exposure, imaginal exposure may be stopped as soon as reported discomfort has declined from its peak level by a sufficient amount for a client to be well aware of the difference. Ideally, a 50% reduction is desirable; however, this may be difficult to achieve for some individuals, especially those who report high baseline levels of anxiety. Certainly, a scene should not be terminated when anxiety is climbing or has just reached peak levels, since this experience may serve to sensitize the client both to the content of the image and to the experience of imaginal exposure itself. The result is likely to be a highly anxious individual who refuses further treatment.

Scenes should be repeated in subsequent sessions until peak anxiety has diminished substantially. Usually, this will require no more than two or three presentations before it is time to move on to the next scene on the hierarchy. A scene may be presented in its entirety more than once in a session, but it is probably preferable simply to dwell at length on those aspects of the image that are most disturbing until discomfort reduces. Since time can stand still in imagination, it is not at all difficult for the therapist simply to rotate the commentary among sensory perceptions, emotional responses, physiological reactions, behaviors, thoughts, and ideas until discomfort diminishes.

Aids to Habituation

Occasionally, the clinician will encounter situations in which clients report minimal or no reduction in their discomfort, despite lengthy presentations of imagined scenes. In such cases, it may be helpful to include some humorous elements in the images that are consonant with the exposure experience. The therapist should probably wait some time (e.g., 45 minutes) before doing so, to determine first whether natural processes induce anxiety reduction. If used, humor should not divert attention from the uncomfortable aspects of an obsessive image; rather, potentially amusing aspects of the situation can be emphasized. For example, feared germs can be imagined as Lilliputian creatures marching with guns drawn, ready to attack. Clients fearful of forgetting to secure the parking brake might picture an unchecked auto mowing down an entire town. Individuals who point accusing fingers at these clients, emphasizing their experienced guilt, might wear ridiculous clothing or behave in an odd manner. Again, the therapist must use humor judiciously to avoid distracting clients, and it may be preferable to allow clients to generate their own funny aspects of the scene.

Some clinical researchers have employed relaxation prior to commencement of exposure in imagery in treating other anxiety problems (e.g., Keane & Kaloupek, 1982; Foa, Rothbaum, Murdock, & Riggs, 1991, for PTSD). Possibly the use of relaxation increases initial attention to and vividness of imagery. It is unlikely, however, that it significantly reduces discomfort during imaginal exposure, since the anxiety provoked is typically substantial—considerably more than can be reduced by even well-practiced relaxation procedures. Relaxation is therefore not recommended during this type of exposure. Its value as an adjunct to flooding has not been demonstrated empirically, nor has it been used in clinical trials that demonstrate the efficacy of imaginal exposure for OCD clients. Unless the clinician has a good rationale for using relaxation, it does not appear to be advantageous.

Example of an Imaginal Exposure Scene

The following scene includes the therapist's narration of details provided by the client as an image unfolded. It is considerably shorter in written form than was required in reality, since the therapist dwelled on disturbing elements of the image and repeated these over and over with minor variations, as needed. The client, Mary, was fearful of contamination from bacteria or microorganisms acquired from dead animals, dog feces, garbage, animal hair, human feces, and flies. The scene below is from midway through treatment.

Now, sit back and make yourself comfortable. Mary, what's your discomfort level before we start? [Mary reported a 40.] That's a little high for you; are you worrying about what we're about to do with the imagery? [Mary indicated that she had been dreading it all day.] I'm not exactly surprised, but I suspect that although you won't enjoy it, you'll survive just fine, and we both know you're trying hard to get better. Are you ready anyway? [She agreed.] O.K., here we go.

I'd like you to start by imagining that you're driving down Route 9 on your way home from work in the afternoon. It's raining out, and the windshield wipers are going on the middle speed. You see them brushing in front of your view of the road, and you can hear the "whip, whip" as they go back and forth. Can you see the wipers clearly? Uh-huh. Can you hear the sound they make? Mmm. Look through the windshield now and tell me what you see in front of you.

Mary was asked to report in present tense, using the first-person pronoun "I." If she resorted to the use of "you" (e.g., "You can see a tree on the right") or past tense (e.g., "I turned left in front of the school"), the therapist corrected the grammar immediately with "You mean, '*I* can see a tree on the right,' " or "You mean, '*I am turning* left in front of the school.' " Therapists may need to make such corrections several times before clients become accustomed to thinking of the image as if it is happening in the present to themselves directly. Mary's therapist continued:

So you see the tree and the school. Describe them briefly. Uh-huh. Hear the sound of the rain on the roof of the car and the tires on the wet pavement. Do you smell anything because of the rain?

You are thinking about the fact that you really hate it when it rains, because it might splash on you with all that bacteria from the roadside garbage or dead animals or heaven only knows what. You are hoping to avoid getting splashed on today particularly, because the clothes you're wearing have to be dry-cleaned and you're never confident that they get out all the bacteria.

The therapist used information acquired from previous discussions with Mary about her fears and rituals.

What are you doing now? Where are you on the highway? O.K., what's your anxiety level right now as you picture the image? [She reported 50 because of the rain she disliked.] Now, suddenly you feel the car become very sluggish, and you think you have just heard the sound of a muffled blowout. It's noisy with all the rain, but it's very clear that the car is leaning to the right and you can feel an odd motion as the wheels go round. You've slowed way down and it's even more pronounced. It's obvious you've got to stop and see what happened. You hate to get out in this rain. What are you thinking?

Mary spoke about trying to figure out how to avoid getting splashed. The therapist interrupted before this train of avoidance thoughts could progress to imagined action.

You get out of the car with your umbrella in hand. The air is damp and you feel a few drops of rain. Just as you're closing the car door, a small truck goes by a little too close to you and sends up a spray of water all over the side of the car and on your skirt and legs. It's not that dirty-looking, but you think immediately about germs, and you can't get the idea out of your head. Ugh! You're covered with street water. What's your anxiety now? [Mary reported a 70.] Feel the wetness on your legs. What are you thinking? [After Mary's response:] How do you feel inside your body? Any other reactions?

The therapist now had to make a decision about how much exposure to include in the image for this session. In the first and second imaginal exposure, the therapist could end the progression of contamination here, repeating the details of the scene up to this point until some habituation of anxiety occurred. In latter sessions, the image could continue with more intense contamination and a corresponding increase in anxiety up to 80 and even 90 on the SUD scale. Mary was also fearful of touching the tires on her car and especially of direct contact with dead animals. In the scene, she might go on to having to change the tire herself, which would entail considerable exposure. To include the next higher item on the hierarchy, she might discover as the rain slowed and she could see better that there was a dead animal just a few yards up the road. The tire she just changed was in fact contaminated directly from the water running past the animal, and she would now be covered with this water. This last and highest-ranking scenario was selected for this session. The therapist proceeded with the scene as follows:

So now you're completely covered with dirty water from the tire, and you can see the dead animal—it's small, maybe a rabbit or a squirrel—just up the road. It's probably been killed by a car several days ago. How could you have missed it, you wonder? What are you thinking? [Mary reported feeling horrified and disgusted. She felt unable to move, since she couldn't imagine getting back into the car, because that would contaminate the interior so badly that it would be impossible to clean.] But you've got to get home. You're already late by at least 30 minutes and your husband will be upset, since you're both supposed to visit his father in the hospital tonight.

The therapist had to find a convincing way to require Mary to get inside the car, since this was part of the contamination fear. Mary suggested that in the image she walk to a phone to call her husband to come get her in his car, so she wouldn't have to dirty hers. She was also thinking about showering thoroughly as soon as she got home. The therapist interceded immediately to foil Mary's desired avoidance and washing efforts.

But you realize there is no phone within walking distance. There's also no traffic, and you doubt you could get a ride. You're thoroughly wet and getting cold. You're going to have to get back into the car. You can see the animal out of the corner of your eye. It looks very dead, and you feel the dirty water all over you. You got it on your dress and legs, and on your hands from touching the tire; it's also on your face and hair from touching them by mistake while changing the tire. You're as thoroughly contaminated as you can be. You're completely covered with dead animal dirt. How do you feel? [Mary responded with "Tired and very upset."] You feel tired, upset, and chilly. You get up to go around the car to get inside.

A therapist should not describe how clients feel without first verifying this with them, lest the description be inaccurate and the therapist miss an important opportunity to help clients examine feelings closely.

You get into the car gingerly, and as you do so another car goes by, splashing again, but this time onto the car seat and the steering wheel. The water lands on your face and hair too. Boy, this is your lucky day! You couldn't have gotten more contaminated if you'd tried. You're worrying now about the consequences of this contamination. What are you thinking?

The therapist thus blocked Mary's wish to avoid contaminating the interior of the car, and turned the image toward her fears of disease. She had already reported that these fears were not elaborate and did not extend past becoming ill. She did not believe she would die from this contamination and did not fear spreading it to others. Therefore, the therapist only asked her to think about becoming ill as a result of the dead animal, and in the next session to include the image of herself falling ill the next morning.

At this point, the therapist continued to alternate between commentary about concrete cues and sensory experiences, about internal sensations and emotional reactions, and about ideas about (but not yet the experience of) feared consequences (i.e., getting sick). As Mary's reported anxiety declined during the exposure, the therapist determined to end the scene—at the point where discomfort was moderate and stable. This scene was repeated several times in later sessions, with modifications to match her reported fears (e.g., adding her illness) and with the heaviest emphasis on parts that provoked the greatest anxiety. Tape recordings of each session's scene served as homework, to be played daily until the next exposure session. When no part of the scene provoked more than mild discomfort, the imaginal exposures were discontinued.

As is apparent from the details of the above-described image, Mary was also participating in direct exposure concurrent with flooding in imagination. Her hierarchy included touching sidewalks, streets, soles of shoes, water in the street, tires, parts of the street near a dead animal, and even a dried carcass of a long-dead animal. (She was not asked to touch a recently killed animal directly, since this was considered potentially dangerous in reality.) Thus, Mary's treatment sessions consisted of about 1 hour of imaginal scenes followed by 45 minutes of direct exposure. Like most patients, she responded very well to this regimen.

10

Preventing Rituals

Chapters 8 and 9 discuss the implementation of exposure *in vivo* and in imagination, respectively, to treat the obsessive and avoidance symptoms of OCD. Both methods require concurrent blocking of rituals for treatment to be effective (e.g., Foa, Steketee, & Milby, 1980; Mills et al., 1973). Rituals must be prevented because they interrupt the experience of prolonged exposure, and probably keep clients from developing coping methods that are more adaptive for managing obsessive fears. Many clients have come to use rituals to relieve discomfort from various stressors not necessarily connected to obsessive fears, so preventing rituals may also require clients to develop other coping strategies to manage this stress from other sources. The therapist will need to be attentive to this issue during the maintenance period.

Several variants of response prevention have been applied to OCD clients, though none have been formally tested in controlled trials. Response prevention alternatives range from instructions to stop ritualizing, gradual methods (with response delay being perhaps the most gradual), self-controlled procedures, and strict supervision. These variations of response prevention are discussed briefly below; the remainder of this chapter is focused on the application of stricter methods, which have been used very successfully in controlled trials.

Supervised versus Self-Controlled Response Prevention

Several studies have employed supervisors for ritual prevention, including hospital staff members for inpatient treatment (e.g., Meyer et al., 1974; van den Hout et al., 1988) and family members for outpatient therapy (e.g., Foa et al., 1984; Emmelkamp & DeLange, 1983; Emmelkamp, de Haan, & Hoogduin, 1990; Mehta, 1990). Regardless of the context, constant supervision of rituals is rarely possible even in an inpatient setting; supervisors cannot always be present, nor are they unfailingly vigilant when they are. Furthermore, the finding that self-controlled treatment led to better long-term improvement than therapist-controlled methods (Emmelkamp & Kraanen, 1977) suggests that clients' involvement in limiting rituals is likely to be important for maintenance of gains. This is a skill they must learn to prevent relapse after treatment ends. The research findings point to a need to maximize clients' involvement while at the same time ensuring that rituals are in fact blocked in a consistent manner.

In inpatient settings, staff members vary considerably in their style of interaction with clients on the ward. Those whose behavior conveys respect and a wish to be helpful are best suited to help supervise the blocking of rituals. The role of a supervisor is akin to that of a therapist, and the same criteria are likely to apply. That is, supervisors should be respectful, understanding, interested, encouraging, challenging, and explicit. However, a few hospital staff members tend to treat clients in a somewhat condescending manner because of the authority of their positions. Such staff members should not serve as the primary supervisors of ritual prevention. Even clients who acknowledge the need for supervision are likely to rebel if treated in an authoritarian manner.

Many outpatients have come for therapy at their own initiative, and are strongly motivated to overcome their obsessive and compulsive symptoms. They view their ritualistic behaviors as unnecessary and embarrassing. Supervisors may not be needed at all for these individuals, though some clients may prefer to have designated family members or friends assist them at times of high anxiety and strong urges to ritualize. On the other hand, for outpatients whose motivation to follow treatment guidelines is not at optimal levels, the therapist may wish to involve trusted family members as supervisors. However, if clients' relationships with potential supervisors are conflictual, marked by criticism and hostility, the clients' needs will be better served without involving these people. The therapist should search for others who might play this role, such as friends, teachers, neighbors, or the like. Obviously, confidentiality issues require involving a client in selecting a supervisor if one is available.

If supervisors are involved in helping prevent rituals, the therapist will need to maximize the clients' role in decision making about not carrying out compulsions. Some clients are relieved of obsessive discomfort whenever they can assign responsibility for decision making to other trusted persons. For example, one client found that she could easily block her checking rituals whenever the therapist was present, since she believed that the therapist would never allow her to make a major mistake in turning off the stove or other appliance that might lead to harm. Alone, however, she had much more difficulty with not returning to be sure the stove was off. In this case, the therapist accomplished more by restricting rituals from another room or by telephone. Likewise, for such clients, family supervisors should not be present in the room during exposure and ritual prevention practice. The goal is to foster clients' trust in their own judgments about the need not to ritualize.

Strict versus Gradual Methods

Decisions about how abruptly to curtail rituals depend largely on clients' reports of their ability to tolerate discomfort. Like phobics, most OCD clients can accurately estimate their probable efficacy in confronting fears, as well as limiting compulsions. The clinician can describe the various strategies for limiting rituals, proposing that according to the research literature, stricter efforts have generally been associated with more improvement in both the numbers of clients who benefited and the amount of their benefit. Clients should be encouraged strongly to tolerate the maximum degree of restriction in rituals, since this will maximize gains from therapy.

The ideal is a "cold turkey" arrangement in which all rituals are eliminated from the outset. This method has been used by Foa, myself, and our colleagues (e.g., Foa et al., 1984, 1992) in studies yielding high rates of successful outcomes with intense treatment on a daily basis. For example, clients in these studies who had washing and cleaning compulsions were required to stop all handwashing (except in unusual circumstances, as in the case of spilling grease or ink) and to take a shower for 10 minutes only once or twice a week; no cleaning was allowed (again, except in unusual circumstances). Clearly, such a requirement restricts washing to a level not considered acceptable by most people; social standards of acceptability can be at least partly maintained by the use of extra deodorant and avoidance of activities that provoke perspiration and contact with dirt. Also according to this "cold turkey" method, clients with checking rituals were not to check at all, unless a potentially dangerous situation required a single check or (as in the case of a security guard) a client's job depended on brief checking. Those with repeating or ordering rituals or other miscellaneous or mental rituals were not allowed to engage in any such ritual under any circumstance. Of course, not all clients will agree to carry out such a strict regimen from the beginning of treatment, desirable though it may be. Some clients require somewhat more gradual blocking of rituals; even so, the maximum possible reduction of rituals in a graduated context is most desirable, for reasons discussed below.

In addition to potentially lower effectiveness, *very* gradual methods have other drawbacks. Trying to gradually reduce the time taken or the number of repetitions of rituals requires clients to keep track of continually changing rules for daily behaviors, under fluctuating levels of discomfort, depending on the exposure circumstances. This effort entails remaking the decision rules from day to day or week to week. This may be more difficult than adopting rigid rules from the outset, particularly since many clients report general difficulties in making decisions in everyday life.

Another graduated method used in some treatment programs is to eliminate rituals during exposure to items low on the hierarchy, while allowing rituals in situations higher on the list that have not yet been addressed during treatment. For example, after exposure to leaving small kitchen appliances plugged in, no checking of small appliances is allowed, but checking of the stove and heater is still permitted. Later on, concurrent with exposure to fears of fire from the stove and heater, checking of these large appliances is blocked. Although a few clients find it difficult to comply with frequently changing rules, most are able to follow this progression of increasingly fewer situations in which rituals are allowed.

A potential problem with this method of preventing rituals in selective situations is that rituals allowed in some situations may serve to relieve discomfort from other obsessive fears for which compulsions have already been proscribed. Washing permitted after more disturbing contaminants may relieve discomfort provoked earlier by deliberate exposure to lower-level hierarchy items. Repeating an action compulsively to prevent a very upsetting idea from coming to pass may also serve as a neutralizing ritual for an earlier obsessive idea already included in the exposure treatment practice. A good solution to this dilemma is to require immediate re-exposure to the most recently confronted items on the hierarchy following the use of a ritual for higher situations. For example, a man who is allowed to wash his hands after defecating but no longer after urinating can be asked to touch his penis (but not anal) area immediately after handwashing. (For readers who are worried about the potentially unsanitary or dangerous nature of this requirement, see the discussion later in this chapter of possible dangers inherent in some exposures and ritual prevention.) For a client fearful of chemicals, handwashing allowed after using lighter fluid for barbecuing can be followed by immediate exposure to touching a (low-discomfort) household cleanser container.

Probably the strictest method acceptable to most clients is a modified form of the "cold turkey" ritual prevention strategy described above. According to this method, most types of compulsions are immediately severely restricted to normal or near-normal levels, though the frequency of compulsions may be somewhat higher than normal. For example, clients with washing rituals are asked to shower no more than daily and preferably on alternate days for a maximum of 10 minutes (though this may be modified to 15 minutes for clients with extreme showering rituals). They are allowed to wash their hands minimally, if at all, but for no more than 30 seconds on any occasion. It is preferable that they avoid feared contaminants high on their hierarchy rather than wash in response to touching them, until they and the therapist are ready to commence deliberate exposure to those items. Clients with checking rituals are asked to check only once, briefly (a few seconds), after all situations from the start, with plans to eliminate checking during treatment in situations where most people do not normally check. Again, avoiding highly feared situations is preferred to exceeding the checking limit until clients confront those items during therapy. Other types of rituals require discussion of the best method for minimizing or eliminating rituals from the beginning of therapy. This method is used in the detailed discussion of the application of response prevention that constitutes the remainder of the chapter.

Planning Ritual Prevention

During the information-gathering phase of treatment, a comprehensive list of exposure situations is constructed (see Chapters 6 and 7). At the same time, the procedure for eliminating rituals is planned, and the rituals that may continue until later in therapy are specified. General guidelines for response prevention are given in Table 10.1, though these usually require modification to suit individual cases.

The most restrictive method that clients can tolerate is likely to be the most effective. Clients should be pressed firmly on this issue; the therapist should emphasize the importance of limiting rituals severely as soon as possible, and should remind clients about their commitment to overcome OCD symptoms and the necessity of stopping even minor rituals to accomplish this goal. The difficulty of carrying out this part of the program should be discussed, since clients will need to feel strongly supported by the therapist as well as the supervisor (if one is selected) in order to endure the discomfort and to resist sometimes powerful urges to engage in compulsions. Clients with multiple rituals should also be warned that sometimes blocking one ritual exacerbates others, but that eventually they will gain control of all ritualistic actions.

Clients should self-record their rituals prior to and throughout the exposure process on the homework form (see Chapter 8, Figure 8.2), to enable themselves and the therapist to follow their progress. The plan for ritual prevention can be discussed in the first treatment session as follows:

So we've planned the list of situations, and we're ready to start on touching the floor, wastepaper baskets, and doorknobs. That means no washing after touching any of these items, either today during our session, or after the practice homework that you do tomorrow and the next day. We've agreed that you can wash briefly after situations we haven't yet worked on, like using the toilet at work. But remember that any washing

TABLE 10.1. Rules for Response Prevention

Washing rituals:

Avoid using water on your body (showering, swimming, bathing, handwashing, rinsing, use of wet washcloths or towels) unless explicitly agreed upon with your therapist.

When you brush your teeth, try not to get water on your face or hands.

The use of creams and other toiletry articles (bath powder, deodorant, etc.) is allowed unless you find that using them reduces feelings of contamination. Discuss this with your therapist.

Shave with an electric shaver, not with water.

Showers should not be more than 10–12 minutes long, depending on your agreement with your therapist. Be careful not to wash any part of the body repeatedly or compulsively during your shower. Be sure to time your showers.

When handwashing is allowed by your therapist near the end of treatment, restrict it to the following times: before meals, after using the bathroom, and after handling greasy or visibly dirty things. Do not exceed six handwashes per day, and do not wash for more than 30 seconds each time.

Check with your therapist for exceptions to these rules in cases of medical conditions or other problems.

Checking rituals:

Beginning with the first session of exposure treatment, you are not permitted to engage in any checking rituals in relation to any items that you and your therapist have worked on during any previous treatment session.

Checking only *once* is allowed in situations where most people might do so (locking a door, using a stove or oven, etc.). For items or situations that are not ordinarily checked (empty envelopes, passing a pedestrian in the car), no checking is allowed. Exceptions must be discussed with your therapist.

Repeating rituals:

Beginning with the first session of treatment, you are not permitted to engage in any repeating rituals in relation to any items that you and your therapist have worked on during any previous treatment session.

General rules for everyone:

At home when you have an urge to ritualize that you are afraid you can't resist, talk to a supportive person before doing the ritual. Ask him or her to remain with you or to go somewhere with you until the urge decreases to a manageable level.

If you have agreed to allow a relative or friend to supervise you, he or she should report any violations of these rules to your therapist after telling you about it. He or she should try to keep you from violating the rules by asking you firmly to stop, without using any physical force or arguing with you. Your supervisor can physically prevent or stop you from ritualizing only if you have given prior consent to a specific plan or action in this regard.

(continued)

TABLE 10.1. (*continued*)

Continue to expose yourself deliberately on a weekly basis to objects or situations that have disturbed you prior to treatment. Do not avoid situations even if they still cause you some discomfort. If you notice a tendency to avoid a situation, make it a point to confront it deliberately at least twice a week until your anxiety level lessens.

Special instructions:

---

that is allowed can be no more than 30 seconds long, including soaping up, rinsing, and drying. You can take one 10-minute shower every other day as long as your husband is timing you. We need to be very strict about this, or treatment will progress very slowly or not at all. Are you game? This is going to be hard on you, but you'll survive, I promise.

There's another thing we need to be clear about from the start. If you *are* allowed to wash because you have to deal with something higher on our list, you'll need to recontaminate yourself immediately afterward with whatever we were working on last. So, beginning today, when you're at work and use the bathroom and wash your hands, you need to go back to your office right away, handle doorknobs, touch the floor, and pick something out of the trash. It's important that you not wait to do the exposure, or the relief you get from the allowed handwashing will make it harder to do this later and will interfere with progress. Do you agree to this requirement?

In cases where the therapist questions clients' motivation to follow through on these restrictions, written contracts can be drawn up and signed. Ordinarily, however, this is not necessary, since most OCD clients are scrupulously honest and will report any infractions of the agreement.

Involvement of a family member as a supervisor requires that this person attend sessions periodically or participate in discussions by phone, preferably with the client listening on another extension, so that everyone is clear on the plans. Generally, the spouse or relative is invited to the first treatment session and might be addressed as follows:

Thanks for coming today, John [the client's husband]. We need to agree on exactly what washing is allowed when, and what role you'll play. You already know that Kristen is allowed to take one shower for 10 minutes every other day, and that you'll supervise this by timing it and calling out times periodically. We won't know how this works out until you try it once or twice, and then you both can call me to tell me what happened. We should all agree on how to do this. Usually, the supervisor sits in or just outside the bathroom reading a book or whatever, and starts timing from the beginning of the shower—when Kristen gets under the water. Then it seems to help to call the time out at 2 minutes, 5 minutes, 7 minutes, 9 minutes, and finally at 10 minutes. Figure that the first time is practice to get used to the method, so if Kristen goes over the time by 1 or 2 minutes, don't worry. Kristen, is this O.K., or would you prefer a different arrangement?

If she agrees, the therapist continues:

If Kristen becomes frustrated or upset with the timing, or is unable to stop right on time, try to stay calm and matter-of-fact. Don't try to stop her with physical force at any point. Don't even turn off the water without getting her permission first. Try to remind yourself that Kristen doesn't wash compulsively because she likes to; she feels trapped by her fears, unreasonable though they may be. You can always say something like "This is what we agreed on with Dr. X," or "The therapist said it would be hard, especially at first," or whatever you like to acknowledge that it's a struggle but has to be done. Don't hesitate to blame me for being a meany and insisting on these limits. And of course, you can call me immediately if there's any confusion or problem. It might be a good idea to find out from you now, Kristen, what you think is likely to happen, and the same with you, John. How might it go?

The clinician has outlined an expected role for the supervisor, suggesting an appropriate attitude and behavioral responses, and enjoining him from using force of any kind. Although clients and supervisors may not be correct in their expectations, the therapist can at least troubleshoot potential difficulties before treatment starts. Supervisors are helpful only if they succeed in making clients' tasks easier. The therapist continues to suggest approaches during and after exposure homework:

Now, Kristen has also said she thinks it would help if you were around in the house when she does her homework practice for the day. You don't need to be in the room with her. She's assigned to do at least 2 hours of exposure each day to whatever items we're working on then in sessions. By way of example, let's say she's supposed to handle the garbage under the sink and touch the toilet seat. [Turning to Kristen after she shudders:] I know that seems hard to imagine, but actually, you'll probably be doing that at the beginning of next week, according to our plan. Anyway, if she gets upset because she's having trouble tolerating the discomfort and has strong urges to wash, I've asked her to work with you to figure out how to manage it. You could sympathize with her and comfort her, or suggest some distracting activities to keep her busy while her anxiety declines. Whatever you do, please don't divert her attention from the fact that she's "contaminated," though it's fine to find a way to make time seem to pass more quickly. If you can get her to laugh a little, so much the better, though this may be hard to do right away. Eventually the discomfort decreases, and it's important to find a way to wait it out without ritualizing. Any questions?

Limiting Reassurance Seeking

In addition to suggesting strategies to clients and supervisors to help ensure effective blocking of rituals, the therapist may need to impose limits on clients' requests for reassurance from supervisors, the therapist, hospital staff members, and any others who are important in this regard. Although many clients require no such intervention, some are quite tenacious in their efforts to substitute someone else's judgment for their own, thereby absolving themselves of perceived responsibility. Requests for reassurance may be quite overt (indeed, bordering on obnoxious) repetitions of the same question with endless variations. Often, however, the effort to seek reassurance is subtle; the urge is satisfied by posing a question that receives only a nod of acknowledgment. Some are convinced that if the reassuring person merely hears the question ("Is this safe?") without responding, no danger is in store, or the individual—a responsible person with good judgment—would intercede. Another variant of requests for reassurance takes the form of consultation with "experts" about feared outcomes, such as repeatedly calling the poison control hotline about possible harm to one's children, or visiting the doctor for numerous examinations and tests for feared cancer.

In Kristen's case, her husband, John, is cautioned about providing too much reassurance. Both have already acknowledged that she tries to reduce anxiety by asking John to make judgments about what is "dirty" and therefore "dangerous."

Now, the other thing I wanted to talk about is how John should handle your requests for reassurance. We've all agreed that they work for you just like a ritual, and therefore they need to be blocked along with the washing. John, would you give me a couple of examples of what Kristen might say that you think is unnecessary reassurance seeking?

The examples will help define what constitutes seeking reassurance, as distinct from reasonable questions that should be answered. Making this discrimination is important: If supervisors refuse to answer *any* questions, clients will become rightfully upset, and the supervisory arrangement will cease to be helpful. The therapist clarifies what constitutes seeking reassurance and proceeds:

If Kristen asks you for reassurance that it's O.K. to touch the trash, then you'll ask her to try to answer the question herself from what she knows about trash and about other people's attitudes and behavior. Of course, it's important to do this in a straightforward way, without snide comments or an irritated tone of voice. You can also remind her that I've asked you not to answer that type of question since it's part of her ritual, and she needs to learn to trust her own knowledge about it. If she's persistent in her questioning, you'll have to be firm and try not even to nod "yes" or give any other nonverbal indication. You may even need to leave the room, but we can talk about that further if the problem arises.

It's really hard for people like Kristen, since they can't trust their instincts about a situation. Their gut reaction is fear, but the fear is unreasonable and therefore can't be trusted. Instead, they have to go by their intellectual understanding, their logic. Unfortunately, feelings are usually much more powerful than logical thought processes in guiding people's actions. So this is a case of not being able to trust a natural reaction because it's wrong. [Turning to Kristen:] It will take a while before what you *know* to be true also *feels* true. In the situation of asking for reassurance, then, it's all the more important to learn to rely on your own intellectual knowledge and not depend on someone else's judgment. Learning to trust your knowledge should facilitate getting your feelings in line with what you already know. Again, if there's any confusion about this issue, call me for clarification. Are there any other things you wanted to discuss at this point?

The therapist then arranges a time for the supervisor to be in contact again, either by phone or by attending the latter part of a later session.

Use of "Mini" Rituals

It is just as important to block the brief rituals that clients use to reduce discomfort as it is to prevent the elaborate ones, such as handwashing, checking, or repeating actions. The therapist needs to be alert to—and ask specifically about—wiping or rinsing to decontaminate, quick glances to check, and so forth. The best question to ask may be this: "Do you find yourself resorting to any other little actions or thinking patterns to reduce your fear, now that we've agreed you can't wash your hands [check, clean, etc.] after touching the trash?" These "mini" rituals will need to be clarified and prevented as well.

Mental Rituals

As noted in Chapters 2 and 6, mental or cognitive rituals are relatively common in OCD—certainly more common than was reported in descriptions of OCD a decade or more ago. The clinician's assessment of symptoms by means of standard interview questions and the YBOCS Symptom Checklist (Appendix A) will ideally have identified any mental rituals that reduce discomfort, in contrast to obsessions that increase it. Examples include prayers, numbers, songs, phrases, and thoughts or images repeated in particular patterns, such as saying "good" phrases to cancel "bad" ones, or picturing a loved one in a healthy state to neutralize an image of the person dying of cancer. Occasionally, an individual will engage in rapid alternations between obsessions and mental rituals; the two may be distinguishable only by the reported discomfort associated with the former and very brief relief from the latter.

The therapist is advised to be alert for mental rituals that occur during the exposure and response prevention process. If clients appear briefly lost in thought or unusually slow to respond to a question or comment, they may be engaged in mental rituals. One therapist noticed that this happened especially at the end of therapy sessions' when some clients simply sat quietly in the chair for a few moments. When asked to report what they were doing or thinking, they indicated that they were trying to "make things right" or to reassure themselves before leaving the room. Brief additional questioning will clarify for the therapist whether such thinking constitutes mental ritualizing. Discrimination of mental compulsions from obsessions is critical to successful treatment, since obsessions require exposure treatment (e.g., exposure to the image of the loved one with cancer), whereas cognitive compulsions require response prevention (e.g., blocking or replacing the image of the same person in a healthy state).

Blocking mental rituals can be difficult, since they are not directly observable. We suggest enlisting clients' aid in finding creative strategies. Strong distractions from the compulsive thoughts (but not the obsessions) may be helpful in some cases. Generally, the best distractions are those that are meaningful to a client, such as an important memory or the use of logical argument about why the ritual is unnecessary. The therapist and client must be careful, however, that the "logical argument" does not itself turn into a mental ritual.

Alternatively, a mental ritual can be foiled by immediately rethinking the obsessive thought that led to the ritual. For example, a client who interpolated thoughts or reminders of the devil with "good" thoughts to undo potential damage was exposed to written and imagined "evil" words, such as "satanic," "devil," "forbidden," and "hell." She was asked to focus on these whenever she noticed herself engaging in "good" thoughts. If 13 is a "bad" number, replaced mentally by a "good" one like 10, the client can deliberately put 13 back into the sequence to short-circuit a compulsion. This is somewhat akin to re-exposure to the items being worked on as homework whenever a ritual has been allowed in response to a more disturbing item.

A variant of this approach is to use an endless-loop audiotape for continuous exposure to obsessions. The loop tape allows exposure to obsessive thoughts for prolonged periods without allowing time for the mental rituals to occur. Essentially, rituals are blocked by constant exposure. This method is particularly appropriate for clients whose obsessions and mental rituals take the form of thoughts or ideas, rather than images or impulses. Salkovskis and

Westbrook (1989) have employed this strategy very successfully in several cases.

Another possible method for blocking mental compulsions (but not obsessions) is thought stopping. Clients are taught to say "Stop!" in an emphatic tone, first aloud and then subvocally. This is startling, especially when accompanied at first by a loud noise or the snap of a rubber band on the wrist. It tends to stop the ritual, if only temporarily. Of course, since the onset of mental compulsions is known only to clients, clinicians must rely on them to signal the beginning of a ritual and then apply the thought-stopping procedure. It needs numerous repetitions, often more than 10 or 20, for lasting effect. This strategy seems to serve both as a distraction procedure and as an aversive consequence for the ritual.

The suggestions above may be useful in designing blocking strategies for mental rituals. It is difficult to provide specific guidelines, since there is little uniformity across clients in the manner by which such rituals appear. Discussing with clients the methods they believe will be most effective is likely to yield the most efficient and effective strategies.

New Rituals

Occasionally, new rituals arise to take the place of former ones, especially in the case of repeating rituals or "mini" rituals described earlier. These need not be cause for alarm, since it seems quite reasonable that frustrated and still fearful clients are merely seeking yet more ways to feel more comfortable. The therapist should reassure clients and family members that these will be incorporated into the treatment program and will also respond to response prevention. As treatment progresses and fears decline, the search for new anxiety-reducing mechanisms will cease.

Family Members' Participation in Rituals and Avoidance

Relatives of many clients have long participated in performing rituals or parts of rituals in order to minimize the time these rituals consume or the clients' discomfort. Other relatives take over ordinary tasks in the clients' stead, allowing the latter to avoid a situation altogether. Relatives' motives for their participation are often admirable, but unfortunately it inadvertently fosters obsessive fears. During treatment, relatives accustomed to performing rituals or doing tasks for clients must be asked to return the responsibility to the clients. This will require the therapist to meet with these significant others (who may or may not also serve as supervisors) to discuss the treatment plan as it pertains to their involvement in avoidance or rituals. Dates should be designated after which clients take back parts of tasks gradually or all at once (e.g., doing laundry, closing up the house for the evening), and relatives no longer perform rituals (e.g., washing hands or showering on return from work to "decontaminate" before entering the house; checking for ants in the corners of the kitchen).

Concerns about Dangers of Blocking Rituals

Most washing and checking rituals are designed to restore a state of safety or to prevent harm. They are extreme versions of normal behaviors, carried out in reaction to exaggerated fears. Nonetheless, most obsessive fears have some basis in reality. Pesticides really are dangerous chemicals; some germs can cause serious diseases; carelessness while driving can result in serious injury or death; fires can result from short-circuits in electrical appliances. How *do* people decide what is safe versus dangerous behavior, or reasonable rather than exaggerated caution? Clients undergoing exposure and response prevention will have genuine concerns about these distinctions; they will usually prefer to err on the side of caution, though no longer to the degree represented by their OCD symptoms. Thus, the therapist will be faced with earnest questions posed about safety and harm, such as the following:

Why do I have to touch the toilet seat? Other people don't go around touching toilet seats in public bathrooms. It's disgusting, and it's not safe. My mother always told me to put paper on the seat, and I know other people do that too. Why else would there be those paper seats in a lot of toilet stalls?

Or, in a very similar vein:

Most people wash after using the bathroom. You always see those signs in bathrooms in restaurants saying, "Employees must wash hands before returning to work." I've seen that kind of sign in other places, too, warning people about infection if they don't wash their hands.

Other variations of legitimate fears include the following:

But you see lots of articles in the paper and magazines about salmonella. You're supposed to be careful of it because it's dangerous.

That's why there's a poison control hotline, because there are a lot of chemicals in the house that are dangerous—especially for kids, who are more vulnerable than us adults.

You read almost every day in the paper about somebody's house going up in flames because of some electrical thing going wrong. Most people check stuff before they leave the house.

How do you know that you didn't miss something when you weren't looking at the road? The other day, a pedestrian got hit near the shopping mall. That driver couldn't have been paying close enough attention.

Behind some of these fears is genuine confusion about what constitutes adequate caution to prevent real damage or harm. Many clients have grown up with authoritative injunctions from parents, teachers, nuns, and so forth, that led to or reinforced their now-automatic thoughts and beliefs. These include "Better safe than sorry," "You can never be sure . . . ," "A good mother would never have allowed . . . ," and "You never know when. . . ."

The therapist must contend with these fears and attitudes, reminding clients that so far their beliefs and behaviors have caused substantial impairment in their ability to function in their own and others' best interests. Their fears and behaviors have obviously become exaggerated and no longer serve the real purpose of protecting others, since the clients have lost their ability to judge accurately how much caution is needed to prevent harm. The therapist might try to correct overcautious attitudes as follows:

It is impossible to live in this world without taking some risks. We all take risks every day when we drive, cross the street, visit sick relatives in the hospital, and so on. There are no guarantees that any activity won't lead to serious harm. Most of us just don't think about it; we assume that whatever will happen will happen, unless we can really see it coming and need to jump out of the way of a speeding car, for example. At those times, though, there is no confusion whatsoever that we're in a dangerous situation. We are 100% sure that something is happening, and we take corrective action as best we can. That's quite different from what you're describing, where you are confused about whether you hit somebody or left the stove on. In these cases, you're not *sure* you did it; you have doubts. Fear interferes with your judgment about the real dangerousness, and instead you seem to focus more on whether people will think you were careful enough than on the actual situation. From what you've told me, I bet that comes from some of the things you remember your mother saying.

Some discussion of clients' mental processes when fear arises is essential to help them decide when to ignore their fearful or guilty thoughts and behave as if the situation did not require avoidance or a compulsion. Clients can be urged to decide that if they are not 100% sure, then it didn't happen. When clients express genuine confusion about the dangerousness of a situation, consultation can be arranged with experts selected by the therapist with clients' input. The therapist should select expert consultants for their knowledge of the topic and, if possible, for their awareness of exaggerated fears about the issue at hand. The clinician can emphasize to the expert consultants that clients are likely to interpret information about danger very literally. The therapist should attend consultations with their clients to help clarify any mistaken impressions that they may obtain. Such consultants (e.g., chemists, public health physicians, and rabbis or priests) might be contacted to clarify such questions as behavior with pesticides or other chemicals, the chances of acquiring AIDS from blood and secretions, and religious rituals or beliefs about God or sin.

Whether or not consultants are involved, the therapist may need to remind clients of the following during difficult exposures and blocking of rituals:

During therapy, our task is to err on the side of risk, not caution. You've been being cautious too long, and it has caused you serious problems or you wouldn't be here now. Many of the exposures that we'll do are probably not typical of most people's behavior. Of course, neither have your obsessive fears and rituals been typical of most people's behaviors. After treatment, when you are much less fearful [or guilty], then you can use your judgment to decide what you want to touch [or check, etc.] and when you want to wash [or check, etc.]. You'll be in a much better position to do this when you are calmer and able to think more rationally. So for now, we need to do it the way we know works for people with OCD. Agreed?

When Treatment Instructions Become Rituals

My colleagues and I have observed several situations in which clients carried out treatment instructions so precisely that they too became ritualized. For example, one woman was obsessed about being a "bad" person whenever she had a "bad" thought (such as swearing or imagining someone dead) about another person. Previously, she had tried to correct her obsessive fears by using a positive word that rhymed with the "bad" one or by changing the image to a pleasant one. She was assigned homework of exposing herself deliberately to "bad" thoughts when serving customers in her job as a salesperson in a shop. The therapist asked her to stop the positive substitutions after specific types of thoughts (hierarchically arranged according to degree of difficulty); to retain the "bad" thoughts; and to remind herself that even good people have "bad" thoughts, as she and the therapist had discussed. Soon she converted this last assignment to a ritualized self-statement: "You're still a nice person. You're still a good person." The therapist finally asked her to revert to only the "bad" thoughts, and to allow any mean or nasty thoghts about others and herself to continue until they declined of their own accord *without* her self-reassurance. Some cognitive intervention did occur in sessions, however, as the therapist helped her clarify her real views about the meaning of "bad" thoughts and those who had them.

Ending Ritual Prevention

As therapy progresses and clients gain control over their urges to ritualize, the degree of supervision required can be reduced accordingly. Again, consultation with clients will determine the strictness of blocking of behaviors that is needed. Even after formal therapist-accompanied exposures are discontinued, it is important to keep rules in place for restricting ritualistic behaviors until it is clear that the *urges* to do so have declined to low levels. Often clients report that although they can control their behavior early on, the urges to wash or to check excessively remain strong for some time thereafter. Since stressors may occur at any point and interfere with tenuous control, rigid rules should be kept in place until clients are confident of their control.

11

Managing Complications and Maintaining Treatment Gains

This chapter focuses on managing complications, as well as on helping OCD clients to maintain gains after the intensive phase of treatment has ended. First, general treatment complications not already mentioned in the preceding treatment chapters are considered. Next, plans for reducing therapist involvement in exposure and ritual prevention, and for transferring responsibility for continued application of these procedures, are discussed. After this, a review of findings from studies examining predictors of outcome is provided, with brief commentary regarding potential strategies for addressing such problems, if intervention is appropriate. Since the therapist is often called upon by clients or relatives to answer questions about prognosis, this didactic information is useful, if only to reassure clients. Finally, planning for a future without OCD symptoms may involve attention to any comorbid difficulties, use of additional forms of treatment, and strategies for preventing relapse.

Complications during Exposure and Response Prevention

Some complications during treatment have already been discussed in earlier chapters, such as problems with generalization of fear reduction; what to do when therapeutic instruction are converted by clients to rituals; use of "mini" rituals; reassurance seeking; and so forth. A few additional potential difficulties are noted here.

Refusal and Arguments

Arguments during exposure treatment are never helpful to the therapy process. It is better to step back from the exposure at hand and discuss the treatment contract between the therapist and client than to engage in a tug-of-war over what the client should do. Obviously, the therapist needs to be attuned to genuine concerns about danger (see Chapters 8 and 10) and about socially appropriate behavior. If overvalued ideas and mistaken beliefs are central to the dispute, these must be directly addressed to correct misconceptions or increase flexibility in thinking about the situation. Motivational factors must also be considered: Does the client have too much to lose if OCD symptoms improve? In some cases, however, anxiety is simply too high for clients to proceed. To resolve this problem, the addition of serotonergic drugs can be considered, and treatment can begin with exposures to items very low on the hierarchy of feared situations. A few clients have made excellent progress in this manner, though at a snail's pace.

Failure to Habituate

If anxiety/discomfort fails to decline during exposure, the therapist should consider whether the client is highly reactive as a result of overarousal or severe depression. Either may respond to pharmacotherapy. It is also possible that the client may have been distracted from the feared exposure situation and therefore is not processing information so that fear decreases. Efforts to maintain attention focused on the exposure content (imaginal or *in vivo*) may be helpful. Alternatively, habituation may not occur if intermittent rituals are occurring, especially undetected minor behavioral rituals, mental rituals, or ritualistic self-reassurance. The therapist can inquire carefully and, with the client, can plan strategies to prevent this.

Undetected Avoidance

Slow recovery may be a result of clients' failure to expose themselves *fully* to feared situations and of continued unreported avoidance of minor exposures. Although some uncommitted clients may be deliberately self-protective in this way, many are unaware of the avoidance because they (and even their parents before them) have always behaved this way. Often the therapist's only clue to avoidance behaviors comes from observing clients as they conduct exposures in their own natural settings. Careful questioning as to why a client does something (e.g., holds an object in the left hand when the client is right-handed) can clarify avoidance problems that allow fears to persist.

New Obsessive Fears

It is not rare for new obsessive fears to appear partway through therapy, after anxiety in response to some items on the hierarchy has already reduced. Usually these obsessions have a similar thematic content and respond readily to continued treatment via exposure and blocking of rituals. As noted in an early report of several cases (Foa & Steketee, 1977), in the case of one man who avoided items from a major city, new fears of contamination by animal hair were actually based on the same underlying catastrophic idea of feared physical debilitation and helplessness resulting from disease, accompanied by pity from others. This theme had not been initially apparent to the therapist. A strategy that is helpful in such a case is to investigate carefully (in the role of detective) and always to ask questions whenever something does not seem quite right.

Fading Therapist Involvement in Treatment

Research by Emmelkamp and Kraanen (1977) showed that clients who controlled a large portion of their treatment, with the therapist advising them regularly about what exposures to carry out and how to prevent rituals, fared significantly better at follow-up than those whose treatment was entirely therapist-controlled. Their findings argue strongly for the need to fade the therapist's involvement during the course of behavioral treatment. It seems advisable to continue intensive exposure sessions (twice weekly or more) for a limited period—probably not more than 8–10 weeks, unless OCD symptoms are unusually complex and severe. Continued intense treatment is likely to increase clients' dependence on the therapist. Even during this phase, the therapist should assign to clients all responsibility for completing homework assignments.

Thereafter, exposure sessions should be decreased to once a week for another 4–6 weeks. These subsequent sessions can be held entirely in the therapist's office for discussion of the week's activities and exposure experiences. In these sessions, discussion also begins to shift to other problems that require specific attention to minimize their potential for provoking OCD symptoms in the future. Such concerns include marital or family communication problems, assertiveness or social anxiety, employment or avocational plans, and time management. Other problematic psychiatric symptoms can also be addressed at this point. If the client has been on psychotropic medications for OCD, fading of these medications can be planned as well: such fading usually begins only after the client's symptoms have been minimal for 3 months or more. All of these issues are discussed later in this chapter.

Predictors of Outcome

As detailed in Chapter 3, treatment by exposure and response prevention benefits about two-thirds to three-quarters of the obsessive compulsives who undergo it; this still leaves a significant number who do not improve or who relapse over time. Several researchers have attempted to identify specific factors that may affect short- and long-term outcome. The findings presented below include those from epidemiological studies of the course of illness of OCD; results of studies using retrospective analyses to identify predictors of treatment outcome; and findings from studies using prospective designs (e.g., outcome comparisons for clients with high vs. low depression, or for adolescents vs. adults).

Demographic Variables

In many ways, it is relieving to learn that demographic factors, over which therapists and patients have no control, have not been found to be important in treatment outcome. According to most studies searching for predictive factors, biographical variables, including age, gender, marital status, intelligence, and education level, have rarely been predictive, with some exceptions noted below (Basoglu, Lax, Kasvikis, & Marks, 1988; Boulougouris, 1977; Foa, Grayson, et al., 1983; Hoogduin & Duivenvoorden, 1988; Mawson et al., 1982). Clients with higher socioeconomic status did show better immediate outcome in these studies.

Although type of religion was not predictive in one study, more devout clients fared more poorly (Steketee et al., 1985). This finding suggests that rigid religious or moral beliefs accompanying excessive devotion may be legitimate targets for modification during exposure treatment, if effective methods for doing so can be found. For example, one client refused to park his car facing a church, even if the church was blocks away, on the off-chance that he might have a blasphemous thought while doing so. The clinician may wish to consult with the appropriate religious leaders (priests, rabbis, ministers, etc.) to verify that the targeted beliefs are in fact inaccurate personal interpretations rather than core denominational beliefs.

Aspects of OCD

A chronic, unremitting course of illness has been associated with males who had early onset of OCD symptoms (Rasmussen & Tsuang, 1986). However, in studies of behavioral treatment, early onset (without attention to gender) actually predicted a better long-term outcome (Foa, Steketee, et al., 1983; Steketee et al., 1985). Clients who are fearful that they will not benefit because of the lengthy duration of their symptoms can be reassured that their chronic symptoms are still highly likely to respond to treatment.

Nonetheless, *current* age may be a problem, in that adolescents tend to benefit less from treatment than adults; gender differences were not reported. In a prospective study, Cox, Merkel, and Pollard (1987) reported that in-patient exposure and response prevention administered to 13 adults and 13 matched adolescents led to improvement in both groups, but that the adults improved significantly more than the adolescents, who tended to withdraw prematurely from treatment. Adolescents appear to have less tolerance for the restrictions of response prevention and the discomfort of exposure. How best to assist them in overcoming their fears is not clear at this point, but therapists should be alert to managing potential refusal to cooperate.

Surprisingly, several studies have failed to find a relationship between outcome and either duration or severity of symptoms (Boulougouris, 1977; Foa, Steketee, et al., 1983; Meyer et al., 1974; Rachman et al., 1973). In most of these studies, clients had chronic and severe symptoms; those with mild symptoms were not included. In a sample with a wider range of severity and duration, these two factors might well be associated with outcome. Of potential relevance to this issue is Walton and Mather's (1963) finding that clients with recent onset (and possibly less severe symptoms) responded well to systematic desensitization, which has otherwise proven ineffective for OCD. Still, there is ample evidence that clients with very severe symptoms usually improve with exposure and response prevention.

Some studies have observed that clients with contamination fears and washing rituals have a better prognosis than those with checking rituals (Boulougouris, 1977; Rachman et al., 1973). However, Foa, I, and our colleagues have failed to find such an association (Foa & Goldstein, 1978; Foa, Steketee, et al., 1983), suggesting that type of ritual does not affect improvement rates. Clients with "pure obsessions" without overt rituals do appear to fare more poorly than those with overt rituals, according to several reports (see Salkovskis & Westbrook, 1989; Steketee & Cleere, 1990). As noted previously, however, it seems very likely that many such clients will respond well to exposure to obsessions (e.g., via an endless-loop audiotape) and prevention of associated *mental* rituals.

Cognitive Factors

In a paper examining treatment failure among 21 OCD clients, Foa (1979) observed that those who held fixed beliefs, labeled "overvalued ideation," did not benefit from treatment. Their mistaken assumptions about the actual dangerousness of obsessive situations appeared to interfere with habituation of fear across exposure treatment sessions; clients' reactivity to feared situations failed to decline as expected from one session to the next. In addition, Perse (1988) observed that OCD clients with overvalued ideation did not respond to antidepressant medication. This issue of insight into the unreasonableness of obsessions is considered by many investigators to be an important predictor of outcome, though at least one subsequent study has failed to find a significant association (Hoogduin & Duivenvoorden, 1988).

McKenna (1984) noted that overvalued ideas also occur in other disorders (several of them closely related to OCD), including morbid jealousy, hypochondriasis, and anorexia nervosa. Body dysmorphic disorder also seems to fit into this group. The reputation of these conditions as difficult to treat seems to derive in large part from the firmly held convictions. It is not surprising that the more strongly clients adhere to mistaken beliefs, the more difficult it will be to dislodge such beliefs merely with exposure. Unfortunately for clinicians, the effect of behavioral treatments on changing the strength of overvalued beliefs has not been adequately studied, nor have successful efforts to rectify such beliefs been reported to date. This is an important area in which further research can inform clinical practice.

There is widespread belief among clinical researchers that many OCD clients hold erroneous beliefs and attitudes that impede progress unless they are modified during the course of treatment (e.g., Rasmussen & Eisen, 1990). Surprisingly, in contrast to such work with depressed clients, specific beliefs and attitudes of OCD sufferers have received little attention (see Chapter 4). Ongoing work by Freeston, Ladouceur, and colleagues (e.g., Freeston et al., 1991), among others, on subclinical and clinical populations may shed light on such issues in the near future.

Depression

Several early studies suggested that high initial depression predicted failure after treatment (e.g., Boulougouris, 1977; Foa, 1979; Foa, Grayson, et al., 1983; Marks et al., 1980), though not necessarily at follow-up (Foa, Grayson, et al., 1983; Mawson et al., 1982). However, more recent evidence consistently contradicts this finding (e.g., Basoglu et al., 1988; Emmelkamp et al., 1985; Hoogduin & Duivenvoorden, 1988; Mavissakalian et al., 1985; Mawson et al., 1982; O'Sullivan et al., 1991; Steketee et al., 1985; Steketee, 1987). Indeed, a prospective comparison (Foa et al., 1992) of depressed and nondepressed OCD clients who received either antidepressant medication or placebo prior to behavior therapy indicated that nondepressed clients did not fare better than depressed ones, and that amelioration of depression via drugs had no impact on treatment outcome. In fact, as OCD symptoms improved with behavior therapy, so did depressed mood. It seems very likely, then, that benefits from behavioral treatment will not be impeded by the moderate levels of depression that many (if not most) clients complain of.

However, clinical experience, along with one case report (Foa, Steketee, & Groves, 1979), suggests that clients suffering from severe depression that leads to suicidal ideation, retardation of activity, and substantial interference with cognitive processing should be treated for depression prior to entering behavior therapy for OCD. Treatment via antidepressant drugs is probably most expedient, though cognitive therapy for depressive cognitions could also be employed, as well as electroconvulsive treatment (ECT). One client, a woman who experienced severe rituals and was also suicidal, was unable to follow instructions for exposure. She underwent a series of ECT treatments that led to near-complete remission of her depressed mood, but had no effect on her OCD symptoms. A subsequent trial of exposure and response prevention led to very substantial reductions in her obsessive fears and compulsions. It appears that without such antidepressant treatment, severely depressed clients have difficulty engaging in exposures and processing information from the experience.

Anxiety

With regard to general anxiety prior to therapy, the weight of the evidence indicates no association with outcome, particularly at follow-up (e.g., Boulougouris, 1977; Emmelkamp et al., 1985; Mawson et al., 1982; O'Sullivan et al., 1991; Steketee et al., 1985). Interestingly, I observed (Steketee, 1988) that high levels of anxiety and depression *after* exposure and blocking of rituals strongly predicted poor outcome. Most clients show substantial general anxiety prior to treatment, which appears to be a result of their OCD fears and usually decreases during exposure. Clients who remain highly anxious at the end of treatment are likely to be both less optimistic about their ability to maintain gains, and more subject to the negative effects of life stressors; these factors tip the scales in favor of relapse.

It is obvious that whatever the therapist can do to reduce both depression and anxiety during behavior therapy will assist clients in the future. Again, cognitive beliefs and attitudes may have much to do with elevating anxiety and depression, and thus with maintenance of gains. Unfortunately, without further research information, there are no clear answers at this time as to how to intervene to resolve persistent mood problems.

Treatment Aspects

In a path analysis of several variables, we (Foa, Grayson, et al., 1983) noted that clients who reacted with more anxiety (reactivity) during exposure to feared situations tended to show less reduction (habituation) of anxiety during, as well as between, exposure sessions. All three of these factors were associated with poorer outcome, indicating that clients who react very strongly to most exposure situations and whose anxiety does not decrease readily may not benefit from treatment. Additional intervention that facilitates these processes will be needed. What the additional intervention should be will probably depend on other factors, such as mood state, personality traits, comorbidity, and problematic cognitions.

Two groups of investigators observed that greater posttest gains on OCD measures (i.e., at least 67% improvement) reduced the risk of relapse at follow-up (Foa, Grayson, et al., 1983; O'Sullivan et al., 1991). Conversely, clients who were only partly improved at the end of behavior therapy tended to relapse. However, data from another study did not support these findings: Of 18 clients who were rated only moderately improved (31–69% improved) after treatment, 13 (nearly 75%) continued to improve further at follow-up (Emmelkamp et al., 1985). Explanations for these discrepant results are unclear.

Nonetheless, the weight of the evidence suggests that it is difficult for clients to continue to improve after intensive exposure and response prevention have ended unless they have made considerable strides during treatment. For this reason, therapists are urged to continue intensive treatment for clients who are improving steadily until the therapists and clients agree that at least 80% of symptoms are eliminated. This degree of gain provides some buffering against the inevitable stressors that reduce resistance to anxiety and urges to ritualize. Even if some relapse occurs, clients with substantial benefits are more likely to be able to recoup losses on their own (or, if necessary, with booster sessions).

Social Functioning Outside the Home

With respect to the prognostic value of aspects of social functioning, studies of satisfaction in employment have been conflicting. Although one study found that higher job satisfaction at pretest was related to *poorer* outcome (Steketee et al., 1985), another showed that better posttest work adjustment predicted more long-term gains (Steketee, 1988). More consistent findings are evident for social relationships: *Improvement* in social functioning at posttreatment was related to better long-term outcome (Steketee et al., 1985), whereas poorer social adjustment after treatment predicted relapse (Steketee, 1988). However, social anxiety and social skill showed no association with outcome. It is apparent to most clinicians that clients who enter or exit treatment with stable work and social relationships have a distinct edge over those who must now struggle to address these problems. Continued assistance by the therapists or referral to other clinicians or agencies (e.g., employment counseling, assertiveness training groups, social skills groups) may be critical in putting clients on the road to recovery from both OCD symptoms and the impairment resulting from them. As discussed below, planning with clients how to use the time that is newly available from not ritualizing will be important in helping them maintain their gains.

Family and Marital Factors

Family and marital factors that influence outcome have been studied through both retrospective examination of predictors of outcome, and prospective studies in which spouses or family members are included in behavioral treatment. Tables 11.1 and 11.2 summarize results of single- and multiple-case studies and group investigations in which behavior therapy for OCD was combined with marital and parental involvement, respectively. Some of these studies are described more fully in this section. Among retrospective studies of pretreatment variables, Hafner (1982) found that OCD clients with more satisfactory marriages improved more, but in three other reports marital adjustment failed to predict outcome (Emmelkamp & DeLange, 1983; Emmelkamp et al., 1990; Steketee, 1988). Similarly, I found (Steketee, 1987) that the size, perceived adequacy, and availability of the social support network were not associated with outcome.

Although some clinicians have suggested that family members' reactions to obsessive compulsive clients' symptoms during and after treatment are important in recovery, few data on this issue are available. We (Steketee & Foa, 1985) have noted that some family members are impatient, expecting

TABLE 11.1. OCD Marital Relationship and Outcome of Treatment

Study	n	Findings
Hafner (1982)	5 F	Relapse on return home to conflictual marriages
Hafner (1988)	5 F	Improved with spouse-aided behavior therapy
Cobb et al. (1980)	12 OCDs and phobics	Improved with spouse-aided behavior therapy
Emmelkamp & DeLange (1983)	12	No advantage of spouse-aided behavior therapy over behavior therapy alone at 6-month follow-up
Emmelkamp et al. (1990)	50	No advantage of spouse-aided behavior therapy over behavior therapy alone at 1-month follow-up; no effect on marriage quality

TABLE 11.2. OCD Parental Relationship and Outcome of Treatment

Study	n	Findings
Dalton (1983)	1 (age 9)	Instructions for behavior modification to parents only led to improvement
Fine 1973	2 (ages 9, 11)	Behavioral treatment (ritual prevention) and joint family meetings led to improvement
Hafner et al. (1981)	2 (ages 16, 24)	Individual behavior therapy failed; family therapy led to improvement
Hoover & Insel (1984)	10 adults	Improved patients relapsed partly on return home; separation from parents led to improvement
Mehta (1990)	30 adults	Family-assisted therapy > therapy alone; firm, nonanxious family members were most helpful

treatment to result in rapid and complete symptom remission, whereas others continue to "protect" the clients from formerly upsetting situations and thereby reinforce avoidance behaviors. Years of accommodation to the clients' peculiar requests have established patterns that are difficult to break and may foster relapse. Consistent with these observations, I observed (Steketee, 1987) that clients were more likely to relapse if their close relatives were critical, reacted angrily to symptoms, or held a firm belief that clients could in fact control their obsessive and compulsive symptoms if they wished. Somewhat similar findings have been reported by Emmelkamp et al. (1985). Interventions directed at these attitudinal family difficulties may be helpful in fostering maintenance of gains. This suggestion is supported by findings that for clients with other disorders, treatments that included participation of family members led to better posttreatment outcome and reduced relapse (e.g., Barlow, O'Brien, & Last, 1984; Mermelstein, Lichtenstein, & McIntyre, 1983; Falloon et al., 1982).

Two studies on a large group of OCD clients have indicated that including spouses as assistants during treatment did not improve upon the benefits derived from behavioral treatment in which spouses were not included (Emmelkamp & DeLange, 1983; Emmelkamp et al., 1990). However, very different findings were reported by Mehta (1990), who conducted a similar study in India, comparing OCD clients treated with or without the assistance of family members (not necessarily spouses). In that study, family assistance led to significantly more benefit, both after treatment and at follow-up (see Figure 11.1).

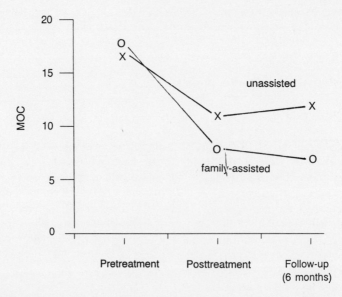

FIGURE 11.1. Comparison of family-assisted versus unassisted exposure treatment for OCD. MOC, Maudsley Obsessional–Compulsive Inventory scores. Data from Mehta (1990).

Including a spouse or a family member as cotherapist may be detrimental when this person's interaction with the client is marked by conflict or strong dependence (Emmelkamp, 1982; Mathews, Gelder, & Johnston, 1981). These conflicts may be temporarily suppressed while the therapist is directing the treatment, but are likely to manifest themselves during the follow-up phase, impeding further progress and possibly leading to decline. Studies of "expressed emotion" (EE; criticism, hostility, emotional over-involvement) in families of schizophrenic and depressed clients show that inpatients who return home to family members who are high in EE relapse after treatment at two to three times the rate of patients from low-EE families (see Hooley, 1985, for a review). The research findings reported for OCD families suggest that EE variables may also be relevant to outcome for OCD clients. Further study of this issue will be needed to determine whether this is indeed an important predictor of gains from exposure and response prevention, and, if so, what treatment strategies may be beneficial. At present, it seems likely that psychoeducational interventions for families and clients to increase knowledge about how OCD symptoms affect behavior may help reduce family members' critical reactions and negative interactions with clients. Therapists are urged to invite significant others to sessions early in treatment, to assess (and, if necessary, to intervene in) family members' responses to clients during the treatment process.

Comorbid Complications during Treatment

Substance Abuse

Comorbidity of OCD with alcohol or drug abuse can seriously impair a client's ability to follow through with the planned behavioral treatment. As with treatment of most other Axis I disorders, a diagnosis of alcohol or drug abuse requires that a client first be treated for substance abuse before exposure and prevention of rituals are begun. Use of substances to self-medicate during exposure will undoubtedly interfere with normal habituation of obsessive fear and with clients' development of confidence in their ability to cope with high levels of obsessive anxiety when under stress in the future. Alcohol and drug use should be at a minimum or absent during the period of exposure and blocking of rituals. For those accustomed to managing anxiety with alcohol or nonprescription drugs, alternative methods of anxiety management (e.g., relaxation, exercise, or other activity) should be sought. Clients are in the best position to identify which strategies will be most fruitful.

Panic Disorder

Comorbid panic disorder (*without* agoraphobia) can be treated concurrently with OCD symptoms, but coping skills for managing panic symptoms should be taught early in the treatment process. Failure to address the panic symptoms can lead to anxiety attacks during exposure and homework sessions, prompting clients to refuse further exposures. This is particularly likely later in therapy, when the most anxiety-provoking exposures are planned. Treatment for panic may include diaphragmatic breathing and relaxation exercises, as well as cognitive forms of treatment (e.g., identifying and correcting faulty assumptions, attention focusing, thought stopping, and possibly paradoxical intention).

Comorbid panic disorder with agoraphobia adds substantially to the complexity of treatment, since exposure is required both for the feared obsessive situations and for places that are avoided because they may provoke a panic attack. The clinician should probably work on exposures for only one disorder at a time to avoid confusion, unless obsessive and panic situations overlap. For behavioral and cognitive treatment of panic symptoms, the reader is referred to Barlow and Cerny's (1988) excellent treatment guide.

Social Anxiety

Mild or even moderate social anxiety is not likely to interfere with exposure therapy. However, severe anxiety that prevents a client from expressing himself or herself to the therapist or to others in exposure contexts is likely to hinder progress. During information-gathering and treatment-planning sessions, the therapist and client will need to consider whether exposure requires contact with feared social situations. If it does, some effort to address the social anxiety directly prior to treatment may be essential. Unfortunately, social contacts are impossible for some clients because of obsessive fears (usually of contamination) that prevent them from entering the situations required for behavioral treatment of social fears. In such cases, concurrent treatment of both sets of anxiety symptoms will be needed, carefully interfaced to allow for gradual reduction of discomfort in both social and OCD contexts. Imaginal exposure is likely to be required, and treatment will require considerably more than the usual time needed for uncomplicated OCD treatment.

Personality Variables

Studies of personality variables in OCD have focused on traits, as well as diagnostic categories of personality disorders. Despite extensive study of obsessional personality traits in OCD, few have attempted to relate these traits to course of illness or outcome of treatment. Lo (1967) reported that premorbid obsessional personality predicted a more favorable course 4 years later, and premorbid compulsive personality style was also associated with better outcome immediately after behavioral treatment in one study (Rabavilas, Boulougouris, Perissaki, & Stefanis, 1979). However, a formal diagnosis of obsessive compulsive personality disorder (OCPD) did not predict outcome (Baer & Jenike, 1990; Steketee, 1990).

This accords with clinical experience, with some caveats. Some clients' OCD symptoms are extensions of obsessional traits, and because of their ego-syntonic nature (they are overvalued ideas of a sort), they are difficult for clients to give up. For example, one accountant prided himself on his carefulness in financial matters, which he believed had both served his clients well and saved him money. When he sought treatment to help reduce the excessive hours of checking financial records that had cost him his job, it was difficult for the therapist to arrive at an agreement with him about how much checking would be allowed. Despite the severe interference of checking rituals in his life, he was unable to change his attitude toward these behaviors and eventually relapsed after tenuous gains.

Such compulsive personality traits can lead to arguments with the therapist about the need for particular exposure experiences or for blocking of certain rituals. Problematic traits include perfectionism, fears of making mistakes, overconscientiousness or refusal to allow others to assume responsibility for daily activities, and inability to discard unneeded objects because they might someday be useful (hoarding). In extreme cases, clients can be encouraged to discontinue treatment, returning at a later point when they feel more able to comply with requirements.

The presence of personality disorders *in general* has been related to a poor prognosis in studies of course of illness in OCD (Ingram, 1961; Kringlen, 1970; Lo, 1967), but not necessarily for behavioral treatment outcome (Steketee, 1990). Particular personality diagnoses have predicted poor outcome following treatment. Borderline clients responded poorly to treatment, according to one study (Hermesh, Shahar, & Munitz, 1987), and I found (Steketee, 1990) that clients with pronounced passive–aggressive personality traits benefited less from behavioral treatment at follow-up. Jenike and associates found that OCD clients with schizotypal personality disorder improved much less often after appropriate behavioral or medication treatment than those without this disorder (Jenike et al., 1986; Minichiello et al., 1987).

It is clear from this summary that there is as yet little agreement across studies regarding which personality traits or disorders are most seriously problematic for successful behavioral treatment of OCD clients. Still, the fairly consistent association of personality disturbance with poor outcome in other anxious clients (e.g., Mavissakalian & Hamann, 1986) suggests that personality disorders of several types may be problematic for treatment outcome.

What can or should the therapist do to address this concern? Unfortunately, the answer is not at all clear at this point. Predictive capacity does not indicate unequivocally that all clients who have certain personality disorders (e.g., borderline, schizotypal, or passive–aggressive) will not benefit from exposure treatment. It is unreasonable, then, to exclude such clients from behavioral treatment. Additional methods may be needed to help manage severe personality disturbances. Neuroleptics may be useful for schizotypal clients, who tend to exhibit overvalued beliefs in obsessive fears. Intensive behavioral treatment (e.g., Linehan's [1993] dialectical behavior therapy) and possibly medications may be required to help those with borderline traits to manage their extreme mood fluctuations and parasuicidal behaviors. It is particularly important to be aware that anxiety-provoking exposures may exacerbate such symptoms, requiring careful monitoring and probably less intense exposures.

Some personality traits and disorders that are not associated with poor outcome, such as dependent and avoidant personality disorders, may nevertheless complicate the therapy. Problematic symptoms include general risk avoidance, extreme sensitivity to perceived criticism by the therapist (even when no criticism is intended), excessive dependency on the therapist or family members (especially spouses) to make decisions the clients should be learning to make alone, and lack of assertiveness with the therapist in planning how to structure treatment to accommodate the clients' emotional needs.

Although there are no clear guidelines for managing these problems, the therapist must obviously intervene to prevent these traits from interfering with the execution of behavior therapy and with maintenance of gains. The latter is particularly threatened if such individuals suffer from unassertiveness in employment or social contexts, which produces frustration, self-criticism, and anger that clients cannot resolve. As a therapist becomes aware of significant problems in these areas, concurrent therapy or referral for intensive work on these issues should be considered.

Combining Behavior Therapy with Other Treatments

Marital Therapy

Marks (1981) has suggested that exposure therapy is indicated for OCD clients with marital problems. His contention is supported by research showing that marital adjustment did not predict behavioral treatment outcome (Emmelkamp & DeLange, 1983; Emmelkamp et al., 1990). In a study of this issue, Cobb et al. (1980) compared the differential effects of exposure and marital therapy on marital problems and on OCD symptoms in a crossover design. Twelve couples, each of which had severe marital problems and one partner with OCD symptoms, were randomly assigned to either marital or OCD treatment during phase 1, followed by 3 months of no treatment, and then by the other treatment during phase 2. Exposure treatment using the nonsymptomatic partner as a cotherapist produced significant improvement in both OCD and marital problems. By contrast, marital therapy alone led to changes only in the marital symptoms. Improvements were maintained at a 13-month follow-up. Although exposure is obviously recommended over marital therapy for treatment of OCD, the possible advantages of combining both treatments for clients with *severe* marital problems obviously merits further investigation (see Cobb & Marks, 1979). The therapist may need to combine treatments when marital difficulties interfere with a client's ability to execute exposure and blocking procedures.

Assertiveness Training

With respect to social dysfunction, assertiveness training produced favorable results with clients who had obsessions about harming others, and was found to be at least as effective as thought stopping (Emmelkamp & van der Heyden, 1980). However, since thought stopping was not very effective, the comparability of assertiveness training does not necessarily recommend it as an effective strategy, particularly since it was not tested against exposure treatment. Clinical impressions suggest that assertiveness training and marital therapy may be useful as *adjuncts* to exposure and response prevention procedures (e.g., Queiroz, Motta, Madi, Sossai, & Boren, 1981), but they cannot substitute for the latter. They may be particularly helpful in preventing relapse.

Cognitive Therapy

It is clear that many clients with OCD suffer from faulty beliefs and mistaken assumptions that appear to be directly or indirectly related to the genesis and persistence of obsessions and compulsions. As discussed in Chapter 4, research on self-instructional training indicated no benefit from this cognitive therapy modality (Emmelkamp et al., 1980). Although rational–emotive therapy led to gains in OCD symptoms, it did not add to the benefits of exposure treatment (Emmelkamp & Beens, 1991; Emmelkamp et al., 1988). Treatment using Beck's model of cognitive therapy (Beck et al., 1985) has not yet been tested, though this strategy would seem potentially very beneficial for identifying and challenging specific cognitions leading to OCD symptoms. As discussed previously, considerably more research is needed to help identify the thoughts, beliefs, and assumptions that commonly underlie obsessive fears and are therefore appropriate targets for cognitive therapies (see Freeston et al., 1991, 1993). The degree to which these cognitions change during exposure and ritual prevention without deliberate cognitive intervention is of considerable interest in determining whether such treatment is needed and for whom. Certainly, the field is likely to move in this direction in the near future. In the interim, the therapist has little to lose by seeking to identify problematic thoughts during exposures and determining whether they shift during treatment.

Drug Treatments

As discussed in Chapter 5, several medications, all of which affect the serotonin system, have been found helpful for OCD. Use of these medications is definitely indicated when clients appear unable to tolerate even mildly uncomfortable exposures to obsessive situations. In such cases, any of the effective medications (clomipramine, fluoxetine, fluvoxamine) can be prescribed for a sufficient period of time to obtain the full effect from the drug. Most psychopharmacologists experienced in treating OCD suggest that patients be given the highest doses readily tolerated, in order to determine the maximum benefit that the drug can produce. Treatment for approximately 8–10 weeks is likely to be necessary for the full antiobsessive effects of these drugs.

If medications prove beneficial, clients can then begin exposure and response prevention in the format suggested in Chapters 8 through 10. Since withdrawal of medications has been found to lead to relapse in nearly 90% of patients in some studies (e.g., Pato et al., 1988), it is important to allow clients to remain on the prescribed drugs for a considerable period of time (at least 6 months, and preferably a year or more) after intensive behavioral treatment has ended. When OCD symptoms have been in remission for several months, clients can be weaned slowly from the medications, with very gradual reductions in dosage over several months. If symptoms worsen following medication reduction, behavioral interventions can be reinstituted briefly until clients' symptoms are again reduced. Further medication withdrawal should proceed very slowly, commensurate with clients' ability to manage obsessive fears and urges to ritualize.

Preventing Relapse

Managing Life Stressors

It is inevitable that all clients will eventually encounter life stressors that will lower their tolerance for anxiety-provoking experiences. Common stressors include a change in residence, bereavement, major physical illness, separation or divorce, financial problems, and serious problems among relatives that require substantial helping efforts. It is essential that therapists use sessions at the end of treatment to review which options for stress management are likely to be useful to—and, perhaps more importantly, *used* by—clients. Stress management strategies include anxiety reduction methods (such as relaxation and meditation), exercise, assertive behaviors to procure needed resources, and possibly additional therapy. Clients with few social resources will undoubtedly require therapeutic efforts to bolster regularly available supports; such efforts may include advocacy for clients with various social service agencies.

Regardless of the methods chosen, advance consideration of what clients *plan* to do when stressors occur can be invaluable in preventing difficulty. Particularly useful are step-by-step strategies for behaviors in which to engage when stressful events provoke strong urges to ritualize. For example, clients might agree to ask themselves a series of predetermined (written) questions to help identify the source of upset; to call a relative or friend (especially a self-help group member—see below) who can encourage abstinence from rituals and help distract them; to leave the feared situation to escape temptation until anxiety is manageable; or to call the therapist for a special session to address the uncomfortable feelings.

Joining a Support Group

Some clients with OCD are interested in becoming members of self-help or support groups in which other members share similar symptoms. This is recommended especially for those who have already completed intensive treatment programs and seek to consolidate gains. A support group provides easy access to a social system whose members can readily empathize with the struggle to overcome powerful obsessive fears and compulsive urges. Often the problem is locating such a group. Interested individuals are urged to contact the OC Foundation (see Chapter 1) if no support groups can be identified in the local area. In making referrals to such groups, clinicians should be aware that many members may not have received behavioral treatment, and may thus be unaware of the coping mechanisms clients have already been taught to tolerate discomfort.

Filling the Time Void

Successful treatment leaves many clients, especially those who were more debilitated at the beginning, with much time on their hands that needs to be put to more appropriate uses. Maintenance sessions after intensive treatment ends can be used to identify appropriate activities to occupy this time in a nonobsessive or compulsive manner that is satisfying to clients. It should be apparent that the new activities must be both reinforcing to clients and less anxiety-provoking that the original obsessively feared ones. Otherwise, these activities will be avoided, and the risk of the return of OCD symptoms will remain high.

Clinicians are cautioned against urging unemployed individuals to begin job training or to apply for work immediately, since this may constitute a major stressor for which the clients are ill equipped. Particularly for those who will immediately lose state or federal benefits if able to work, progress toward employment should proceed slowly, lest the threat of financial loss disrupt the therapeutic relationship.

Exploration of substitute activities should begin as intensive treatment is nearing an end; the therapist should always follow clients' leads regarding interests and capabilities. Gradual involvement in outside activities can include volunteer work in an area of interest, or planned activities at home (preferably leading to self-satisfaction for a task accomplished, as well as reinforcement from others). As clients gain confidence and skill, the clinician can suggest progressively more challenging work options, strongly supporting clients' personal goals in the process.

One Final Note

It is undoubtedly clear from the discussion above that recovery from debilitating OCD symptoms via behavioral treatment is rarely a smooth process. The more collaborative and respectful the relationship between therapist and client, the more likely it is that the client will make steady (if fitful) progress toward a nonobsessive and noncompulsive lifestyle.

Appendices

APPENDIX A. Yale–Brown Obsessive–Compulsive Scale (YBOCS) Symptom Checklist

Name _____ Date _____

Check all that apply, but clearly mark the principal symptoms with a "P."
(Rater must ascertain whether reported behaviors are bona fide symptoms of OCD, and not symptoms of another disorder such as simple phobia or hypochondrias. Items marked "*" may or may not be OCD phenomena.)

Current   Past

Aggressive obsessions

____   ____   Fear might harm self

____   ____   Fear might harm others

____   ____   Violent or horrific images

____   ____   Fear of blurting out obscenities or insults

____   ____   Fear of doing something else embarrassing*

____   ____   Fear will act on unwanted impulses (e.g., to stab friend)

____   ____   Fear will steal things

____   ____   Fear will harm others because not careful enough (e.g., hit/run motor vehicle accident)

____   ____   Fear will be responsible for something else terrible happening (e.g., fire, burglary)

____   ____   Other _____

Contamination obsessions

____   ____   Concerns or disgust with bodily waste or secretions (e.g., urine, feces, saliva)

____   ____   Concerns with dirt or germs

____   ____   Excessive concern with environmental contaminants (e.g., asbestos, radiation, toxic waste)

____   ____   Excessive concern with household items (e.g., cleansers, solvents)

____   ____   Excessive concern with animals (e.g., insects)

____   ____   Bothered by sticky substances or residues

____   ____   Concerned will get ill because of contaminant

____   ____   Concerned will get others ill by spreading contaminant (aggressive)

____   ____   No concern with consequences of contamination other than how it might feel

____   ____   Other _____

Sexual obsessions

___   ___ Forbidden or preverse sexual thoughts, images, or impulses
___   ___ Content involves children or incest
___   ___ Content involves homosexuality*
___   ___ Sexual behavior toward others (aggressive)*
___   ___ Other_____

Hoarding/saving obsessions

___   ___ [distinguish from hobbies and concern with objects of monetary or
           sentimental value] _____

Religious obsessions (scrupulosity)

___   ___ Concerned with sacrilege and blasphemy
___   ___ Excess concern with right/wrong, morality
___   ___ Other _____

Obsession with need for symmetry or exactness

___   ___ Accompanied by magical thinking (e.g., concerned that mother will
           have accident unless things are in the right place)
___   ___ Not accompanied by magical thinking

Miscellaneous obsessions

___   ___ Need to know or remember
___   ___ Fear of saying certain things
___   ___ Fear of not saying just the right thing
___   ___ Fear of losing things
___   ___ Intrusive (nonviolent) images
___   ___ Intrusive nonsense sounds, words, or music
___   ___ Bothered by certain sounds/noises*
___   ___ Lucky/unlucky numbers
___   ___ Colors with special significance
___   ___ Superstitious fears
___   ___ Other_____

Somatic obsessions

___   ___ Concern with illness or disease*
___   ___ Excessive concern with body part or aspect of appearance (e.g.,
           dysmorphophobia)*
___   ___ Other_____

Cleaning/washing compulsions
___   ___ Excessive or ritualized handwashing
___   ___ Excessive or ritualized showering, bathing, toothbrushing, groom-
            ing, or toilet routine
___   ___ Involves cleaning of household items or other inanimate objects
___   ___ Other measures to prevent or remove contact with contaminants
___   ___ Other _____

Checking compulsions
___   ___ Checking locks, stove, appliances, etc.
___   ___ Checking that did not/will not harm others
___   ___ Checking that did not/will not harm self
___   ___ Checking that nothing terrible did/will happen
___   ___ Checking that did not make mistake
___   ___ Checking tied to somatic obsessions
___   ___ Other _____

Repeating rituals
___   ___ Rereading or rewriting
___   ___ Need to repeat routine activities (e.g., in/out door, up/down from
            chair)
___   ___ Other _____

Counting compulsions
___   ___ _____

Ordering/arranging compulsions
___   ___ _____

Hoarding/collecting compulsions
[distinguish from hobbies and concern with objects of monetary or
sentimental value (e.g., carefully reads junk mail, piles up old
newspapers, sorts through garbage, collects useless objects)]
___   ___ _____

Miscellaneous compulsions
___   ___ Mental rituals (other than checking/counting)
___   ___ Excessive listmaking

—   — Need to tell, ask, or confess
—   — Need to touch, tap, or rub*
—   — Rituals involving blinking or staring*
—   — Measures (not checking) to prevent harm to self __, harm to others
            __, terrible consequences__
—   — Ritualized eating behaviors*
—   — Superstitious behaviors
—   — Trichotillomania*
—   — Other self-damaging or self-mutilating behaviors*
—   — Other_____

APPENDIX B. Yale–Brown Obsessive–Compulsive Scale (YBOCS)

Patient Name _____

Patient ID _____

YBOCS TOTAL (add items 1–10) ☐

Date _____

Rater _____

	None 0	Mild 1	Moderate 2	Severe 3	Extreme 4
1. Time spent on obsessions	0	1	2	3	4
1b. Obsession-free interval (do not add to subtotal or total score)	No Symptoms 0	Long 1	Moderately Long 2	Short 3	Extremely Short 4
2. Interference from obsessions	0	1	2	3	4
3. Distress of obsessions	0	1	2	3	4
4. Resistance	Always Resists 0	1	2	3	Completely Yields 4
5. Control over obsessions	Complete Control 0	Much Control 1	Moderate Control 2	Little Control 3	No Control 4

Obsession subtotal (add items 1–5) ☐

	None 0	Mild 1	Moderate 2	Severe 3	Extreme 4
6. Time spent on compulsions					
6b. Compulsion-free interval (do not add to subtotal or total score)	No Symptoms 0	Long 1	Moderately Long 2	Short 3	Extremely Short 4
7. Interference from compulsions	0	1	2	3	4
8. Distress from compulsions	0	1	2	3	4
9. Resistance	Always Resists 0	1	2	3	Completely Yields 4
10. Control over compulsions	Complete Control 0	Much Control 1	Moderate Control 2	Little Control 3	No Control 4

Compulsion subtotal (add items 6–10) ☐

	Excellent 0	1	2	3	Absent 4
11. Insight into O-C symptoms					

	None 0	Mild 1	Moderate 2	Severe 3	Extreme 4
12. Avoidance	0	1	2	3	4
13. Indecisiveness	0	1	2	3	4
14. Pathologic responsibility	0	1	2	3	4
15. Slowness	0	1	2	3	4
16. Pathologic doubting	0	1	2	3	4

17. Global severity	0	1	2	3	4	5	6
18. Global improvement	0	1	2	3	4	5	6

19. Reliability: Excellent = 0 Good = 1 Fair = 2 Poor = 3

From Goodman, Price, Rasmussen, Mazure, Fleischman, et al. (1989). Copyright 1989 by the American Medical Association. Reprinted by permission.

APPENDIX C. Maudsley Obsessional–Compulsive
Inventory (MOC)

Instructions: Please answer each question by putting a circle around the "TRUE" or the "FALSE" following the question. There are no right or wrong answers, and no trick questions. Work quickly and do not think too long about the exact meaning of the question.

1. I avoid using public telephones because of possible contamination.   TRUE   FALSE
2. I frequently get nasty thoughts and have difficulty in getting rid of them.   TRUE   FALSE
3. I am more concerned than most people about honesty.   TRUE   FALSE
4. I am often late because I can't seem to get through everything on time.   TRUE   FALSE
5. I don't worry unduly about contamination if I touch an animal.   TRUE   FALSE
6. I frequently have to check things (e.g., gas or water taps, doors, etc.) several times.   TRUE   FALSE
7. I have a very strict conscience.   TRUE   FALSE
8. I find that almost every day I am upset by unpleasant thoughts that come into my mind against my will.   TRUE   FALSE
9. I do not worry unduly if I accidentally bump into somebody.   TRUE   FALSE
10. I usually have serious doubts about the simple everyday things I do.   TRUE   FALSE
11. Neither of my parents was very strict during my childhood.   TRUE   FALSE
12. I tend to get behind in my work because I repeat things over and over again.   TRUE   FALSE
13. I use only an average amount of soap.   TRUE   FALSE
14. Some numbers are extremely unlucky.   TRUE   FALSE
15. I do not check letters over and over again before mailing them.   TRUE   FALSE
16. I do not take a long time to dress in the morning.   TRUE   FALSE
17. I am not excessively concerned about cleanliness.   TRUE   FALSE
18. One of my major problems is that I pay too much attention to detail.   TRUE   FALSE
19. I can use well-kept toilets without any hesitation.   TRUE   FASLE
20. My major problem is repeated checking.   TRUE   FALSE
21. I am not unduly concerned about germs and diseases.   TRUE   FALSE
22. I do not tend to check things more than once.   TRUE   FASLE

23. I do not stick to a very strict routine when doing ordinary things.   TRUE   FALSE
24. My hands do not feel dirty after touching money.   TRUE   FALSE
25. I do not usually count when doing a routine task.   TRUE   FALSE
26. I take rather a long time to complete my washing in the morning.   TRUE   FALSE
27. I do not use a great deal of antiseptics.   TRUE   FALSE
28. I spend a lot of time every day checking things over and over again.   TRUE   FALSE
29. Hanging and folding my clothes at night does not take up a lot of time.   TRUE   FALSE
30. Even when I do something very carefully I often feel that it is not quite right.   TRUE   FALSE

SCORING KEY

Instructions: Score 1 when a response matches that of this key and 0 when it does not; maximum scores for the five scales are, therefore, respectively 30, 9, 11, 7, 7. Factor 5 (i.e., ruminations) has not been scored, since only Q2 and Q8 loaded on it. A "TRUE" response to these two items is possibly a sign of ruminations. Only the checking, washing, and total obsessional scores have been validated; the "slowness–repetition" and "doubting–conscientious" factors need replication and validation.

	Total Obsessional Score	Checking	Washing	Slowness–Repetition	Doubling–Conscientious
Q1	True	—	True	—	—
Q2	True	True	—	False	—
Q3	True	—	—	—	True
Q4	True	—	True	True	—
Q5	False	—	False	—	—
Q6	True	True	—	—	—
Q7	True	—	—	—	True
Q8	True	True	—	False	—
Q9	False	—	False	—	—
Q10	True	—	—	—	True
Q11	False	—	—	—	False
Q12	True	—	—	—	True
Q13	False	—	False	—	—
Q14	True	True	—	—	—
Q15	False	False	—	—	—
Q16	False	—	—	False	—
Q17	False	—	False	—	—

Q18	True	—	—	—	True
Q19	False	—	False	—	—
Q20	True	True	—	—	—
Q21	False	—	False	—	—
Q22	False	False	—	—	—
Q23	False	—	—	False	—
Q24	False	—	False	—	—
Q25	False	—	—	False	—
Q26	True	True	True	—	—
Q27	False	—	False	—	—
Q28	True	True	—	—	—
Q29	False	—	—	False	—
Q30	True	—	—	—	True

APPENDIX D. Compulsive Activity Checklist—Revised (CAC-R)

INSTRUCTIONS: Below is a rating scale and a list of activities that people sometimes have problems with. In front of each item, please write the number that best describes how much difficulty you have had with that activity in the past week.

0— I have *no problem* with this activity. It takes me about the same time as an average person. I don't need to repeat or avoid it.

1— This activity takes me about twice as long as most people, or I have to repeat it twice, or I tend to avoid it.

2— This activity takes me about *three* times as long as most people, or I have to repeat it three or more times, or I usually avoid it.

3— I am unable to complete or attempt this activity.

____ 1. Retracing steps
____ 2. Having a bath or shower
____ 3. Washing hands and face
____ 4. Care of hair (washing, combing, brushing)
____ 5. Brushing teeth
____ 6. Dressing and undressing
____ 7. Using toilet to urinate or defecate
____ 8. Touching people or being touched
____ 9. Handling garbage or wastebasket
____ 10. Washing clothes
____ 11. Washing dishes
____ 12. Handling or cooking food
____ 13. Cleaning the house
____ 14. Keeping things neat and orderly
____ 15. Bedmaking
____ 16. Cleaning shoes
____ 17. Touching door handles
____ 18. Touching genitals or sexual activity
____ 19. Switching lights or faucets on or off
____ 20. Locking or closing doors or windows
____ 21. Checking electrical appliances
____ 22. Getting to work
____ 23. Doing my work
____ 24. Filling out forms
____ 25. Mailing letters
____ 26. Touching the floor
____ 27. Using public restrooms
____ 28. Throwing things away

Total ____

APPENDIX E. Obsessive Thoughts Checklist (OTC)

NAME: AGE:
DATE: SEX:

For some people, certain thoughts may seem to occur against their will, and they cannot get rid of them.

Could you rate the thoughts listed below from 0 to 4, according to the degree of disturbance during the past week:

0: This thought does not trouble me at all.
1: This thought rarely troubles me.
2: This thought often troubles me.
3: This thought troubles me very often.
4: This thought troubles me continuously.

____ 1. I think I could be "contaminated."
____ 2. I am very concerned that objects and furniture should always be in the same position.
✕ 3. I am afraid of having forgotten something, so I need to always remind myself what I have done.
____ 4. I think that I am responsible for what is going wrong in the world.
____ 5. I need to be forgiven.
____ 6. I think I could make embarrassing gestures in the presence of other people.
✕ 7. I feel responsible for what may happen to others (accidents, illness . . .).
____ 8. I am concerned about the fact that things must all be correct and in order.
____ 9. There are intrusive words that constantly enter my mind.
____ 10. I have to say words or to count in order to prevent disasters from occurring.
____ 11. I must always reach perfection.
____ 12. If laundry just being washed touches my clothes or slips from my fingers, I feel compelled to wash it again.
____ 13. As soon as I think I could have forgotten to turn off the water or the gas, to lock the doors, or to switch off the light, I have to check.
____ 14. I get the feeling that if an object is touched or used by someone else, then the object is dirty.
____ 15. When I see a knife or any other cutting object, I cannot help thinking I could hurt someone.
____ 16. I feel I have done a great deal of damage to others.
____ 17. I think that my thought may cause my own or others' death.
____ 18. I feel compelled to wash all that comes from outside.

___ 19. I think I could hurt someone or even kill someone without wanting it.

___ 20. I feel compelled to wash myself as soon as I think of dirtiness or contamination.

___ 21. I am compelled to read again or write again to be sure of what I have read or written.

___ 22. Because I am not sure of what I do, I have to check more than one time.

___ 23. I think that just one contact with secretions from the body (sweat, saliva, urine, sperm) can be dangerous and can contaminate my clothes and all that belongs to me.

___ 24. I feel bad if I think I have not been able to do something exactly as I wanted to do it.

___ 25. I feel compelled to remove the dust on furniture or dirt on the ground as soon as I see it.

___ 26. I think I could cause harm to myself or somebody else, and this thought occurs without reason.

___ 27. I am excessively concerned about germs and illnesses.

___ 28. I feel compelled to mentally count or enumerate things.

___ 29. Any other thought that disturbs you (write it and give it a score).

APPENDIX F. Belief Inventory

The statements below describe the attitudes people may have toward their own thoughts. Please mark the space next to each statement according to how strongly you believe that it is true or false for you. Please mark every one.

6: I believe **strongly** that this statement is **true**.
5: I believe that this statement is **true**.
4: I believe that this statement is **probably true**, at least more true than false.
3: I believe that this statement is **probably false**, at least more false than true.
2: I believe that this statement is **false**.
1: I believe **strongly** that this statement is **false**.

_____ 1. Thoughts are in themselves harmless.
_____ 2. Uncertainty should not disturb.
_____ 3. It is unforgivable to be responsible for an error that makes oneself look bad.
_____ 4. Guilt is an appropriate response to unacceptable thoughts.
_____ 5. Danger is always a terrible thing.
_____ 6. If one believes that there is even the slightest possibility of having caused harm, then one must act so as not to be blamed.
_____ 7. One should avoid at any price any activity that runs the possibility of being held personally responsible for a loss.
_____ 8. Loss is always a terrible thing.
_____ 9. One should feel guilty if thoughts are not controlled.
_____ 10. Not being able to control thoughts will harm no one
_____ 11. Enduring unpleasant thoughts without doing anything is dangerous for the person who has them.
_____ 12. Generally speaking, it is preferable to carry responsibility alone.
_____ 13. Punishing oneself for errors that may have been made will enable future errors to be avoided.
_____ 14. Enduring unpleasant thoughts without doing anything can lead to their disappearance.
_____ 15. A responsible person does not let unpleasant thoughts occur without trying to control them.
_____ 16. The loss of someone dear is always unbearable.
_____ 17. One is to blame if something happens that one has thought about.
_____ 18. To be uncertain about having caused possible harm is unbearable even if the possibility is very unlikely.
_____ 19. Uncertainty is a source for concern.
_____ 20. One should feel very guilty if there is the slightest possibility that one is responsible for an unfortunate event.

Translation of L'Inventaire de Croyances Reliées aux Obsessions by M. H. Freeston, in Freeston, Ladouceur, Gagnon, and Thibodeau (1993). Reprinted by permission of the authors.

APPENDIX G. Target Symptoms Rating Form O-C

Patient's Name_____ Rater_____

Date_____

    Below, please rate the degree of fear and/or avoidances of the main situations that the patient has difficulty with. Use the following scale:

0	1	2	3	4	5	6	7	8
None		Mild		Moderately severe		Marked		Extremely severe

	Situation	Rating
1.	_____	_____
2.	_____	_____
3.	_____	_____

Please rate the frequency and/or duration of the ritualistic (compulsive) behavior(s) for which the patient has sought psychological help. Use the following scale:

0	1	2	3	4	5	6	7	8
No problem, no more than normal		Twice as often as normal, requires 30 minutes per day		Three times as often as normal, requires 1 hour per day		Four times as often as normal, requires 1½ hours per day		Five or more times as often as normal, requires 2 or more hours per day

	Ritual	Rating
1.	_____	_____
2.	_____	_____

APPENDIX H. List of Readings on OCD

Books for Professionals

Beech, H. R. (Ed.). (1974). *Obsessional states.* London: Methuen.

Emmelkamp, P. M. G. (1982). *Phobic and obsessive compulsive disorders: Theory, research, and practice.* New York: Plenum Press.

Jenike, M. A., Baer, L., & Minichiello, W. E. (Eds.). (1990). *Obsessive–compulsive disorders: Theory and management.* Chicago: Year Book Medical.

Mavissakalian, M., Turner, S. M., & Michelson, L. (Eds.). (1985). *Obsessive–compulsive disorder: Psychological and pharmacological treatment.* New York: Plenum Press.

Pato, M. T., & Zohar, J. (Eds.). (1990). *Current treatments of obsessive–compulsive disorder.* Washington, DC: American Psychiatric Press.

Rachman, S. J., & Hodgson, R. J. (1980). *Obsessions and compulsions.* Englewood Cliffs, NJ: Prentice-Hall.

Turner, S. M., & Beidel, D. C. (1988). *Treating obsessive–compulsive disorder.* New York: Pergamon Press.

Zohar, J., Insel, T., & Rasmussen, S. (Eds.). (1991). *The psychobiology of obsessive–compulsive disorder.* New York: Springer.

Books for OCD Sufferers and Their Families

Baer, L. (1991). *Getting control.* Boston: Little, Brown.

DeSilva, P. & Rachman, S. (1992). *Obsessive compulsive disorder: The facts.* Oxford: Oxford University Press.

Foa, E. B., & Wilson, R. (1991). *Stop obsessing!* New York: Bantam.

Neziroglu, F., & Yaryura-Tobias, Y. A. (1990). *Over and over again: Understanding obsessive–compulsive disorder.* Lexington, MA: Lexington Books.

Steketee, G., & White, K. (1990). *When once is not enough.* Oakland, CA: New Harbinger Press.

References

Akhtar, S., Wig, N. A., Verma, V. K., Pershad, D., & Verma, S. K. (1975). A phenomenological analysis of symptoms in obsessive–compulsive neurosis. *British Journal of Psychiatry, 114,* 342–348.

Allen, J. J., & Tune, G. S. (1975). The Lynfield Obsessional Compulsive Questionnaire. *Scottish Medical Journal, 20* (Suppl. 1), 21–24.

American Psychiatric Association. (1993, March). *DSM-IV draft criteria.* Washington, DC: Author.

Ananth, J., Pecknold, J. C., Van den Steen, N., & Englesmann, F. (1981). Double-blind comparative study of clomipramine and amitriptyline in obsessive neurosis. *Progress in Neuropsychopharmacology, 5,* 257–262.

Baer, L. (1991). *Getting control.* Boston: Little, Brown.

Baer, L., & Jenike, M. A. (1990). Personality disorders in obsessive compulsive disorder. In M. A. Jenike, L. Baer, & W. E. Minichiello (Eds.), *Obsessive–compulsive disorders: Theory and management.* Chicago: Year Book Medical.

Baer, L., Jenike, M. A., Ricciardi, J. N., Holland, A. D., Seymour, R. J., Minichiello, W. E., & Buttolph, M. L. (1990). Standardized assessment of personality disorders in obsessive–compulsive disorder. *Archives of General Psychiatry, 47,* 826–830.

Baer, L., & Minichiello, W. E. (1990). Behavior therapy for obsessive–compulsive disorder. In M. A. Jenike, L. Baer, & W. E. Minichiello (Eds.), *Obsessive–compulsive disorders: Theory and management.* Chicago: Year Book Medical.

Balslev-Olesen, T., & Geert-Jorgensen, E. (1959). The prognosis of obsessive–compulsive disorder. *Acta Psychiatrica Scandinavica, 34,* 232–241.

Ballantine, H. T., Bouckoms, A. J., Thomas, E. K., & Giriunas, I. E. (1987). Treatment of psychiatric illness by stereotactic cingulotomy. *Biological Psychiatry, 22,* 807–819.

Ballerini, A., & Stanghellini, G. (1989). Phenomenological question about obsession and delusion. *Psychopathology, 22,* 315–319.

Barlow, D. H., & Cerny, J. A. (1988). *Psychological treatment of panic.* New York: Guilford Press.

Barlow, D. H., DiNardo, P. A., & Vermilyea, B. B. (1986). Comorbidity and depression among the anxiety disorders. *Journal of Nervous and Mental Disease, 174,* 63–72.

Barlow, D. H., O'Brien, G. T., & Last, C. G. (1984). Couples treatment of agoraphobia. *Behavior Therapy, 15,* 41–58.

Basoglu, M., Lax, T., Kasvikis, Y., & Marks, I. (1988). Predictors of improvement in obsessive–compulsive disorder. *Journal of Anxiety Disorders, 2,* 299–317.

Bass, B. A. (1973). An unusual behavioral technique for treating obsessive ruminations. *Psychotherapy: Theory, Research, and Practice, 10,* 191–192.

Baxter, L. R., Schwartz, J. M., & Guze, B. H. (1991). Brain imaging: Toward a neuroanatomy of OCD. In J. Zohar, T. Insel, & S. Rasmussen (Eds.), *The psychobiology of obsessive–compulsive disorder.* New York: Springer.

Baxter, L. R., Schwartz, J. M., Mazziotta, J. C., Phelps, M. E., Pahl, J. J., Guze, B. H., & Fairbanks, L. (1988). Cerebral glucose metabolic rates in nondepressed obsessive–compulsives. *American Journal of Psychiatry, 145,* 1560–1563.

Beck, A. T., Epstein, N., Brown, G., & Steer, R. A. (1988). An inventory for measuring clinical anxiety: The Beck Anxiety Inventory. *Journal of Consulting and Clinical Psychology, 56,* 893–897.

Beck, A. T., Emery, G., & Greenberg, R. L. (1985). *Anxiety disorders and phobias: A cognitive perspective.* New York: Basic Books.

Beck, A. T., Ward, C. H., Mendelson, M., Mock, J., & Erbaugh, J. (1961). An inventory for measuring depression. *Archives of General Psychiatry, 4,* 561–571.

Beech, H. R., Ceiseilski, K. T., & Gordon, K. T. (1983). Further observations of evoked potentials in obsessional patients. *British Journal of Psychiatry, 142,* 605–609.

Beech, H. R., & Liddell, A. (1974). Decision making, mood states, and ritualistic behavior among obsessional patients. In H. R. Beech (Ed.), *Obsessional states.* London: Methuen.

Beech, H. R., & Vaughn, M. (1978). *Behavioral treatment of obsessional states.* New York: Wiley.

Beidel, D. C., & Bulik, C. M. (1990). Flooding and response prevention as a treatment for bowel obsessions. *Journal of Anxiety Disorders, 4,* 247–256.

Benkelfat, C., Murphy, D. L., Zohar, J., Hill, J. L., Grover, G., & Insel, T. R. (1989). Clomipramine in obsessive–compulsive disorder: Further evidence for a serotonergic mechanism of action. *Archives of General Psychiatry, 46,* 23–28.

Berg, C. Z., Rapoport, J. L., Whitaker, A., Davies, M., Leonard, H., Swedo, S. E., Braiman, S., & Lenane, M. (1989). Childhood obsessive compulsive disorder: A two-year prospective follow-up of a community sample. *Journal of the American Academy of Child and Adolescent Psychiatry, 8,* 528–533.

Black, A. (1974). The natural history of obsessional neurosis. In H. R. Beech (Ed.), *Obsessional states.* London: Methuen.

Black, D. W., Noyes, R., Goldstein, R. B., & Blum, N. (1992). A family study of obsessive–compulsive disorder. *Archives of General Psychiatry, 49,* 362–368.

Black, D. W., Yates, W. R., Noyes, R., Jr., Pfohl, B., & Kelley, M. (1989). DSM-III personality disorder in obsessive–compulsive study volunteers: A controlled study. *Journal of Personality Disorders, 3,* 58–62.

Boersma, K., Den Hengst, S., Dekker, J., & Emmelkamp, P. M. G. (1976). Exposure and response prevention: A comparison with obsessive compulsive patients. *Behaviour Research and Therapy, 14,* 19–24.

Boulougouris, J. C. (1977). Variables affecting the behaviour modification of obsessive–compulsive patients treated by flooding. In J. C. Boulougouris & A. D. Rabavilas (Eds.), *The treatment of phobic and obsessive–compulsive disorders.* Oxford: Pergamon Press.

Boulougouris, J. C., & Bassiakos, L. (1973). Prolonged flooding in cases with obsessive–compulsive neurosis. *Behaviour Research and Therapy, 11,* 227–231.

Boulougouris, J. C., Rabavalis, A. D., & Stefanis, C. (1977). Psychophysiological responses in obsessive compulsive patients. *Behaviour Research and Therapy, 15,* 221–230.

Bouvard, M., Mollard, E., Cottraux, J., & Guerin, J. (1989). Étude préliminaire d'une liste de pensées obsédantes. *L'Encéphale, 15,* 351–354.

Brady, K. T., Austin, L., & Lydiard, R. B. (1990). Body dysmorphic disorder: The relationship to obsessive–compulsive disorder. *Journal of Nervous and Mental Disease, 178,* 538–539.

Breier, A., Charney, D. S., & Heninger, G. R. (1986). Agoraphobia and panic disorder: Development, diagnostic stability, and course of illness. *Archives of General Psychiatry, 43,* 1029–1036.

Capstick, N., & Seldrup, J. (1973). Phenomenological aspects of obsessional patients treated with clomipramine. *British Journal of Psychiatry, 122,* 719–720.

Carey, G., & Gottesman, I. I. (1981). Twin and family studies of anxiety, phobic, and obsessive disorders. In D. F. Klein & J. G. Rabkin (Eds.), *Anxiety: New research and changing concepts.* New York: Raven Press.

Carr, A. I. (1974). Compulsive neurosis: A review of the literature. *Psychological Bulletin, 8,* 311–318.

Catts, S., & McConaghy, N. (1975). Ritual prevention in the treatment of obsessive–compulsive neurosis. *Australian and New Zealand Journal of Psychiatry, 9,* 37–41.

Cawley, R. (1974). Psychotherapy and obsessional disorders. In H. R. Beech (Ed.), *Obsessional states.* London: Methuen.

Ceiseilski, H. R., Beech, H. R., & Gordon, P. K. (1981). Some electrophysiological observations in obsessional states. *British Journal of Psychiatry, 138,* 479–484.

Chiocca, E. A., & Martuza, R. L. (1990). Neurosurgical therapy of obsessive–compulsive disorder. In M. A. Jenike, L. Baer, & W. E. Minichiello (Eds.), *Obsessive–compulsive disorders: Theory and management.* Chicago: Year Book Medical.

Christensen, H., Dadzi-Pavlovic, D., Andrews, G., & Mattick, R. (1987). Behavior therapy and tricyclic medication in the treatment of obsessive–compulsive disorder: A quantitative review. *Journal of Consulting and Clinical Psychology, 55,* 701–711.

Cloninger, C. R., Martin, R. L., Guze, S. B., & Clayton, P. (1981). A blind follow-up and family study of anxiety neurosis: Preliminary analysis of the St. Louis 500. In D. F. Klein & J. Rabkin (Eds.), *Anxiety: New research and changing concepts.* New York, Raven Press.

Cobb, J. P., McDonald, R., Marks, I. M., & Stern, R. (1980). Marital versus exposure therapy: Psychological treatments of co-existing marital and phobic obsessive problems. *Behavioural Analysis and Modification*, 4, 3–16.

Cobb, J. P., & Marks, I. M. (1979). Morbid jealousy featuring as obsessive–compulsive neurosis: Treatment by behavioural psychotherapy. *British Journal of Psychiatry*, 134, 301–305.

Cooper, J. E. (1970). The Leyton Obsessional Inventory. *Psychological Medicine*, 1, 48–64.

Cooper, J. E., Gelder, M. G., & Marks, I. M. (1965). The results of behaviour therapy in 77 psychiatric patients. *British Medical Journal*, i, 1222–1225.

Coryell, W. (1981). Obsessive–compulsive disorder and primary unipolar depression. *Journal of Nervous and Mental Disease*, 169, 220–224.

Cottraux, G., Bouvard, M., Defayolle, M., & Messy, P. (1988). Validity and factorial structure study of the Compulsive Activity Checklist. *Behavior Therapy*, 19, 45–53.

Cottraux, J., Mollard, E., Bouvard, M., Marks, I., Sluys, M., Nury, A. M., Douge, R., & Cialdella, P. (1989). A controlled study of fluvoxamine and exposure in obsessive compulsive disorder. *International Clinical Psychopharmacology*, 5, 1–14.

Cox, G. L., Merkel, W. T., & Pollard, C. A. (1987, November). *Age-related differences in response to exposure and response prevention: A comparison of adolescents and adults with OCD.* Paper presented at the annual meeting of the Association for Advancement of Behavior Therapy, Boston.

Dalton, P. (1983). Family treatment of an obsessive–compulsive child: A case report. *Family Process*, 22, 99–108.

Denckla, M. B. (1988). Neurological examination. In J. L. Rapoport (Ed.), *Obsessive compulsive disorder in children and adolescents*. Washington, DC: American Psychiatric Press.

Dent, H. R., & Salkovskis, P. M. (1986). Clinical measures of depression, anxiety and obsessionality in nonclinical populations. *Behaviour Research and Therapy*, 24, 689–691.

DeVeaugh-Geiss, J. (1991). Pharmacologic treatment of obsessive–compulsive disorder. In J. Zohar, T. Insel, & S. Rasmussen (Eds.), *The psychobiology of obsessive–compulsive disorder*. New York: Springer.

DiNardo, P. A., & Barlow, D. H. (1988). *Anxiety Disorders Interview Schedule—Revised (ADIS-R)*. Albany: Graywind Publications.

Dollard, J., & Miller, N. E. (1950). *Personality and psychotherapy: An analysis in terms of learning, thinking and culture*. New York: McGraw-Hill.

Doppelt, H. (1983). *A typological investigation of the MMPI scores of clients with and obsessive compulsive disorder and the relationship of the MMPI scores to behavioral treatment outcome.* Unpublished doctoral dissertation, Adelphi University.

Dowson, H. H. (1977). The phenomenology of severe obsessive–compulsive neurosis. *British Journal of Psychiatry*, 131, 75–78.

Edwards, S., & Dickerson, M. (1987). Intrusive unwanted thoughts: A two-stage model of control. *British Journal of Medical Psychology*, 60, 317–328.

Eisen, J. L., & Rasmussen, S. A. (1989). Coexisting obsessive compulsive disorder and alcoholism. *Journal of Clinical Psychiatry, 50,* 96–98.

Elsarrag, M. E. (1968). Psychiatry in the northern Sudan: A study in comparative psychiatry. *British Journal of Psychiatry, 114,* 945–948.

Emmelkamp, P. M. G. (1982). *Phobic and obsessive compulsive disorders: Theory, research, and practice.* New York: Plenum Press.

Emmelkamp, P. M. G., & Beens, H. (1991). Cognitive therapy with obsessive–compulsive disorder: A comparative evaluation. *Behaviour Research and Therapy, 29,* 293–300.

Emmelkamp, P. M. G., de Haan, E., & Hoogduin, C. A. L. (1990). Marital adjustment and obsessive–compulsive disorder. *British Journal of Psychiatry, 156,* 55–60.

Emmelkamp, P. M. G., & DeLange, I. (1983). Spouse involvement in the treatment of obsessive–compulsive patients. *Behaviour Research and Therapy, 21,* 341–346.

Emmelkamp, P. M. G., Hoekstra, R. J., & Visser, S. (1985). The behavioral treatment of OCD: Prediction of outcome at 3.5 years follow-up. In P. Pichot, P. Berner, R. Wolf, & K. Thau (Eds.), *Psychiatry: The state of the art.* New York: Plenum Press.

Emmelkamp, P. M. G., & Kraanen, J. (1977). Therapist-controlled exposure *in vivo* versus self-controlled exposure *in vivo:* A comparison with obsessive–compulsive patients. *Behaviour Research and Therapy, 15,* 491–495.

Emmelkamp, P. M. G., & Kwee, K. G. (1977). Obsessional ruminations: A comparison between thought stopping and prolonged exposure in imagination. *Behaviour Research and Therapy, 15,* 441–444.

Emmelkamp, P. M. G., van den Heuvell, C. V. L., Rüphan, M., & Sanderman, R. (1989). Home-based treatment of obsessive–compulsive patients: Intersession interval and therapist involvement. *Behaviour Research and Therapy, 27,* 89–93.

Emmelkamp, P. M. G., & van der Helm, M., van Zanten, B. L., & Plochg, I. (1980). Contributions of self-instructional training to the effectiveness of exposure *in vivo:* A comparison with obsessive compulsive patients. *Behaviour Research and Therapy, 18,* 61–66.

Emmelkamp, P. M. G., & van der Heyden, H. (1980). The treatment of harming obsessions. *Behavioural Analysis and Modification, 4,* 28–35.

Emmelkamp, P. M. G., Visser, S., & Hoekstra, R. J. (1988). Cognitive therapy vs. exposure *in vivo* in the treatment of obsessive–compulsives. *Cognitive Therapy and Research, 12,* 103–114.

Esquirol, J. E. D. (1838). *Des maladies mentales* (Vol. 2). Paris: Baillière.

Falloon, I. R. H., Boyd, J. L., McGill, G. W., Razani, J., Moss, H. B., & Gilderman, A. M. (1982). Family management in the prevention of exacerbations of schizophrenia: A controlled study. *New England Journal of Medicine, 306,* 1437–1440.

Farid, B. T. (1986). Obsessional symptomatology and adverse mood states. *British Journal of Psychiatry, 149,* 108–112.

Fenichel, O. (1945). *The psychoanalytic theory of neurosis.* New York: Norton.

Fine, S. (1973). Family therapy and a behavioral approach to childhood obsessive–compulsive neurosis. *Archives of General Psychiatry, 28,* 695–697.

Fitz, A. (1990). Religious and familial factors in the etiology of OCD: A review. *Journal of Psychology and Theology, 18,* 141–147.

Foa, E. B. (1979). Failure in treating obsessive–compulsives. *Behaviour Research and Therapy, 17,* 169–176.

Foa, E. B., & Chambless, D. L. (1978). Habituation of subjective anxiety during flooding in imagery. *Behaviour Research and Therapy, 16,* 391–399.

Foa, E. B., & Goldstein, A. (1978). Continuous exposure and complete response prevention of obsessive–compulsive disorder. *Behavior Therapy, 9,* 821–829.

Foa, E. B., Grayson, J. B., Steketee, G. S., Doppelt, H. G., Turner, R. M., & Latimer, P. R. (1983). Success and failure in the behavioral treatment of obsessive–compulsives. *Journal of Consulting and Clinical Psychology, 51,* 287–297.

Foa, E. B., & Kozak, M. J. (1985). Treatment of anxiety disorders: Implications for psychopathology. In A. H. Tuma & J. Maser (Eds.), *Anxiety and the anxiety disorders.* Hillsdale, NJ: Erlbaum.

Foa, E. B., & Kozak, M. J. (1986). Emotional processing of fear: exposure to corrective information. *Psychological Bulletin, 44,* 99, 20–35.

Foa, E. B., Kozak, M. J., Steketee, G. S., & McCarthy, P. R. (1992). Imipramine and behavior therapy in the treatment of depressive and obsessive–compulsive symptoms: Immediate and long-term effects. *British Journal of Clinical Psychology, 31,* 279–292.

Foa, E. B., McNally, R., Steketee, G. S., & McCarthy, P. R. (1991). A test of preparedness theory in anxiety-disordered patients using an avoidance paradigm. *Journal of Psychophysiology, 5,* 159–163.

Foa, E. B., Rothbaum, B. O., Murdock, T., & Riggs, D. S. (1991). The treatment of PTSD in rape victims. *Journal of Consulting and Clinical Psychology, 59,* 715–723.

Foa, E. B., & Steketee, G. S. (1977). Emergent fears during treatment of three obsessive–compulsives: Symptom substitution or deconditioning? *Journal of Behavior Therapy and Experimental Psychiatry, 8,* 353–358.

Foa, E. B., & Steketee, G. S. (1979). Obsessive–compulsives: Conceptual issues and treatment interventions. In M. Hersen, R. M. Eisler, & P. M. Miller (Eds.), *Progress in behavior modification* (Vol. 8). New York: Academic Press.

Foa, E. B., Steketee, G. S., & Grayson, J. B. (1985). Imaginal and *in vivo* exposure: A comparison with obsessive–compulsive checkers. *Behavior Therapy, 16,* 292–302.

Foa, E. B., Steketee, G. S., Grayson, J. B., & Doppelt, H. G. (1983). Treatment of obsessive–compulsives: When do we fail? In E. B. Foa & P. M. G. Emmelkamp (Eds.), *Failures in behavior therapy.* New York: Wiley.

Foa, E. B., Steketee, G. S., Grayson, J. B., Turner, R. M., & Latimer, P. R. (1984). Deliberate exposure and blocking of obsessive–compulsive rituals: Immediate and long term effects. *Behavior Therapy, 15,* 450–472.

Foa, E. B., Steketee,. G. S., & Groves, G. A. (1979). Use of behavioral therapy and imipramine: A case of obsessive–compulsive neurosis with severe depression. *Behavior Modification, 3,* 419–430.

Foa, E. B., Steketee, G. S., & Milby, J. B. (1980). Differential effects of exposure and response prevention in obsessive compulsive washers. *Journal of Consulting and Clinical Psychology, 48,* 71–79.

Foa, E. B., Steketee, G. S., Turner, R. M., & Fischer, S. C. (1980). Effects of imaginal exposure to feared disasters in obsessive compulsive checkers. *Behaviour Research and Therapy, 18,* 449–455.

Foa, E. B., & Tillmanns, A. (1980). The treatment of obsessive compulsive neurosis. In A. Goldstein & E. B. Foa (Eds.), *Handbook of behavioral interventions: A clinical guide.* New York: Wiley.

Foa, E. B., & Wilson, R. (1991). *Stop obsessing!* New York: Bantam.

Fontaine, R., & Chouinard, G. (1985). Fluoxetine in the treatment of obsessive compulsive disorder. *Progress in Neuro-Psychopharmacology and Biological Psychiatry, 9,* 605–608.

Fowler, R. D. (1986, May). Howard Hughes: A psychological autopsy. *Psychology Today,* pp. 22–33.

Freeston, M. H., Ladouceur, R., Gagnon, F., & Thibodeau, N. (1993). Beliefs about obsessional thoughts. *Journal of Psychopathology and Behavioral Assessment, 15,* 1–21.

Freeston, M. H., Ladouceur, R., Thibodeau, N., & Gagnon, F. (1991). Cognitive intrusions in a non-clinical population: I. Response style, subjective experience, and appraisal. *Behaviour Research and Therapy, 29,* 585–597.

Freeston, M. H., Ladouceur, R., Thibodeau, N., & Gagnon, F. (1992). Cognitive intrusions in a non-clinical population: II. Associations with depressive, anxious, and compulsive symptoms. *Behaviour Research and Therapy, 30,* 263–272.

Freud, S. (1924). Notes upon a case of obsessional neurosis. In *Collected papers III.* London: Institute of Psycho-Analysis and Hogarth Press.

Freund, B., Steketee, G. S., & Foa, E. B. (1987). Compulsive Activity Checklist (CAC): Psychometric analysis with obsessive–compulsive disorder. *Behavioral Assessment, 9,* 67–79.

Frost, R. O., Steketee, G. S., Cohn, L., & Griess, K. E. (1991, November). *Familial and background characteristics of nonclinical compulsives.* Paper presented at the annual convention of the Association for Advancement of Behavior Therapy, New York.

Gertz, H. O. (1966). Experience with the logotherapeutic technique of paradoxical intention in the treatment of phobic and obsessive–compulsive patients. *American Journal of Psychiatry, 123,* 548–553.

Gittelson, N. L. (1966). The effect of obsessions on depressive psychosis. *British Journal of Psychiatry, 112,* 253–259.

Gojer, J., Khanna, S., & Channabasavanna, S. M. (1987). Obsessive compulsive disorder, anxiety and depression. *Indian Journal of Psychological Medicine, 10,* 25–30.

Goktepe, E. O., Young, L. B., & Bridges, P. K. (1975). A further review of the results of stereotactic subcaudate tractotomy. *British Journal of Psychiatry, 126,* 270–280.

Goodman, W. K., Price, L. H., Delgado, P. L., Palumbo, J., Krystal, J. H., Nagy, L. M., Rasmussen, S. A., Heninger, G. R., & Charney, D. S. (1990).

Specificity of serotonin reuptake inhibitors in the treatment of obsessive–compulsive disorder. *Archives of General Psychiatry, 47,* 577–585.

Goodman, W. K., Price, L. H., Rasmussen, S. A., Delgado, P. L., Heninger, G. R., & Charney, D. S. (1989). Efficacy of fluvoxamine in obsessive–compulsive disorder. *Archives of General Psychiatry, 46,* 36–44.

Goodman, W. K., Price, L. H., Rasmussen, S. A., Mazure, C., Delgado, P., Heninger, G. R., & Charney, D. S. (1989). The Yale–Brown Obsessive Compulsive Scale: II. Validity. *Archives of General Psychiatry, 46,* 1012–1016.

Goodman, W. K., Price, L. H., Rasmussen, S. A., Mazure, C., Fleischman, R. L., Hill, C. L., Heninger, G. R., & Charney, D. S. (1989). The Yale–Brown Obsessive Compulsive Scale: I. Development, use, and reliability. *Archives of General Psychiatry, 46,* 1006–1011.

Goodman, W. K., Price, L. H., Woods, S.W., & Charney, D. S. (1991). Pharmacological challenges in obsessive–compulsive disorder. In J. Zohar, T. Insel, & S. Rasmussen (Eds.), *The psychobiology of obsessive–compulsive disorder.* New York: Springer.

Goodwin, D. W., Guze, S. B., & Robins, E. (1969). Follow-up studies in obsessional neurosis. *Archives of General Psychiatry, 20,* 182–187.

Grayson, J. B., Foa, E. B., & Steketee, G. S. (1982). Habituation during exposure treatment: Distraction versus attention focusing. *Behaviour Therapy and Research, 20,* 323–328.

Grayson, J. B., Steketee, G. S., & Foa, E. B. (1986). Exposure *in vivo* of obsessive–compulsives under distracting and attention-focusing conditions: Replication and extension. *Behaviour Research and Therapy, 24,* 475–479.

Green, R. C., & Pitman, R. K. (1990). Tourette syndrome and obsessive–complusive disorder: Clinical relationships. In M. A. Jenike, L. Baer, & W. E. Minichiello (Eds.), *Obsessive–compulsive disorders: Theory and management.* Chicago: Year Book Medical.

Greenberg, D. (1987). Compulsive hoarding. *American Journal of Psychotherapy, 41,* 409–416.

Greenberg, D., Witztum, E., & Pisante, J. (1987). Scrupulosity: Religious attitudes and clinical presentations. *British Journal of Medical Psychology, 60,* 29–37.

Greist, J. H. (1990). Treatment of obsessive compulsive disorder: Psychotherapies, drugs, and other somatic treatment. *Journal of Clinical Psychiatry, 51*(8, Suppl.), 44–50.

Greist, J. H., Jefferson, J. W., Rosenfeld, R., Gutzman, L. D., March, J. S., & Barklage, N. E. (1990). Clomipramine and obsessive compulsive disorder: A placebo-controlled double-blind study of 32 patients. *Journal of Clinical Psychiatry, 51,* 292–297.

Guidano, V. L., & Liotti, G. (1983). *Cognitive processes and emotional disorders.* New York: Guilford Press.

Gurnani, P. D., & Wang, M. (1987). Letter to the editor. *Behavioural Psychotherapy, 15,* 101–103.

Hafner, R. J. (1982). Marital interaction in persisting obsessive–compulsive disorders. *Australian and New Zealand Journal of Psychiatry, 16,* 171–178.

Hafner, R. J. (1988). Obsessive–compulsive disorder: A questionnaire survey of a self-help group. *International Journal of Social Psychiatry, 34,* 310–315.

Hafner, R. J., Gilchrist, P., Bowling, J., & Kalucy, R. (1981). The treatment of obsessional neurosis in a family setting. *Australian and New Zealand Journal of Psychiatry, 15,* 145–151.

Hafner, R. J., & Marks, I. M. (1972). Physiological habituation to continuous phobic stimulation. *Behaviour Research and Therapy, 10,* 269–278.

Hasin, D. S., & Grant, B. F. (1987). Psychiatric diagnosis of patients with substance abuse problems: A comparison of two procedures, the DIS and the SADS-L. *Journal of Psychiatric Research, 21,* 7–22.

Headland, K., & MacDonald, B. (1987). Rapid audio-tape treatment of obsessional ruminations: A case report. *Behavioural Psychotherapy, 15,* 188–192.

Hembree, E. A., Kozak, M. J., Foa, E. B., Cohen, A., Freund, B. V., & Riggs, D. S. (1991, November). *Long term efficacy of behavior therapy vs. serotonergic drugs in the treatment of obsessive compulsive disorder.* Paper presented at the annual meeting of the Association for Advancement of Behavior Therapy, New York.

Henderson, J. G., & Pollard, C. A. (1988). Three types of obsessive compulsive disorder in a community sample. *Journal of Clinical Psychology, 44,* 747–752.

Hermesh, H., Shahar, A., & Munitz, H. (1987). Obsessive–compulsive disorder and borderline personality disorder [Letter to the editor]. *American Journal of Psychiatry, 144,* 120–121.

Hodgson, R. J., & Rachman, S. (1972). The effects of contamination and washing in obsessional patients. *Behaviour Research and Therapy, 10,* 11–117.

Hodgson, R. J., & Rachman, S. (1977). Obsessional compulsive complaints. *Behaviour Research and Therapy, 15,* 389–395.

Hodgson, R. J., Rachman, S., & Marks, I. M. (1972). The treatment of chronic obsessive–compulsive neurosis: Follow-up and further findings. *Behaviour Research and Therapy, 10,* 181–189.

Hollander, E., Liebowitz, M. R., & Rosen, W. G. (1991). Neuropsychiatric and neuropsychological studies in obsessive–compulsive disorder. In J. Zohar, T. Insel, & S. Rasmussen (Eds.), *The psychobiology of obsessive–compulsive disorder.* New York: Springer.

Hollander, E., Liebowitz, M. R., Winchel, R., Klumker, A., & Klein, D. F. (1989). Treatment of body-dysmorphic disorder. *American Journal of Psychiatry, 146,* 768–770.

Honjo, S., Hirano, C., Murase, S., Kaneko, T., Sugiyama, T., Ohtaka, K., Aoyama, T., Takel, Y., Inoko, K., & Wakabayashi, S. (1989). Obsessive–compulsive symptoms in childhood and adolescence. *Acta Psychiatrica Scandinavica, 80,* 83–91.

Hoogduin, C. A. L., & Duivenvoorden, H. J. (1988). A decision model in the treatment of obsessive–compulsive neuroses. *British Journal of Psychiatry, 152,* 516–521.

Hoogduin, C. A. L., & Hoogduin, W. A. (1984). The outpatient treatment of patients with an obsessional–compulsive disorder. *Behaviour Research and Therapy, 22,* 455–459.

Hooley, J. M. (1985). Expressed emotion: A review of the critical literature. *Clinical Psychology Review, 5,* 119–139.

Hoover, C., & Insel, T. R. (1984). Families of origin in obsessive–compulsive disorder. *Journal of Nervous and Mental Disease, 172,* 207–215.

Hornsveld, R. H. J., Kraaimaat, F. W., & van Dam-Baggen, R. M. J. (1979). Anxiety/discomfort and handwashing in obsessive compulsive and psychiatric control patients. *Behaviour Research and Therapy, 17,* 223–228.

Hudson, J. I., Pope, H. G., Yurgelun-Todd, D., Jonas, J. M., & Frankenburg, F. R. (1988). Phenomenologic relationship of eating disorders to major affective disorder. *Psychiatry Research, 9,* 345–354.

Ingram, I. M. (1961). Obsessional illness in mental hospital patients. *Journal of Mental Science, 107,* 382–402.

Insel, T. R., & Akiskal, H. S. (1986). Obsessive–compulsive disorder with psychotic features: A phenomenological analysis. *American Journal of Psychiatry, 143,* 1527–1533.

Insel, T. R., Hoover, C., & Murphy, D. L. (1983). Parents of patients with obsessive compulsive disorder. *Psychological Medicine, 13,* 807–811.

Insel, T. R., & Winslow, J. T. (1990). Neurobiology of obsessive–compulsive disorder. In M. A. Jenike, L. Baer, & W. E. Minichiello (Eds.), *Obsessive-compulsive disorders: Theory and management.* Chicago: Year Book Medical.

Janet, P. (1903). *Les obsessions et la psychosthenie.* Paris: Baillière.

Jenike, M. A. (1990). Drug treatment of obsessive–compulsive disorder. In M. A. Jenike, L. Baer, & W. E. Minichiello (Eds.), *Obsessive–compulsive disorders: Theory and management.* Chicago: Year Book Medical.

Jenike, M. A., Baer, L., Ballantine, H. T., Martuza, R. L., Tynes, S., Giriunas, I., Buttolph, M. L., & Cassem, N.H. (1991). Cingulotomy for refractory obsessive–compulsive disorder. *Archives of General Psychiatry, 48,* 548–555.

Jenike, M. A., Baer, L., & Minichiello, W. E. (Eds.). (1990). *Obsessive–compulsive disorders: Theory and management,* Chicago: Year Book Medical.

Jenike, M. A., Baer, L., Minichiello, W. E., Schwartz, C. E., & Carey, R. J. (1986). Concomitant obsessive–compulsive disorder and schizotypal personality disorder. *American Journal of Psychiatry, 143,* 530–532.

Jenike, M. A., Baer, L., Summergrad, P., Weilburg, J. B., Holland, A., & Seymour, R. (1989). Obsessive–compulsive disorder: A double-blind, placebo-controlled trial of clomipramine in 27 patients. *American Journal of Psychiatry, 146,* 1328–1329.

Jenike, M. A., Buttolph, L., Baer, L., Ricciardi, J., & Holland, A. (1989). Open trial of fluoxetine in obsessive–compulsive disorder. *American Journal of Psychiatry, 146,* 909–911.

Jenike, M. A., Hyman, S., Baer, L., Holland, A., Minichello, W. E., Buttolph, L., Summergrad, P., Seymour, R., & Ricciardi, J. (1990). A controlled trial of fluvoxamine in obsessive–compulsive disorder: Implications for a serotonergic theory. *American Journal of Psychiatry, 147,* 1209–1215.

Joffee, R. T., Swinson, R. P., & Regan, J. J. (1988). Personality features of obsessive–compulsive disorder. *American Journal of Psychiatry, 145,* 1127–1129.

Julien, R. A., Rivière, B., & Note, I. D. (1980). Traitement comportemental et cognitif des obsessions et compulsions: Résultats et discussion. *Séance du Lundi, 27 Octobre,* 1123–1133.

Karno, M., Golding, J. M., Sorenson, S. B., & Burnam, M. A. (1988). The epidemiology of obsessive–compulsive disorder in five U.S. communities. *Archives of General Psychiatry, 45,* 1094–1099.

Katon, W. (1984). Panic disorder and somatization. *American Journal of Medicine*, 77, 101–106.

Katz, R. J., DeVeaugh-Geiss, J., & Landau, P. (1990). Clomipramine in obsessive–compulsive disorder. *Biological Psychiatry*, 20, 401–414.

Kazarian, S. S., & Evans, D. R. (1977). Modification of obsessional ruminations: A comparative study. *Canadian Journal of Behavioural Science*, 9, 91–100.

Keane, T. M., & Kaloupek, D. (1982). Imaginal flooding in the treatment of a posttraumatic stress disorder. *Journal of Consulting and Clinical Psychology*, 50, 138–140.

Kearney, C. A., & Silverman, W. K. (1990). Treatment of an adolescent with obsessive–compulsive disorder by alternating response prevention and cognitive therapy: An empirical analysis. *Journal of Behavior Therapy and Experimental Psychiatry*, 21, 39–47.

Kelly, D. (1980). *Anxiety and emotions: Physiologic basis and treatment.* Springfield, IL: Charles C Thomas.

Kenny, F. T., Mowbray, R. M., & Lalani, S. (1978). Faradic disruption of obsessive ideation in the treatment of obsessive neurosis: A controlled study. *Behavior Therapy*, 9, 209–221.

Kettl, P. A., & Marks, I. M. (1986). Neurological factors in obsessive–compulsive disorder: Two case reports and a review of the literature. *British Journal of Psychiatry*, 149, 315–319.

Khanna, S., Kaliaperumal, V. G., & Channabasavanna, S. M. (1986). Reactive factors in obsessive compulsive neurosis. *Indian Journal of Psychological Medicine*, 9, 68–73.

Kirk, J. W. (1983). Behavioural treatment of obsessional–compulsive patients in routine clinical practice. *Behaviour Research and Therapy*, 21, 57–62.

Klass, E. T. (1987). Situational approach to the assessment of guilt: Development and validation of a self-report measure. *Journal of Psychopathology and Behavioral Assessment*, 9, 35–48.

Knight, R. P. (1941). Evaluation of results of psychoanalytic therapy. *American Journal of Psychiatry*, 98, 434–446.

Kozak, M. J., Foa, E. B., & McCarthy, P. R. (1987). Assessment of obsessive–compulsive disorder. In C. Last & M. Hersen (Eds.), *Handbook of anxiety disorders*. Elmsford, NY: Pergamon Press.

Kozak, M. J., Foa, E. B., & Steketee, G. (1988). Process and outcome of exposure treatment with obsessive–compulsives: Psychophysiological indicators of emotional processing. *Behavior Therapy*, 19, 157–169.

Kringlen, E. (1965). Obsessional neurotics: A long-term follow-up. *British Journal of Psychiatry*, 111, 709–722.

Kringlen, E. (1970). Natural history of obsessional neurosis. *Seminars in Psychiatry*, 2, 403–419.

Kullberg, G. (1977). Differences in effects of capsulotomy and cingulotomy. In W. H. Sweet, S. Obrador, & J. G. Rodrigues (Eds.), *Neurosurgical treatment in psychiatry, pain, and epilepsy*. Baltimore: University Park Press.

Laessle, R. G., Wittchen, H. V., Fichter, M. M., & Pirke, K. M. (1989). The significance of bulimia and anorexia nervosa: Lifetime frequency of psychiatric disorders. *International Journal of Eating Disorders*, 8, 569–574.

Lang, P. J. (1977). Imagery in therapy: An information processing analysis of fear. *Behavior Therapy, 8,* 862-886.

Lang, P. J. (1979). A bio-informational theory of emotional imagery. *Psychophysiology, 16,* 495–512.

Last, C., & Strauss, C. C. (1989). Obsessive–compulsive disorders in childhood. *Journal of Anxiety Disorders, 3,* 295–302.

Lenane, M. C., Swedo, S. E., Leonard, H., Pauls, D. L., Cheslow, D. L., & Rapoport, J. L. (1990). Psychiatric disorders in first degree relatives of children and adolescents with obsessive compulsive disorder. *Journal of the American Academy of Child and Adolescent Psychiatry, 29,* 407–412.

Lewis, A. (1936). Problems of obsessional illness. *Proceedings of the Royal Society of Medicine, 29,* 325–336.

Likierman, H., & Rachman, S. (1982). Obsessions: An experimental investigation of thought-stopping and habituation training. *Behavioural Psychotherapy, 10,* 324–338.

Linehan, M. M. (1993). *Cognitive–behavioral treatment of borderline personality disorder.* New York: Guilford Press.

Lipinski, J., White, K., & Quay, S. (1988). *Antiobsessional effects of fluoxtine: An open trial.* Unpublished manuscript.

Lo, W. H. (1967). A follow-up study of obsessional neurotics in Hong Kong Chinese. *British Journal of Psychiatry, 113,* 823–832.

Luff, M. C., & Garrod, M. (1935). The after-results of psychotherapy in 500 adult cases. *British Medical Journal, ii,* 54–59.

Mahoney, M. J. (1971). The self-management of covert behavior: A case study. *Behavior Therapy, 2,* 575–578.

Makhlouf-Norris, F., Jones, H. G., & Norris, H. (1970). Articulation of the conceptual structure in obsessional neurosis. *British Journal of Social and Clinical Psychology, 9,* 264–274.

Makhlouf-Norris, F., & Norris, H. (1972). The obsessive–compulsive syndrome as a neurotic device for the reduction of self-uncertainty. *British Journal of Psychiatry, 121,* 277–288.

Mansuedo, C. S., & Goldfinger, R. I. (1990, November). *Group treatment of trichotillomania with multi-system habit-competition training.* Paper presented at the annual meeting of the Association for Advancement of Behavior Therapy, San Francisco.

Markovitz, P. J., Stagno, S. J., & Calabrese, J. R. (1990). Buspirone augmentation of fluoxetine in obsessive–compulsive disorder. *American Journal of Psychiatry, 147,* 798–800.

Marks, I. M. (1981). *Cure and care of the neuroses.* New York: Wiley.

Marks, I. M. (1986). Genetics of fear and anxiety disorders. *British Journal of Psychiatry, 149,* 406–418.

Marks, I. M., Crowe, E., Drewe, E., Young, J., & Dewhurst, W. G. (1969). Obsessive compulsive neurosis in identical twins. *British Journal of Psychiatry, 15,* 991–998.

Marks, I. M., Hallam, R. S., Connolly, J., & Philpott, R. (1977). *Nursing in behavioural psychotherapy.* London: Royal College of Nursing of the United Kingdom.

Marks, I. M., Hodgson, R., & Rachman, S. (1975). Treatment of chronic obsessive–compulsive neurosis *in vivo* exposure: A 2 year follow-up and issues in treatment. *British Journal of Psychiatry, 127,* 349–364.

Marks, I. M., Lelliott, P., Basoglu, M., Noshirvani, H., Monteiro, W., Cohen, D., & Kasvikis, Y. (1988). Clomipramine, self exposure and therapist-aided exposure for obsessive compulsive rituals. *British Journal of Psychiatry, 152,* 522–534.

Marks, I. M., Stern, R. S., Mawson, D., Cobb, J., & McDonald, R. (1980). Clomipramine and exposure for obsessive–compulsive rituals. *British Journal of Psychiatry, 136,* 1–25.

Mathews, A. M., Gelder, M. G., & Johnston, D. W. (1981). *Agoraphobia: Nature and treatment.* New York: Guilford Press.

Mavissakalian, M. R., & Hamann, M. S. (1986). DSM-III personality disorder in agoraphobia. *Comprehensive Psychiatry, 27,* 471–479.

Mavissakalian, M. R., Hamann, M. S., & Jones, B. (1990). A comparison of DSM-III personality disorders in panic/agoraphobia and obsessive–compulsive disorder. *Comprehensive Psychiatry, 31,* 238–244.

Mavissakalian, M. R., Jones, B., & Olson, S. (1990). Absence of placebo response in obsessive–compulsive disorder. *Journal of Nervous and Mental Disease, 178,* 268–270.

Mavissakalian, M. R., Turner, S. M., Michelson, L., & Jacob, R. (1985). Tricyclic antidepressants in obsessive–compulsive disorder: Anti-obsessional or antidepressant agents. *American Journal of Psychiatry, 142,* 572–576.

Mawson, D., Marks, I. M., & Ramm, L. (1982). Clomipramine and exposure for chronic obsessive–compulsive rituals: Two year follow-up and further findings. *British Journal of Psychiatry, 140,* 11–18.

McCarthy, P. R., & Foa, E. B. (1990). Treatment interventions for obsessive–compulsive disorder. In M. Thase, B. Edelstein, & M. Hersen (Eds.), *Handbook of outpatient treatment of adults.* New York: Plenum Press.

McFall, M. E., & Wollersheim, J. P. (1979). Obsessive–compulsive neurosis: A cognitive behavioral formulation and approach to treatment. *Cognitive Therapy and Research, 3,* 333–348.

McGuire, R. J., & Vallance, M. (1964). Aversion therapy by electric shock: A simple technique. *British Medical Journal, i,* 151–153.

McKenna, P. J. (1984). Disorders with overvalued ideas. *British Journal of Psychiatry, 45,* 579–585.

McKeon, J., Bridget, R., & Mann, A. (1984). Life events and personality traits in obsessive–compulsive neurosis. *British Journal of Psychiatry, 144,* 185–189.

Mehta, M. (1990). A comparative study of family-based and patient-based behavioral management in obsessive–compulsive disorder. *British Journal of Psychiatry, 157,* 133–135.

Mellman, T. A., & Uhde, T. W. (1987). Obsessive–compulsive symptoms in panic disorder. *Americal Journal of Psychiatry, 12,* 1573–1576.

Mermelstein, R., Lichtenstein, E., & McIntyre, K. (1983). Partner support and relapse in smoking-cessation programs. *Journal of Consulting and Clinical Psychology, 51,* 465–466.

Meyer, V., & Levy, R. (1973). Modification of behavior in obsessive–compulsive disorders. In H. E. Adams & P. Unikel (Eds.), *Issues and trends in behavior therapy*. Springfield, IL: Charles C Thomas.

Meyer, V., Levy, R., & Schnurer, A. (1974). A behavioral treatment of obsessive–compulsive disorders. In H. R. Beech (Ed.), *Obsessional states*. London: Methuen.

Milby, J. B., Meredith, R. L., & Rice, J. (1981). Videotaped exposure: A new treatment for obsessive–compulsive disorders, *Journal of Behavior Therapy and Experimental Psychiatry, 12,* 249–255.

Mills, H. L., Agras, W. S., Barlow, D. H., & Mills, J. R. (1973). Compulsive rituals treated by response prevention. *Archives of General Psychiatry, 28,* 524–527.

Milner, A. D., Beech, H. R., & Walker, V. J. (1971). Decision processes and obsessional behaviour. *British Journal of Social and Clinical Psychology, 10,* 88–89.

Minichiello, W., Baer, L., & Jenike, M. A. (1987). Schizotypal personality disorder: A poor prognostic indicator for behavior therapy in the treatment of obsessive–compulsive disorder, *Journal of Anxiety Disorders, 1,* 273–276.

Moergen, S., Maier, M., Brown, S., & Pollard, C. A. (1987). Habituation to fear stimuli in a case of obsessive compulsive disorder: Examining the generalization process. *Journal of Behavior Therapy and Experimental Psychiatry, 18,* 65–70.

Mowrer, O. H. (1960). *Learning theory and behavior*. New York: Wiley.

Myers, J. K., Weissman, M. M., Tischler, G. L., Holzer, C. E., Leaf, P. J., Orvaschel, H., Anthony, J. C., Boyd, J. H., Burke, J. D., Kramer, M., & Stoltzman, R. (1984). Six months prevalence of psychiatric disorders in three communities: 1980–1982. *Archives of General Psychiatry, 41,* 952–967.

Neal, A., & Turner, S. (1991). Anxiety disorders research with African Americans. *Psychological Bulletin, 109,* 400–410.

Neziroglu, F. (1979). A combined behavioral pharmacotherapy approach to obsessive compulsive disorders. In J. Oriols, C. Ballus, M. Gonzales, & J. Prijol (Eds.), *Biological psychiatry today*. Amsterdam: Elsevier/North-Holland.

Neziroglu, F., & Yaryura-Tobias, Y. A. (1990). *Over and over again: Understanding obsessive–compulsive disorder*. Lexington, MA: Lexington Books.

Niler, E. R., & Beck, S. J. (1988). The relationship among guilt, dysphoria, anxiety and obsessions in a normal population. *Behaviour Research and Therapy, 27,* 213–220.

Noonan, J. R. (1971). An obsessive–compulsive reaction treated by induced anxiety. *American Journal of Psychotherapy, 25,* 293–295.

Okasha, A., Kamel, M., & Hassan, A. H. (1968). Preliminary psychiatric observations in Egypt. *British Journal of Psychiatry, 114,* 949–955.

O'Sullivan, G., Noshirvani, H., Marks, I., Monteiro, W., & Lelliott, P. (1991). Six-year follow-up after exposure and clomipramine therapy for obsessive compulsive disorder. *Journal of Clinical Psychiatry, 52,* 150–155.

Parkinson, L., & Rachman, S. (1981). Intrusive thoughts: The effects of an un-contrived stress. *Advances in Behaviour Research and Therapy, 3,* 111–118.

Pato, M. T., Zohar-Kadouch, R., Zohar, J., & Murphy, D. (1988). Return of symptoms after discontinuation of clomipramine in patients with obsessive–compulsive disorder. *American Journal of Psychiatry, 145,* 1521–1527.

Pauls, D. L., Raymond, C. L., & Robertson, M. (1991). The genetics of obsessive–compulsive disorder: A review. In J. Zohar, T. Insel, & S. Rasmussen (Eds.), *The psychobiology of obsessive–compulsive disorder*. New York: Springer.

Pauls, D. L., Towbin, K. E., Leckman, J. G., Zahner, G. E. P., & Cohen, D. J. (1986). Gilles de la Tourette syndrome and obsessive compulsive disorder: Evidence supporting an etiological relationship. *Archives of General Psychiatry, 43*, 1180–1182.

Perse, T. L. (1988). Obsessive–compulsive disorder: A treatment review. *Journal of Clinical Psychiatry, 49*, 48–55.

Perse, T. L., Greist, J. H., Jefferson, J. W., Rosenfeld, R., & Dar, R. (1987). Fluvoxamine treatment of obsessive–compulsive disorder. *American Journal of Psychiatry, 144*, 1543–1548.

Persons, J. B., & Foa, E. B. (1984). Processing of fearful and neutral information by obsessive–compulsives. *Behaviour Research and Therapy, 22*, 259–265.

Pfohl, B., Black, D., Noyes, R., Kelley, M., & Blum, N. (1990). A test of the tridimensional personality theory: Association with diagnosis and platelet imipramine binding in obsessive–compulsive disorder. *Biological Psychiatry, 28*, 41–46.

Phillips, K. A. (1990, May). *Body dysmorphic disorder: The distress of imagined ugliness*. Paper presented at the annual meeting of the American Psychiatric Association, New York.

Philpott, R. (1975). Recent advances in the behavioral measurement of obsessional illness: Difficulties common to these and other instruments. *Scottish Medical Journal, 20*(Suppl.), 33–40.

Pitman, R. K. (1987). A cybernetic model of obsessive–compulsive psychopathology. *Comprehensive Psychiatry, 28*, 334–343.

Pitman, R. K., Green, R. C., Jenike, M. A., & Mesulam, M. M. (1987). Clinical comparison of Tourette's disorder and obsessive–compulsive disorder. *American Journal of Psychiatry, 144*, 1166–1171.

Pollitt, J. (1957). Natural history of obsessional states: A study of 150 cases. *British Medical Journal, i*, 194–198.

Price, L. H., Goodman, W. K., Charney, D. S., Rasmussen, S. A., & Heninger, G. R. (1987). Treatment of severe obsessive–compulsive disorder with fluvoxamine. *American Journal of Psychiatry, 144*, 1050–1061.

Queiroz, L. O. S., Motta, M. A., Madi, M. B. B. P., Sossai, D. L., & Boren, J. J. (1981). A functional analysis of obsessive–compulsive problems with related therapeutic procedures. *Behaviour Research and Therapy, 19*, 377–388.

Rabavilas, A. D., & Boulougouris, J. C. (1974). Physiological accompaniments of ruminations, flooding and thought-stopping in obsessive patients. *Behaviour Research and Therapy, 12*, 239–243.

Rabavilas, A. D., Boulougouris, J. C., Perissaki, C., & Stefanis, C. (1979). Premorbid personality traits and responsiveness to flooding in obsessive–compulsive patients. *Behaviour Research and Therapy, 17*, 575–580.

Rabavilas, A. D., Boulougouris, J. C., & Stefanis, C. (1976). Duration of flooding sessions in the treatment of obsessive–compulsive patients. *Behaviour Research and Therapy, 14*, 349–355.

Rachman, S. (1971). Obsessional ruminations. *Behaviour Research and Therapy, 9*, 229–235.

Rachman, S. (1976a). The modification of obsessions: A new formulation. *Behaviour Research and Therapy, 14,* 437–443.

Rachman, S. (1976b). Obsessional–compulsive checking. *Behaviour Research and Therapy, 14,* 269–277.

Rachman, S. J. (1977). The conditioning theory of fear acquisition: A critical examination. *Behaviour Research and Therapy, 15,* 375–387.

Rachman, S. (1980). Emotional processing. *Behaviour Research and Therapy, 18,* 51–60.

Rachman, S., & DeSilva, P. (1978). Abnormal and normal obsessions. *Behaviour Research and Therapy, 16,* 233–248.

Rachman, S., & Hodgson, R. (1980). *Obsessions and compulsions.* Englewood Cliffs, NJ: Prentice-Hall.

Rachman, S., Hodgson, R., & Marks, I. M. (1971). The treatment of chronic obsessive–compulsive neurosis. *Behaviour Research and Therapy, 9,* 237–247.

Rachman, S., Marks, I. M., & Hodgson, R. (1973). The treatment of obsessive–compulsive neurotics by modelling and flooding *in vivo. Behaviour Research and Therapy, 11,* 463–471.

Rachman, S., & Wilson, G. T. (1980). *The effects of psychological therapy.* Oxford: Pergamon Press.

Rasmussen, S. A., & Eisen, J. L. (1989). Clinical features and phenomenology of obsessive compulsive disorder. *Psychiatric Annals, 19,* 67–73.

Rasmussen, S. A., & Tsuang, M. T. (1984). Epidemiology of obsessive compulsive disorder: A review. *Journal of Clinical Psychiatry, 45,* 450–457.

Rasmussen, S. A., & Tsuang, M. T. (1986). Epidemiological and clinical findings of significance to the design of neuropharmacologic studies of obsessive–compulsive disorder. *Psychopharmacological Bulletin, 22,* 723–733.

Reed, G. F. (1968). Some formal qualities of obsessional thinking. *Psychiatria Clinica, 1,* 382–392.

Reed, G. F. (1969). "Under-inclusion"—a characteristic of obsessional personality disorder: I. *British Journal of Psychiatry, 115,* 787–790.

Reed, G. F. (1985). *Obsessional experience and compulsive behavior.* Orlando, FL: Academic Press.

Riddle, M. A., Scahill, L., King, R., Hardin, M. T., Towbin, K. E., Ort, S. I., Leckman, J. F., & Cohen, D. J. (1990). Obsessive compulsive disorder in children and adolescents: Phenomenology and family history. *Journal of the American Academy of Child and Adolescent Psychiatry, 29,* 766–772.

Riemann, B. C., McNally, R. J., & Cox, W. M. (1992). The comorbidity of obsessive–compulsive disorder and alcoholism. *Journal of Anxiety Disorders, 6,* 105–110.

Robertson, J., Wendiggensen, P., & Kaplan, I. (1983). Towards a comprehensive treatment for obsessional thoughts. *Behaviour Research and Therapy, 21,* 347–356.

Roper, G., & Rachman, S. (1976). Obsessional compulsive checking: Experimental replication and development. *Behaviour Research and Therapy, 14,* 23–32.

Roper, G., Rachman, S., & Hodgson, R. (1973). An experiment on obsessional checking. *Behaviour Research and Therapy, 11,* 271–277.

Roper, G., Rachman, S., & Marks, I. M. (1975). Passive and participant modelling in exposure treatment of obsessive–compulsive neurotics. *Behaviour Research and Therapy, 13*, 271–279.

Rosen, I. (1957). The clinical significance of obsessions in schizophrenia. *Journal of Mental Science, 103*, 773–786.

Rosen, J. C., & Leitenberg, H. (1982). Bulimia nervosa: Treatment with exposure and response prevention. *Behavior Therapy, 13*, 117–124.

Rubin, R. D., & Merbaum, M. (1971). Self-imposed punishment versus desensitization. In R. D. Rubin, H. Fensterheim, A. A. Lazarus, & C. M. Franks (Eds.), *Advances in behavior therapy.* New York: Academic Press.

Rudin, G. (1953). Ein Beitrag zur frange der Zwangkran Kheit insobesondere ihre here diatreu beziehungen. *Archiv für Psychiatrie und Nervenkrankheiten, 191*, 14–54.

Salkovskis, P. M. (1983). Treatment of an obsessional patient using habituation to audiotaped ruminations. *British Journal of Clinical Psychology, 22*, 311–313.

Salkovskis, P. M. (1985). Obsessional–compulsive problem: A cognitive–behavioural analysis. *Behaviour Research and Therapy, 23*, 571–583.

Salkovskis, P. M. (1989). Cognitive–behavioural factors and the persistence of intrusive thoughts in obsessive problems. *Behaviour Research and Therapy, 27*, 677–682.

Salkovskis, P. M. (1989). Somatic problems. In K. Hawton, P. M. Salkovskis, J. Kirk, & D. M. Clark (Eds.), *Cognitive behaviour therapy for psychiatric problems.* Oxford: Oxford University Press.

Salkovskis, P. M., & Harrison, J. (1984). Abnormal and normal obsessions: A replication. *Behaviour Research and Therapy, 22*, 549–552.

Salkovskis, P. M., & Warwick, H. M. C. (1986). Morbid preoccupations, health anxiety and reassurance: A cognitive–behavioural approach to hypochondriasis. *Behaviour Research and Therapy, 24*, 597–602.

Salkovskis, P. M., & Westbrook, D. (1989). Behavior therapy and obsessional ruminations: Can failure be turned into success? *Behavior Research and Therapy, 27*, 149–160.

Sanavio, E. (1988). Obsessions and compulsions: The Padua Inventory. *Behaviour Research and Therapy, 26*, 169–177.

Sanderson, W. C., Beck, A. T., & Betz, S. (in press). Prevalence of personality disorders among patients with anxiety disorders. *Journal of Abnormal Psychology.*

Sandler, J., & Hazari, A. (1960). The "obsessional": On the psychological classification of obsessional character traits and symptoms. *British Journal of Medical Psychology, 33*, 113–122.

Sartory, G., & Master, D. (1984). Contingent negative variation in obsessional–compulsive patients. *Biological Psychology, 18*, 253–267.

Schneider, K. (1925). Schwangs zustande in schizophrenie. *Archiv für Psychiatrie und Nervenkrankheiten, 74*, 93–107.

Shagass, C., Roemer, R. A., Straumanis, J. J., & Josiassen, R. C. (1984). Distinctive somatosensory evoked potential features in obsessive compulsive disorder. *Biological Psychiatry, 19*, 1507–1524.

Shahar, A., & Marks, I. M. (1980). Habituation during exposure treatment of compulsive rituals. *Behavior Therapy, 11*, 397–401.

Sher, K. J., Frost, R. O., & Otto, R. (1983). Cognitive deficits in compulsive checkers: An exploratory study. *Behaviour Research and Therapy, 21*, 357–364.

Sher, K. J., Mann, B., & Frost, R. O. (1984). Cognitive dysfunction in compulsive checkers: Further explorations. *Behaviour Research and Therapy, 22*, 493–502.

Solyom, L., Garza-Perez, J., Ledwidge, & Solyom, C. (1972). Paradoxical intention in the treatment of obsessive thoughts: A pilot study. *Comprehensive Psychiatry, 13*, 291–297.

Solyom, L., Zamanzadeh, D., Ledwidge, B., & Kenny, F. (1971). Aversion relief treatment of obsessive neurosis. In R. D. Rubin, H. Fensterheim, A. A. Lazarus, & C. M. Franks (Eds.), *Advances in behavior therapy*. New York: Academic Press.

Spitzer, R. L., Williams, J. B. W., & Gibbon, M. (1987). *SCID: Structured Clinical Interview for DSM-III-R*. New York: New York State Psychiatric Institute.

Stanley, M. A., Turner, A. M., & Borden, J. W. (1990). Schizotypal features in obsessive–compulsive disorder. *Comprehensive Psychiatry, 31*, 511–518.

Steiner, J. (1972). A questionnaire study of risk-taking in psychiatric patients. *British Journal of Medical Psychology, 45*, 365–374.

Steketee, G. S. (1987). *Predicting relapse following behavioral treatment for obsessive–compulsive disorder: The impact of social support*. Ann Arbor, MI: UMI Dissertation Information Service.

Steketee, G. S. (1988). Intra- and interpersonal characteristics predictive of long-term outcome following behavioral treatment of obsessive–compulsive disorders. In H. Wittchen & I. Hand (Eds.), *Treatments of panic and phobias*. New York: Springer-Verlag.

Steketee, G. S. (1990). Personality traits and disorders in obsessive–compulsives. *Journal of Anxiety Disorders, 4*, 351–364.

Steketee, G. S., & Cleere, L. (1990). Obsessive–compulsive disorders. In A. S. Bellack, M. Hersen, & A. E. Kazdin (Eds.), *International handbook of behavior modification and therapy*. New York: Plenum Press.

Steketee, G. S., & Doppelt, H. (1986). Measurement of obsessive–compulsive symptomatology: Utility of the Hopkins Symptom Checklist. *Psychiatry Research, 19*, 135–145.

Steketee, G. S., & Foa, E. B. (1985). Obsessive–compulsive disorder. In D.H. Barlow (Ed.), *Clinical handbook of psychological disorders: A step-by-step treatment manual* (1st ed.). New York: Guilford Press.

Steketee, G. S., Foa, E. B., & Grayson, J. B. (1982). Recent advances in the behavioral treatment of obsessive–compulsives. *Archives of General Psychiatry, 39*, 1365–1371.

Steketee, G. S., & Freund, B. (1993). Psychometric properties of the Compulsive Activity Checklist. *Behavioural Psychotherapy, 21*, 13–25.

Steketee, G. S., Kozak, M. J., & Foa, E. B. (1985, September). *Predictors of outcome for obsessive–compulsives treated with exposure and response prevention*. Paper presented at the 15th Annual Meeting of the European Association for Behaviour Therapy, Munich, West Germany.

Steketee, G. S., & Lam, J. (1993). Obsessive compulsive disorder. In T. R. Giles (Ed.), *Effective psychotherapy: A handbook of comparative research*. New York: Plenum Press.

Steketee, G. S., Quay, S., & White, K. (1991). Religion and guilt in OCD patients. *Journal of Anxiety Disorders, 5*, 359–367.

Steketee, G. S., & Shapiro, L. (1992). Obsessive–compulsive disorder. In A. S. Bellack & M. Hersen (Eds.), *Handbook of behavior therapy in the psychiatric setting*. New York: Plenum Press.

Steketee, G. S., & White, K. (1990). *When once is not enough*. Oakland, CA: New Harbinger Press.

Stern, R. S. (1978). Obsessive thoughts: The problem of therapy. *British Journal of Psychiatry, 133*, 200–205.

Stern, R. S., Lipsedge, M. S., & Marks, I. M. (1975). Obsessive ruminations: A controlled trial of thought stopping technique. *Behaviour Research and Therapy, 11*, 659–662.

Sternberger, L. G., & Burns, G. L. (1990a). Compulsive Activity Checklist and the Maudsley Obsessional–Compulsive Inventory: Psychometric properties of two measures of obsessive–compulsive disorder. *Behavior Therapy, 21*, 117–127.

Sternberger, L. G., & Burns, G. L. (1990b). Maudsley Obsessional–Compulsive Inventory: Obsessions and compulsions in a nonclinical sample. *Behaviour Research and Therapy, 28*, 337–340.

Sternberger, L. G., & Burns, G. L. (1990c). Obsessions and compulsions: Psychometric properties of the Padua Inventory with an American college population. *Behaviour Research and Therapy, 28*, 341–345.

Suess, L., & Halpern, M. S. (1989). Obsessive–compulsive disorder: A religious perspective. In J. L. Rapoport (Ed.), *Obsessive–compulsive disorder in children and adolescents*. Washington, DC: American Psychiatric Press.

Swedo, S. E., Lenane, M. C., Leonard, H. L., & Rapoport, J. L. (1990, November). *Drug treatment of trichotillomania: Two year follow-up*. Paper presented at the meeting of the Association for Advancement of Behavior Therapy, San Francisco.

Swedo, S. E., Rapoport, J. L., Leonard, H. L., Lenane, M. C., & Cheslow, D. L. (1989). Obsessive–compulsive disorder in children and adolescents. *Archives of General Psychiatry, 46*, 335–341.

Teasdale, J. D. (1974). Learning models of obsessional compulsive disorder. In H. R. Beech (Ed.), *Obsessional states*. London: Methuen.

Thoren, P., Asberg, M., Cronholm, B., Jornstedt, L., & Traskman, L. (1980). Clomipramine treatment of obsessive–compulsive disorder: A controlled clinical trial. *Archives of General Psychiatry, 37*, 1281–1285.

Thyer, B. A. (1985). Audiotaped exposure therapy in a case of obsessional neurosis. *Journal of Behavior Therapy and Experimental Psychiatry, 16*, 271–274.

Towbin, K. E., Leckman, J. F., & Cohen, D. J. (1987). Drug treatment of obsessive–compulsive disorder: A review of findings in the light of diagnostic and metric limitations. *Psychiatric Developments, 1*, 25–50.

Turner, S. M., Beidel, D. C., & Nathan, R. S. (1985). Biological factors in obsessive–compulsive disorders. *Psychological Bulletin, 97*, 430–450.

Turner, S. M., Beidel, D. C., Stanley, M. A., & Jacob, R. G. (1988). A comparison of fluoxetine, flooding, and response prevention in the treatment of obsessive compulsive disorder. *Journal of Anxiety Disorders, 2,* 219–225.

Turner, S. M., Hersen, M., Bellack, A. S., Andrasik, F., & Capparell, H. V. (1980). Behavioral and pharmacological treatment of obsessive–compulsive disorders. *Journal of Nervous and Mental Disease, 168,* 651–657.

Tynes, L. L., White, K., & Steketee, G. S. (1990). Toward a new nosology of OCD. *Comprehensive Psychiatry, 31,* 465–480.

van den Hout, M., Emmelkamp, P., Kraaykamp, H., & Griez, E. (1988). Behavioural treatment of obsessive–compulsives: Inpatient vs outpatient. *Behaviour Research and Therapy, 26,* 331–333.

van Oppen, P. (1992). Obsessions and compulsions: Dimensional structure, reliability, convergent and divergent validity of the Padua Inventory. *Behaviour Research and Therapy, 30,* 631–637.

Volans, P. J. (1976). Styles of decision-making and probability appraisal in selected obsessional and phobic patients. *British Journal of Social and Clinical Psychology, 15,* 305–317.

Volavka, J., Neziroglu, F., & Yaryura-Tobias, J. A. (1985). Clomipramine and imipramine in obsessive–compulsive disorder. *Psychiatry Research, 14,* 85–93.

Walker, V. J. (1967). *An investigation of ritualistic behaviour in obsessional patients.* Unpublished doctoral dissertation, Institute of Psychiatry, University of London.

Walton, D. (1960). The relevance of learning theory to the treatment of an obsessive–compulsive state. In H. J. Eysenck (Ed.), *Behaviour therapy and the neuroses.* Oxford: Pergamon Press.

Walton, D., & Mather, M. D. (1963). The application of learning principles to the treatment of obsessive–compulsive states in the acute and chronic phases of illness. *Behaviour Research and Therapy, 1,* 163–174.

Warren, R., & Zgourides, G. D. (1991). *Anxiety disorders: A rational–emotive perspective.* Elmsford, NY: Pergamon Press.

Watts, F. N. (1971). Habituation model of systematic desensitization, *Psychological Bulletin, 86,* 627–637.

Wegner, D. M. (1989). *White bears and other unwanted thoughts.* New York: Viking Penguin.

Weizman, A., Zohar, J., & Insel, T. (1991). Biological Markers in obsessive–compulsive disorder. In J. Zohar, T. Insel, & S. Rasmussen (Eds.), *The psychobiology of obsessive–compulsive disorder.* New York: Springer.

Welner, A., Reich, T., Robins, E., Fishman, R., & Van Doren, T. (1976). Obsessive–compulsive neurosis: Record, follow-up, and family studies. *Comprehensive Psychiatry, 17,* 527–539.

Westphal, K. (1878). Über Zwangsvorstellungen. *Archiv für Psychiatrie und Nervenkrankheiten, 8,* 734–750.

White, K., Steketee, G. S., & Julian, J. (1992). *Course and comorbidity in OCD.* Unpublished manuscript.

Wolpe, J. (1958). *Psychotherapy by reciprocal inhibition.* Stanford, CA: Stanford University Press.

Woodruff, R., & Pitts, F. N. (1964). Monozygotic twins with obsessional illness. *American Journal of Psychiatry, 120,* 1075–1080.

Zohar, J., & Insel, T. R. (1986). Drug treatment of obsessive–compulsive disorder. *Journal of Affective Disorders, 13,* 193–202.

Zohar, J., Insel, T. R., Berman, K. F., Foa, E. B., Hill, J. L., & Weinberger, D. R. (1989). Anxiety and cerebral blood flow during behavioral challenge: Dissociation of central from peripheral and subjective measures. *Archives of General Psychiatry, 46,* 505–510.

Index